A Therapeutic Community Approach
to Care in the Community

Therapeutic Communities
Series editors: Rex Haigh and Jan Lees

The Therapeutic Community movement holds a multidisciplinary view of health which is based on ideas of collective responsibility, citizenship and empowerment. The tradition has a long and distinguished history and is experiencing a revival of interest in contemporary theory and practice. It draws from many different principles - including analytic, behavioural, creative, educational and humanistic – in the framework of a group-based view of the social origins and maintenance of much overwhelming distress, mental ill-health and deviant behaviour. Therapeutic Community principles are applicable in a wide variety of settings, and this series will reflect that.

Introduction to Therapeutic Communities
David Kennard
Therapeutic Communities 1
ISBN 1 85302 603 4

Therapeutic Communities
Past, Present and Future
Edited by Rex Haigh and Penelope Campling
Therapeutic Communities 2
ISBN 1 85302 614 X hb
ISBN 1 85302 626 3 pb

Bion, Rickman, Foulkes and the Northfield Experiments
Advancing on a Different Front
Tom Harrison
Therapeutic Communities 5
ISBN 1 85302 837 1

Therapeutic Communities 3

A Therapeutic Community Approach to Care in the Community

Dialogue and Dwelling

Edited by Sarah Tucker

Jessica Kingsley Publishers
London and Philadelphia

The right of the contributors to be identified as authors of this work has been asserted by them in accordance with the Copyright, Designs and Patents Act 1988.

First published in the United Kingdom in 2000 by
Jessica Kingsley Publishers Ltd
116 Pentonville Road
London N1 9JB, England
and
325 Chestnut Street
Philadelphia, PA 19106, USA

www.jkp.com

© Copyright 2000 Jessica Kingsley Publishers

Library of Congress Cataloging in Publication Data
A therapeutic community approach to care in the community : dialogue
and dwelling / edited by Sarah Tucker.
    p. cm. -- (Therapeutic communities ; 3)
  ISBN 1-85302-751-0 (pbk. : alk. paper)
  1. Therapeutic communities. 2. Community mental health services.
I. Tucker, Sarah. II. Series.
RC489.T67T486   1999
362.2'2--dc21   99-42612
                                                CIP
British Library Cataloguing in Publication Data
A therapeutic community approach to care in the community :
  dialogue and dwelling. - (Therapeutic communities ; 3)
  1. Therapeutic communities
I. Tucker, Sarah
362.2'0425
ISBN 1 85302 751 0

ISBN 1 85302 751 0

Printed and Bound in Great Britain by
Athenaeum Press, Gateshead, Tyne and Wear

Contents

Foreword

This volume is written by members of Community Housing and Therapy (CHT), and the contributions together provide an exposition of our development and application of the therapeutic community approach to working with people with mental health problems in a community setting. The contributions also present an ongoing exploration of our approach which reflects the impulse to question which is so central to our work. All of the ideas in this volume have been either provoked or inspired by John Gale, who has offered his reliable and enduring stimulation, support, advice and criticism during the process of putting our ideas into this volume.

COMMUNITY HOUSING AND THERAPY (CHT)

CHT is a charity that runs six TCs in the community for severely mentally ill people and homeless ex-service men and women: five in South-West London and one in Eastbourne. CHT has historical roots in the Richmond Fellowship, a national voluntary organization pioneered by Elly Jansen in the 1960s and 1970s (see Kennard 1998a, p.75; Kennard 1998b, p.325). Out of the context of the Richmond Fellowship, CHT developed new TC projects and now runs as an independent organization.

Each TC has between nine and fifteen clients with a variety of diagnoses, including schizophrenia, manic depression, personality disorder and depression. Each TC has an educational and therapeutic programme which includes practical groups and individual and group therapy sessions. The progress of each client is reviewed every three to six months at interdisciplinary meetings involving psychiatrists, social workers, CPNs, family and others involved with the client. Staff are recruited from a variety of backgrounds and are usually university graduates, frequently having read psychology and trained in counselling. Staff involved in management have usually studied to Master's degree level either in social psychology or health psychology.

'Citizens in Dialogue' is CHT's in-house three-year training programme in Dialogical Group Therapy for therapeutic community practitioners. The course provides training in theoretical material, supervised practice and experiential self-learning (see Tucker 1998).

REFERENCES

Kennard, D. (1998a) *An Introduction to Therapeutic Communities* (second edition). London: Jessica Kingsley Publishers.

Kennard, D. (1998b) 'Therapeutic communities back – and there's something a little different about them.' *Therapeutic Communities 19*, 4, 323–329.

Tucker, S. (1998) 'Dialogue: Training for active citizenship.' *Therapeutic Communities 19*, 1, 41–53.

Introduction

Why We Need a Therapeutic Community
Approach to Care in the Community

Sarah Tucker

This volume explores Community Housing and Therapy's (CHT's) particular approach to working in Care in the Community with people diagnosed as severely mentally ill. CHT's way of working has its roots in the therapeutic community (TC) approach. In this introduction I frame CHT's approach to Care in the Community within the context of the TC approach. I argue that CHT's TC approach is one which is vitally needed to make a successful implementation of Care in the Community for those diagnosed as severely mentally ill.

I describe how the TC approach is essentially a socio-political one as opposed to an individualist approach. As such it takes as fundamental to an understanding of a person the relations between that person and others in their society. This is by contrast to an individualist approach which takes an understanding of a person to be possible in isolation from their fellows. I contrast the TC socio-political approach with the individualist medical approach and an individualist reading of Freudian psychoanalysis. I move on to argue that while Care in the Community is at root a socio-political policy and not an individualist one, nevertheless in the mental health field it is currently implemented in an individualist fashion. I suggest that this is why those involved experience fundamental problems with the implementation of the policy. I describe how what is needed is a socio-political approach to implementing Care in the Community. This is what CHT's TC approach to Care in the Community provides. With this ground prepared I then describe the underlying theoretical features of CHT's socio-political approach to implementing Care in the Community. Finally, I turn to an introduction to the contributions in this volume which together express the central facets of CHT's innovative TC approach to Care in the Community.

THE HISTORICAL TC APPROACH AS A SOCIO-POLITICAL APPROACH

The TC approach is fundamentally a socio-political approach in the sense that it takes as central a conception of a person whose essential identity is both dependent upon and in some way constituted by their relationships to others. The very person who I am is dependent on and constituted by the relationships I have had and do have with others – be they my family, friends, work colleagues, different social, political, sexual, cultural and racial groups, and so forth. I cannot help but be in responsive relationships to these others. The particular feelings and thoughts I have are dependent upon and constituted by the relationships I have with these others. For this reason I have a responsibility towards myself and others as a citizen.

This approach stands in sharp contrast to an individualist one which says that the essential nature of a person can exist quite independently of other people. The person who I am may depend, but does not necessarily depend, on my relationships to other people. I, the essential me, can exist completely independently of others.

The TC approach has its roots in two separate developments made in response to people suffering from emotional and psychological problems. Both developments have sought to give prominence to a socio-political approach to people rather than an exclusively individualistic one. One development resulted in the contemporary hospital TCs, the other arose out of the anti-psychiatry movement. I will briefly describe each in turn in order to clarify the ways in which the TC approach has grown out of a rejection of an individualist approach to people.

Following a form of 'moral treatment' developed at the Retreat and at various educational establishments for children that were set up in the 1930s, Maxwell Jones at Mill Hill and Tom Main with Bion and Foulkes at Northfields started to implement a TC approach in these hospitals during the Second World War. Tom Main went on to work at the Cassel Hospital and Maxwell Jones at the Henderson Hospital.

Bion echoes Aristotle's thesis that man is essentially a political group animal (Bion 1961), but it is perhaps Foulkes (1948) who gives the clearest exposition of the underlying social-political approach that motivated the work in these early TCs.[1] Foulkes says:

> For Freud, and for the majority of Analysts at the present day still, the social nature of man is a derivative from sexual love, or a reaction formation against incompatible destructive impulses. The infant is thought to be solipsistic, knowing nothing but his own instinctual urges, learning of the 'outside' world only by a painful trial and error method. (Foulkes 1948, p.10)

The view Foulkes attributes to Freud, and goes on to oppose, is individualistic in so far as it is one which allows that 'no psychological state...presupposes the existence of any individual other than the subject to whom that state is ascribed' (Putnam 1975, p.220).[2]

According to Foulkes, Freud's view is that it makes sense to think that we start off as beings whose constitution is completely independent of our relations with other people. It is only afterwards that we have to forge relationships with other people and the outside world. Certainly this view is expressed by Freud when he says:

> Consciousness makes each of us aware only of his own states of mind; that other people, too, possess a consciousness is an inference which we draw by analogy from their observable utterances and actions...the assumption of consciousness in them...rests on an inference and cannot share the immediate certainty which we have of our own consciousness. (Freud 1915, p.169)

Foulkes opposes this view, explaining that we must think of people as essentially constituted and determined, only in the context of the relations they bear to other people. He says:

> ...each individual – itself an artificial, though plausible, abstraction – is basically and centrally determined...by the world in which he lives, by the community, the group, of which he forms a part. (Foulkes 1948, p.10)

> He is part of a social network, a little nodal point, as it were, in this network and can only artificially be considered in isolation like a fish out of water. (Foulkes 1948, p.14)

For Foulkes, Freud's individualistic idea of an 'inner world' or mind, structured with an 'Id', 'Ego' and 'Super-ego', which can exist independently of (and must struggle to form a relationship with) the 'outer world', including other people, does not make sense. For him, the 'inner' and 'outer' are essentially interdependent. 'They at no stage can be separated from each other except by artificial isolation' (Foulkes 1948, p.10).

It is not only this individualistic reading of Freud's psychoanalytic approach which Foulkes rejects in favour of a socio-political one, but also by implication the biological or medical approach most often used in psychiatry. For this approach, too, has at its centre an individualistic conception of a person.

The medical approach is individualistic in the following way. Very basically, it takes the fundamental cause of our emotional and psychological states as they are manifested in the way we feel, think and behave to reside in the functioning of our brains. Thus the cause of mental illness is taken to be some form of malfunctioning of the brain, be this in the form of a deteriorating disease, a genetically determined neurodevelopment disorder or a chemical imbalance. Changing the functioning of the brain by chemical and/or physical intervention results in changes in our feelings, thoughts and behaviour. This is an individualist conception of a person because the fundamental cause of our mental states, and thus the nature of the interventions made in order to change them, is taken to be quite independent of the person's relationships to others. The person's brain, albeit the locus of our mental states, is, in principle, treated quite independently of the person's relationships to their family, friends, work colleagues and their place in society in general. Just as in Foulkes' reading of Freud's psychoanalysis there is an internal structure, the mind, which can be constituted quite independently of its relations to other people and the external world, so in the medical model there is an internal structure, the brain, which is similarly independent.

It is out of a socio-political theoretical framework that the hospital TCs grew. It is out of this context that, for example, the Henderson Hospital and the Cassel Hospital are committed to the following: that the treatment of patients in hospitals focus on relationships of responsibility between people; an attempt to understand the individual in the context of the underlying psychodynamics of the group; non-hierarchical relationships between staff and patients; staff and patients being open to learning from the experience of living and working together in work and therapy groups and in boundaried informal situations; an open culture of debate and inquiry (see Kennard 1998, p.114).

What emerges from this list is a clearly socio-political approach in the sense that the staff and client *group* is seen as a central tool in the therapy. Patients are seen as responsive and responsible people equal in personal status to staff, thus sowing the seeds of citizenship. The treatment is seen to be within the context of doing things together, be they practical, psychological or cerebral. This stands in sharp contrast to a model of treatment which takes the person as an individual, in principle separable from their social context.

The other development in which the TC approach has its roots is the anti-psychiatry movement which revolved around the work of R.D. Laing and others (see Cooper 1967; Laing 1967, 1971; Laing and Esterson 1964). They propose that what goes with an individualistic conception of a person, in the context of psychiatry, is the medical 'treatment of mentally ill' people. The chemical/physical, individualist intervention on the brain – designed to help change the person's feelings, thoughts and behaviour – is placed within a medical paradigm in which people with distressing, emotionally painful and unusual feelings, are treated by psychiatrists as *ill patients*. What the anti psychiatrists take to follow from this is that those suffering emotional distress are treated as inferior, in need and powerless. Further, their emotional states are treated as unwanted and socially unacceptable, to be repressed by medication while the people who have them are banished outside society within the walls of institutions. By being in the position of the 'ill person', emotionally distressed patients give up their integral power to the 'healthy' psychiatrists who take complete control over their lives – leaving the patients passive, stuck with their 'illness' and having their integral rights as citizens stripped from them. Medical *treatment* of the 'mentally ill' is seen to be a grossly immoral and political repression of people. It is thus that Laing says:

> The 'normally' alienated person, by reason of the fact that he acts more or less like everyone else, is taken to be sane. Other forms of alienation are those that are labeled by the 'normal' majority as bad or mad. (Laing 1967, p.24)

The anti-psychiatrists take this to be a political consequence of individualist medical treatment because in their view psychological distress is a social problem, rooted not in the individual but in society at large, in the relationships people have in their families and in the larger socio-political arena. According to them, once we take this seriously, we see that a person's relationships with others are constitutive of them. If this is so, then psychological distress will not be removed by treating the individual outside their social context, and indeed to do so is simply to ignore and even repress a response to dysfunctional relationships between people in families and society. They think that some psychotic states are an involuntary political protest to the ills of society. Thus, hiding that person in an institution and intervening with medication that acts on the individual without regard for their social context and which reduces the intensity of the psychosis is seen to be a political repression of a social problem.

Like Foulkes, the anti-psychiatrists oppose the individualistic detachment of 'inner' structures of the mind from the 'outer' world that they see as prevalent in both the medical model and Freud's psychoanalysis (see Laing 1967, pp.41–42). For them,

> the ground of being of all beings is the relation between them. The relationship is the 'is', the being of all things... (Laing 1967, p.36)

Later, Oakley describes the work of the Philadelphia Association, set up by Laing and others in 1965, as

> evoking the place of the between, thus dissolving the logic of inner and outer... (Oakley 1989a, p.4)

The motivation behind this socio-political approach is the idea that at the heart of being human is the fact that our experiences, thoughts, actions and speech have meaning and purpose (see Skolnick 1999, p.5). It is this meaning and purpose which cannot be accommodated by considering people in isolation, as in principle devoid of their relationships to others – for meaning is something which in principle requires a 'public' space where what is meant can be shared. What we mean, or what is meant, by our experiences, thoughts, actions and speech is not something that is determined 'inside' us, independently of our relations to others, it is not something 'internal' that we communicate by sending 'external' signals to others (see Oakley 1989b, p.121). Rather, it is something that is, at least partially, essentially determined and created by our relationships to each other.[3]

It was within this climate that the Philadelphia Association set up Kingsley Hall, a TC where schizophrenic people lived with others with as little structure as possible. It was a place where there were no staff to police people to behave in socially acceptable ways, a place where some people could guide others through a necessary inner journey back to their earliest experiences and back out again. Here people lived through the turmoil of their psychosis without any medical intervention to control their necessary, if painful, thoughts and experiences. This could be done, only in the context of the belief that these experiences had to do with the sorting out of relationships with others and that the schizophrenic and his others were all responsible to and for each other (see Cooper *et al.* 1989). In addition to the Philadelphia Association, the Site of Contemporary Psychoanalysis and Arbours are descendants of this approach.

Both the developments which have resulted in current hospital TCs and the anti-psychiatry movement are socio-political in the sense that they place as central the social relations that an individual has with others. They were led by different groups of people and at different times. They have resulted in distinct contemporary organizations. The deeper difference lies in their underlying theoretical approaches to the way in which we are to understand what it means to place as central the relations between people. This hinges on whether, in rejecting the individualist idea of an independent 'inner' mind, we completely reject the distinction of 'inner' and 'outer' altogether as senseless, or whether we hold on to this distinction but claim that they cannot be considered independently of each other. The former position is clearly endorsed by Oakley, who, as we have seen, wants to dissolve the logic of inner and outer. It is not fully endorsed by Foulkes. For while he does say on the one hand, 'the old juxtaposition of an inside and outside world…are untenable' (Foulkes 1948, p.10), he goes on to say the following:

> Indeed the family group…is precipitated in the innermost core of the human mind incorporated into the individual's growing ego and super-ego… (Foulkes 1948, p.20)

This suggests that he still holds on to the coherence of a discrete inner and outer world but maintains that they are interdependent. An examination of the respective coherence of these two socio-political views is beyond the scope of this introduction. The main aim here is to put into context the historical development of the TC approach as a broadly socio-political one.

It is this which motivates the TC view that 'interventions' or responses need to occur at the locus of our relationships with others: '[T]he TC is right at the interface of the social and the personal' (Hinshelwood 1987, p.15). It is from this that it follows that in TCs it is possible to give priority to sorting out the relations of responsibility between people. It is in this context that it is possible to break the hierarchical relationship between healthy worker and ill patients, given the recognition of the inherent responsibility we all have to ourselves and others. It is here that rather than being seen as attempting to cure a passive, lacking, ill patient, one can engage in a creative learning experience. It is here, in the context of a community of others, that one can begin to sort out the underlying complex psychodynamics of one's feelings and thoughts literally in relationship to the others in the community and in relationship to others in one's life and society at large. In the struggle to do so, painful emotional and mental states are permitted rather than constantly alleviated or suppressed the moment they arise.

CARE IN THE COMMUNITY AS A SOCIO-POLITICAL POLICY

It cannot help but make sense that Care in the Community, as it relates to the psychiatric services with the policy to treat people suffering psychological distress in the community, should have been motivated, at least in part, by a desire to include as a priority socio-political 'interventions' or responses to those people. Underlying this desire, there may have been a leaning towards a non-individualist socio-political conception of a person. This is because the policy of responding to psychiatric patients or those suffering from psychological distress in the context of the social community of other people, rather than in the exclusive confines of a hospital, reflects the following non-individualist socio-political ideas. The general thesis is that integrating psychologically distressed people with other people and being part of a larger social group is of some value, both for the distressed and the other people. That working out one's relationships with others in the context of others is of value. That these people as citizens have the right to access housing and employment in the way that any other citizens do. That the mentally ill or psychologically distressed should not be excluded and ostracized from the rest of society, that their relationships with the rest of society are in some way important. That these people are anyway by rights equally part of the larger group of society both in the sense that they are at some level responsible for themselves and in the sense that society is responsible for them.

These things seem to be confirmed in the recent White Paper, which says: 'The proposals will support welfare reform and *social inclusion*' (White Paper 1999, p.9, my italics). In relation to this, Anthony Giddens explains:

> Inclusion refers...to citizenship, to the civil and political rights and obligations that all members of society should have, not just formally but as a reality of their lives. It also refers to opportunities and to involvement in public space...access to work is one main context of opportunity. Education is another... (Giddens 1998, pp.102–103)

I think it is clear from the above the ways in which Care in the Community as it relates to the psychiatric services cannot help but be, at least in part, a non-individualist socio-political response to people in psychological distress. The policy would not make sense at all if there were not some belief underlying it that placing people in the community of others was of some value and this is a socio-political belief. For the policy to make any sense,

> The political climate needs to be an enabling one with general unanimity about the values of integration, community, *other-directedness* and altruism... For the U.K. none of these conditions have existed for the last two decades. (Carrier and Kendall 1997, pp.3–4, my italics)

I now turn to an explanation of why none of these socio-political conditions have existed over the last two decades.

THE INDIVIDUALIST IMPLEMENTATION OF CARE IN THE COMMUNITY

It may seem paradoxical that while Care in the Community is wedded to a socio-political ideology, in practice the policy, in many respects, is being implemented in line with an individualist approach and conception of a person. I will describe some of the ways in which this individualist implementation is manifesting itself before identifying what I take to be the cause of this paradoxical situation.

In Care in the Community there is an emphasis placed on individual care plans. Care managers and key workers think about the individual and make plans for them which ideally look at various aspects of the individual's life. However, the emphasis on the individual by its very nature does not reflect a commitment to taking seriously the functioning of the group of others the person has been with, is with now and may want to be with in the future. The emphasis on the individual does not reflect the fact that the person is living in the community.

This is reflected in the recent White Paper in which there are repeated references to 'the individual' without reference to the individual's relations to others in the community. For example, we read that 'Services should meet each individual's specific needs' (White Paper 1999, p.8) and about 'tailoring services to the needs of the individual' (White Paper 1999, p.13). While these references are perhaps well motivated in the sense that they aim at moving away from providing services where 'one size fits all' (White Paper 1999, p.8), even with this motivation it seems to me that they speak of the implementation of an essentially socio-political policy, Care in the Community, in an individualist fashion. This is compounded by the repeated references to 'promoting [people's] independence' (White Paper 1999, p.14) and 'encouraging those who are helped to do what they can for themselves' (White Paper 1999, p.13).

Again, no reference is made at all to people doing things for themselves with the support of other people living in the community. No reference is made to what it would mean for a person to become independent of state support by coming to understand their place in their community or finding a role in the context of others. The equation seems to be that either individuals are dependent on the state or they are independent of it, and the aim is to promote independence of it. Nowhere is there any indication of what it would mean for someone to live in the community in the context of others and to depend on those others for their sense of themselves.

Indeed, we go on to read:

> Promoting independence should not…be at the expense of effective and safe services. In particular, in mental health services people have suffered in the past as a result of being left too much to look after themselves…the Government Strategy for developing safe, sound, supportive mental health services…will aim to promote, health, well being and safety of individuals and the safety of the wider community. (White Paper 1999, p.20)

Here we see that according to the White Paper, the price of 'independence' for people with mental health problems is their safety and the safety of the community who need to be protected from them. If, in line with the underlying theoretical socio-political framework of Care in the Community, 'independence' here meant independent of the state but involved and interdependent with the community in which one lived, perhaps we would not take so much for granted this passion for protecting the community from people with mental health problems.

Whether the media creates or reflects the community's response to those who have been placed in their care by this policy, there is certainly an enormous amount of public anxiety about the risks of having psychiatric patients living freely amongst them. The fact that the tragic fatal cases get so much media attention, while the ongoing quiet lives of many people living as part of Care in the Community receive no attention, is not surprising. However, it does seem to reflect an underlying attitude that psychiatric patients in general are ill, irresponsible and dangerous people who need to be controlled and if possible excluded from everyday society and put back into secure units. The attitude seems to be that where there is a problem, it lies in the psychiatric patient and not in their social relationships with others, and certainly not with the community's response to them. This individualist attitude has led to an implementation of Care in the Community with an individualist emphasis on providing enough secure places for dangerous people and a tightening up on the controlling powers of the Mental Health Act in order to contain the public anxiety and to control the cause of their anxiety rather than an emphasis on changing the community's response.

What lies at the bottom of this paradox of a socio-political policy which seems to be being implemented in an individualist way? It is *not* the fact that an integral part of the implementation of the policy involves, as it does, the *prescription of medication* to people by psychiatrists. Rather, it is the *medical culture*, the particular social and political *attitudes* towards those to whom the medication is prescribed, those of the healthy doctor and ill patient, which guide the individualist implementation of Care in the Community. That is, it is not, as the anti-psychiatrists seemed to suggest, the fact that medication is prescribed and this constitutes a response or intervention at the level of the biological individual that *necessarily* means that a predominately or exclusively individualist approach is being or must be taken. Rather, it is the social, cultural and political *attitudes* of treating disturbed people as ill individuals who need to be cured and excluded, and so forth, that have characteristically accompanied the individualist intervention with medication, that hijack the socio-political implementation of Care in the Community.

The medical culture is an individualist one and it is this culture which in my view dominates the implementation of Care in the Community. The prescription and taking of medication, while being an intervention at the individualist level rather than at the interface between the person in question and the rest of society, need not in and of itself mean that we take an individualist paradigm as guiding or basic in our overall response to psychologically distressed people in Care in the Community. I will now explain these points in more detail.

The use of medication is an intervention at an individualist level because it acts on the brain and not at the point of social and political contact between the person in question and other people. However, responding to a person in this way at a physical or biological level does not exclude, and is indeed perfectly compatible with, a socio-political approach to that person. The fact that we have bodies, that we are biological organisms, does not exclude the idea that we need to also understand ourselves as social beings in terms of the concepts constitutive of relationships with other people. The biological and socio-political paradigms may not be reducible one to the other but this does not entail that they are not dependent on each other or at least interconnected in complex ways. What is important is that the prescription and use of medication is done within the context of a reflective socio-political approach. That is, that it is done with the focus being on the person in the context of their social and political relationships with others rather than the focus being simply on removing that individual's pain from other people. I believe the important place of medication in Care in the Community resides in the former context.

Medical care in the form of medication is not responsible for the apparently individualist implementation of Care in the Community. However, the idea that in providing medical care, in prescribing medication, the healthy professionals are treating ill people who are in some way lacking, who are incapable, is, I believe, responsible for this style of implementation of the policy. This is because, as I have described, treating someone as ill locates the perceived problem in them alone, outside the context of the socio-political arena.

That the individualist medical culture is still predominant in implementing the socio-political Care in the Community is perhaps not surprising given the long history of medical culture in response to people with mental health problems.[4]

Further, this culture may

> reflect the *anxiety* of some professionals concerning the trend toward demedicalisation of the new system of care, and the narrowing role of professionals such as psychiatric nurses and psychiatrists. (Leff 1997, pp.208–209, my italics)

THE NEED FOR THE TC APPROACH IN CARE IN THE COMMUNITY

Whatever the reason for the individualist implementation of Care in the Community, what we need to do, in order to implement Care in the Community with the non-individualist socio-political approach that it ideologically promises, is precisely to re-emphasize that socio-political approach to people in practice. We need to shift the emphasis away from the implementation of an individualist *treatment* of ill patients that continues to captivate psychiatric health professionals (though as I have explained it need not do so) towards the socio-political *approach* to people who are emotionally and psychologically disturbed. It is this theoretical stance that motivates the work of CHT in its implementation of an innovative TC approach to Care in the Community. It is the various aspects of this innovative approach that are presented and explored in this volume.

CHT'S CONTEMPORARY TC APPROACH TO CARE IN THE COMMUNITY

By way of an introduction to the explorations and illustrations of our approach to working with people with mental health and emotional difficulties in the community, I shall present a brief account of the four fundamental themes which underlie it. These are: dialogue, dwelling, care and community. I highlight the way in which we understand each of these themes to reflect a particular kind of socio-political conception of a person. In this way I intend to show how our approach has both grown out of the foundations of the historical TC approach and also represents a vital and innovative stance towards working in the field of Care in the Community.

Dialogue

Dialogue is the spoken word between people. However, dialogue is not any old spoken word that is apparently carried out between people. For example, when someone 'talks at you' without any regard for whether you want to hear what the person is saying (that is, without regard for you) no contact is being made and we would not want to call this dialogue between people. Rather, it is a one-sided monologue. Again, two people may exchange words on a daily basis without ever making any real contact; their words do not reach each other. This is another example of talk or conversation where there is no dialogue *between* the people. True dialogue between people is a fundamental theme underlying CHT's approach to working with people with mental health and emotional difficulties in the community because it provides the medium through which we can begin to make sense of our chaotic, often unconscious, inner lives. It involves response, responsibility, active participation and it provides the basis for education.

The spoken word: Unconscious and conscious language

Dialogue takes place in the spoken word, in language. However, so often our struggle to engage, to become involved, to become agents and to understand ourselves, others and our environment comes in the form of apparently dislocated actions or is spoken in a way which we cannot immediately make sense of. That is, our questions do not always come ready formulated and articulated in an easy to understand spoken dialogue. While we can make sense of our conscious language (and it is in this conscious language that dialogue takes place), these dislocated actions and speech which it is difficult to make sense of are a manifestation of our unconscious language. Often our questions come untranslated from our unconscious language. In our everyday lives we are all constantly faced with the task of translating into conscious language, and thus making sense of, underlying unconscious questions in our interactions with ourselves and others. The process of translation involves finding the underlying questions being asked behind why Jo suddenly flared up in anger at me during the dinner party, why Sue sat in silence throughout the counselling session, why Phil tells me on a daily basis that there is no milk in the fridge, why Fiona gets frightened and believes that agents in cars and street lamps are controlled to see into her mind.

In a sense some dialogues begin outside conscious language and sometimes outside the spoken word altogether. Indeed silence invites us to inquire into the question, the demand that the silent person is unconsciously making. However, it is only in the spoken conscious word, in dialogue, that we can begin to translate the questions asked in the unconscious language into our conscious one. It is only by attempting to do this translation that we can begin to understand and learn about ourselves and to respond in real dialogue to others.

Lacan says:

> ...psychoanalysis has only a single medium: the patient's speech...there is
> no speech without reply, even if it is met by silence, provided it has an
> auditor: this is the heart of its function in psychoanalysis. (Lacan 1977,
> p.40)

In our use of dialogue we follow Lacan with the idea that the unconscious is
structured like a language and is in some sense a language, albeit one that needs
translating. Moreover, we follow him in the idea that it is in language, only in
speech with others, even with its essential punctuations with silence, that the
client creates a meaning out of their experiences, thoughts, actions and words.
It is at the interface between the client and those others that this happens,
because it is only, in principle, in relation to others that words, or silence, can
have meaning. Dialogue forms the heart of our socio-political approach (see
Lacan 1981, pp.74–78).

Response and responsibility

When there is true dialogue between people, each person is 'seen', understood
and acknowledged by the other. What emerges from this is a meeting between
the people at a deep level. When someone speaks to you, honestly from their
centre, having discarded their defences, they are calling to you to respond to
them at a profound human level. They are calling out for you to recognize them
and their particular way of struggling to exist in their everyday lives. When
someone calls out to you in this way it is impossible not to respond, and it is
here that a meeting between you and that person can take place. By responding
to that person you enter into dialogue with them. Meeting the other person by
responding to their call carries a further significance because, in so doing, one
finds that one cannot help but be in a relation of responsibility to the other
person. Once one has responded, one has taken responsibility for the other. It is
in this sense that dialogue involves response and responsibility between people.

Buber said that when a person is really living in dialogue, making dialogue
the basis and centre of their life rather than having momentary conversations
with people, then they feel themselves approached, as it were, for an answer.
One feels this approach in the ordinary course of the day if one is really living in
dialogue. Further, living in dialogue means that one's being receives a harsh but
strong sense of reciprocity, even in moments of extreme dereliction. A life lived
like this stands in fundamental contrast to a life lived in monologue, for when
one lives in monologue one is utterly unable to grope out over the outlines of
oneself, even in moments of tenderness and intimacy (see Buber 1965, p.20).

Following Buber (see also Buber 1937) and Levinas (1969, 1978, 1982),
we take as primitive the ethical relation between people as it is manifested in
dialogical response and responsibility. For these thinkers, this ethical relation-

ship is irreducible and basic. It is not a derivative of a metaphysical Cartesian, solipsistic self who has to forge relationships with the outer world. Rather, this intersubjective ethical relationship is constitutive of a fully authentic human life. In this way, working with this aspect of dialogue forms a further basis for our socio-political approach in which we take it that people cannot be taken outside the context of their relations to others.

Active participation

Plato's Socratic dialogues reflect his view that philosophy is an active ongoing pursuit and inquiry. When we engage with Plato's dialogues we learn that dialogue not only means responding to and being responsible for *others* but also means being responsible for *oneself* in the sense that it essentially involves active participation. For, dialogues begin with questions, be they about oneself, others or the environment around one. In dialogues, these questions get provisional answers as we search to make sense of the questions. These provisional answers in turn lead to further questions. When one asks questions about oneself, others or the environment, one begins to open out the bases upon which one has previously lived one's life and one begins to take responsibility for one's own degree of understanding. In this way, in dialogue, one becomes an agent in the world who moves out of a passive acceptance, disinterest or even rejection of engagement with ourselves, others and the environment. One moves towards an active involvement with a sense of one's own agency.

Education

It is because dialogues take place between people and essentially involve active participation that dialogue is the primary medium for education – the starting point for learning is precisely being able to take an interest in oneself, others or the environment in a way that allows us to become involved in thinking about and understanding these things. We begin to do this when we are able to open out questions and provide provisional answers. Education via dialogue involves taking active responsibility for one's own learning by being able to engage in questions. It does not involve passive learning by rote from an authoritative teacher who is presented as holding a body of official knowledge. This kind of education does not engage students in real understanding – it leaves them only able to regurgitate ready formulated facts. This kind of education does not involve dialogue between teacher and student.

Following Buber (1965), we have developed a 'dialogical' model of education which essentially involves the development of a relation between the student and the teacher. No education can take place when the student is in effect by himself or herself in solitude. Education via dialogue involves the teacher and the student in open inquiry, *together*, where the teacher's skill is the ability both to open out questions and contain the inquiry for the student, rather than to transmit official knowledge. As Heidegger says:

> If the relation between teacher and the taught is genuine...there is never a place for the sway of the authority of the know-it-all or the authoritative sway of the official. (Heidegger 1968, p.15)

Education via dialogue involves an experiential apprenticeship of student to teacher where the student learns, by being in dialogue with the teacher, how to engage in an ongoing active inquiry about themselves, others and their environment.

Dwelling

Heidegger says:

> [H]uman being consists in dwelling and, indeed, dwelling in the sense of the *stay* of mortals on earth. (Heidegger 1971, p.149)

For him, dwelling is a way of being in the world, a way which characterizes our stay in the world. This way of being is *being-with* both our physical environment and the community of other people around us. This being-with is something we need to learn to do (Heidegger 1971, p.161). However, we do not start from a solipsistic, Cartesian position of isolation, completely out of contact with the world and other people and having to forge a relation of being-with from this position. Rather, we start *right in* the world of things and other people. We already dwell in the world, in relation to our environment and others. It is just that, on the whole, in our everyday lives we dwell inauthentically. The relation we have to our environment is one of disregard, lack of concern, and withdrawal, even alienation, concealing our true desires. What we have to learn to do is dwell authentically, and this involves forming a relation of involvement and concern for our physical and social environments. We have to learn to be fully engaged with our environments to 'protect, cherish, preserve and cultivate' them (Heidegger 1971, p.147).

This learning to dwell, to stay and be with our physical and social environments, is something that both therapists and clients at CHT are committed to. This is not only because so many of our clients seem to have lost or forgotten their physical and social dwelling place in the world, but also because the locus of learning to dwell is right at the point *in between* the individual and the world of things and people around them. The belief that we are all already right in the world, dwelling, is precisely what provides meaning to our lack of concern, our inability to dwell in the world with others when that occurs. It is only by placing ourselves intrinsically in the context of our environments that absence of involvement and concern can be meaningful. We believe that the absence of concern – the loss of the ability to dwell – that so often characterizes our clients, does have a meaning. This meaning is precisely expressed in the relationship clients have with their environment and other people. It is within our communities that this meaning can begin to be translated into language and clients can move on to learn to dwell with concern. The essentially contextual nature of dwelling as a way of being, promoted by Heidegger, provides a further tenet of our socio-political approach.

Physical location and physical dwelling

Dwelling in a physical place is much more than simply being physically located in that place. Dwelling in one's room, house, flat or tent involves more than simply putting oneself inside the four walls, the bricks and mortar or canvas. To dwell in a place it is not enough to put oneself in a particular physical space and environment. Certainly, in order to dwell in a room it is necessary to physically be within the four walls of the room; but, further, one has to form a *relationship* to the four walls of the room and the space they contain.

Depending on how much of oneself is engaged with the physical place, one can dwell more or less fully. The more one allows oneself to impinge upon the four walls and bricks and mortar, the more fully one dwells in that place. A person cannot fully dwell in a place unless their relationship with it has become an expression of themselves. Further, one's relationship to one's physical context is an integral part of *becoming* one's true self. On the one hand, the extent to which a person fully dwells in their physical environment depends on how much of himself or herself they are willing or able to put into that environment. On the other hand, one cannot be, or attempt to find oneself, without allowing oneself to be open to, and influenced by, the physical environment.

The more a person is involved in building, constructing, repairing, designing, decorating, choosing colours, furnishings, pictures, objects, arranging furnishing and objects within the physical space, and the more they mark or put themselves into their living space, the deeper is the relationship they form with the physical place and the more fully they dwell in that place. Further, the way in which they choose to do these things is an expression of themselves. The sparsity and tidiness or the clutteredness and chaotic nature of their arrangements is an important part of the relationship they form with the living space. Someone who is homeless, who has no place to dwell, is excluded from forming an integral relationship to their living space and excluded from making choices about self-expression in that space. They are dislocated from their physical environment in more than a literal sense, for they have their liberty to articulate themselves in relation to place curtailed.

A person's physical house provides literal shelter from the elements, but their physical dwelling with its walls delimiting a boundary between their space and that outside, further provides a symbolic refuge or asylum in which they can nurture and create themselves. This is one of the fundamental ways in which the physical environment influences acts and impinges upon us. Without a physical shelter we remain too impervious and vulnerable to begin to develop our essential being. Only within a shelter can we do so and from there conversely develop an active relationship with that physical shelter and begin to dwell in it.

Social location and social dwelling

In addition to forming an integral relationship with one's physical living space, dwelling also has a social aspect to it. Dwelling amongst other people, one's family, one's circle of friends, at work or in society at large as a citizen means finding one's place amongst other people. It means finding a position amongst others in which what one says and what one does has meaning. Just as in order to dwell in a physical location it is not enough simply to put oneself in a particular physical space and environment (one has to form a *relationship* to that environment), so too in order to dwell amongst other people, in order to find one's place amongst others, it is not enough simply to, as it were, 'put oneself near' other people, as one does, for example, when one lives in a densely populated city. Indeed, living in close proximity to other people is neither necessary nor sufficient for dwelling amongst others. Essentially, dwelling amongst others involves forming relationships with others, and one can live in isolation or in a sparsely populated area and sustain important social, employment and political relationships with others either by infrequent face-to-face but rich contact interspersed by longer periods of intense thought and reflection in relation to those others, or interspersed by contact by letter, telephone, fax or e-mail.

The more a person is able to engage in relation to others, the more fully they dwell in relation to them in the sense of having a meaningful place in the context of which to exist. On the one hand, the extent to which one fully dwells in one's social environment depends on how much of oneself one is willing or able to put into that environment. On the other hand, one cannot be, or attempt to find oneself, without allowing oneself to be open to, and influenced by, one's social environment.

The more a person is involved in building, constructing, leaving and repairing relationships with others, in choosing friends, lovers, organizations with whom to work and people with whom to pursue creative, physical, emotional, leisure and political interests within their social environment, and the more they create a meaningful place for themselves, and the deeper are the relationships they form with their social dwelling.

Someone who is isolated from others, struggling in their loneliness to find a way to form relationships with others, has no place to dwell in the sense that they are unable to find their meaningful place amongst others, a place in which they can both respond to others but also take measure of themselves in relation to others. We need to be in relation to others, to construct our ways of interpreting and struggling to understand others, in order to have a place in which to interpret and struggle to give meaning to ourselves and in order to grasp a sense of ourselves as discrete beings. At a basic level, my separateness from you would not make sense except as a feature I have in relation to you. As Heidegger says:

> Indeed the loss of rapport…that occurs in states of depression would be wholly impossible if even such a state were not what it is as a human state: that is a staying with things. Only if the stay already characterises human being can the things among which we are also *fail* to speak to us, *fail* to concern us any longer. (Heidegger 1971, p.157)

Care

Care as the craft of involvement

Being able to care means being able to engage with the world around us, including other people. We need to be able to be moved to engage with the world. We will not care in the sense of being engaged if we are not interested. Being able to be interested enough to engage with the world involves, to start with, being able to perceive the world, including other people, with enough precision and in enough detail to find some part, aspect or quality which inspires us to grasp hold of it. Many of our clients do not seem to care when they arrive at our communities in the sense that, despite intermittent and florid thoughts and actions, they appear disengaged. This is manifested in a blank stare, the smearing of sugar on the kitchen counter, the desire to spend days endlessly sitting alone with nothing to do, the shutting away of others by retreating to inauthentic solitude or actions which alienate them. It is as if the world and other people have become an unarticulated blur, as if there is nothing to catch hold of with which to engage. There is nothing to show concern or care for. It is through dialogue with clients – the opening out of questions – that therapists work with clients to help them to perceive the world with enough articulation for them to be able to re-engage with it and thus to care.

Care as 'being-alongside'

For Heidegger, 'Dasein's Being reveals itself as care' (Heidegger 1962, section 182). As with dwelling, care is a way of being. Indeed, in order to dwell authentically one has to dwell with concern or care for one's environment. One has to learn to 'be-alongside' the world and other people. Again, it is not that we start outside the world, out of relation to it and then have to build interest and concern in order to 'be-alongside' it, in order to care. We are already in the world, in relation to it, but we have to learn to really be with it, in relation to it, alongside it. For Heidegger, this starts with the ability to 'be-towards' our physical environment in a practical way. This involves crafting a reciprocal relationship with objects by finding the qualities they have with which to be creative, in the way that the carpenter does with wood and tools. The same craft is involved in relation to other people. Here the 'tool' is dialogue and the material our responses to each other's actions and speech. Learning to care is about learning to do something new, or different, at the interface between oneself and the world of things and other people. As such it forms a further tenet of our socio-political approach.

Care as active

Learning the craft of care is something we do largely experientially by apprenticeship to others. In one sense, clients who come to our communities are apprentices of the craft of care. So, for us, care is not something which therapists do to or for passive, helpless, ill people. Such a notion of care is not applicable in the context of our communities because it involves a certain reification of the person for whom others perform tasks. Rather, for us, care is something which each of us needs to actively engage in. So, at CHT, we care *for* our clients only by helping them to learn to care *themselves* in the context of the community of others.

Community

In a sense, community is everything which dialogue, dwelling and care create. It is what is created when a person takes seriously the fact that making sense of themselves and finding meaning in their life occurs in dialogue at the point of contact between themselves and others. It is what is created when a person takes seriously the fact that meaning in principle requires a context of other people. It is what is created when a person is mindful of the active response to, and responsibility for, others that engaging in dialogue between themselves and others involves. It is what is created when a person engages in dwelling, in being-with and finding his place amongst others. It is what is created when a person learns to take enough care to be-alongside others, when he learns to live actively with concern for others. In this sense, community is 'life lived towards one another' (Buber 1965, p.31). However, community is also something over and above these things.

Community as commitment to struggle together

> The feeling of community...reigns where the fight that is fought takes place from the point of a community struggling for its own reality as a community. (Buber 1965, p.31)

What creates membership of a community, what binds a group of individuals together and creates a sense of belonging, is a commitment to struggle together. The struggle may be between the community and people or circumstances outside it or, importantly, it may be *amongst* the people who form the community. What makes me part of a community is my commitment to deal with, stay with and engage with, often difficult, feelings towards other individuals in it or the whole group I find myself in. I may do more household chores than anyone else and then resent it. What makes me part of my community is being able to struggle with both my apparent desire to do more than others and my feelings of discomfort when I fulfil this apparent desire. I may find myself drawn to someone in the group who ignores me. What makes both of us part of the community is our ability to struggle with this situation in the context of the rest of the group.

The real struggle which binds individuals in a group together is a commitment on the part of each person to open their hitherto concealed self, both to others and in so doing to themselves. This is something a person can do only in the context of others with an equal commitment, for it is only by risking taking a 'step out' in relation to another that one can discover what it is one has hitherto concealed from oneself. A community of people is not fundamentally constituted by things or attributes they have in common, but rather by a common attitude of commitment to, as it were, have dealings with one another, in all their diversity. In essence, a commitment not to turn their backs on what they find in themselves and others. This struggle to be oneself with others is indeed a struggle, but when there is a real commitment to it, then there is a community.

It is this sense of community which shapes our socio-political approach to working with our clients in our therapeutic communities. It is perhaps each client's courage to make the commitment to struggle with others during their stay with us that provides the bedrock of their passage towards change. It is this courage which underlies the therapeutic nature of our communities.

However, it is perhaps this sense of community that is absent in 'the Community' into which people with mental health problems have been 'released'. A person with mental health problems, living in 'the Community', needs to be committed to struggle with themselves in relation to all those others who do not have a psychiatric diagnosis, both on a practical level in terms of finding housing and employment or finding a way of being in the world without employment, and on an emotional level in terms of finding a place in relation to the rest of the community. But the struggle cannot be a one-way street: each person in 'the Community' needs to enter into an equally difficult struggle to deal with themselves in relation to people with mental health problems. It is for this reason that CHT communities have Project Action Committees specifically aimed at creating dialogue with 'the Community'.

CHT's TC approach to Care in the Community places as fundamental our clients' relations to others by focusing on dialogue, learning to dwell and care, and creating a commitment to struggle with others. We believe that it is these things which should constitute the core of an *implementation* of Care in the Community. Indeed, it is these things which make central the socio-political approach to people promised by the *ideology* of Care in the Community but which is currently implemented in an individualist fashion.

INTRODUCING THE CONTRIBUTIONS

In the contributions which follow, each author explores one or more of the central themes (dialogue, dwelling, care and community) which underlie CHT's TC and essentially socio-political approach to Care in the Community. Thus, together, the contributions unfold the web of interconnections that lie between these central themes. Each author illustrates their theoretical exposition and examination of CHT's approach with clinical case examples. (Where client material has been referred to names, places and other details have been changed to ensure anonymity.) In this way the contributors strive to illustrate the ways in which staff at CHT put the approach into practice. On the whole, the contributors implicitly assume the historical TC literature and take the work of Lacan, Heidegger, Buber and Levinas as their explicit starting point. These thinkers are less often associated with TC work and our aim has been to endeavour both to strengthen the underlying TC theory and to create new avenues for exploration.

In Chapter 1 John Gale discusses some of the ways in which a community is constituted by the word. He argues that meaning is always situated in a community and that by being in a community meaning is uncovered for clients. For Gale, it is because a TC is a community constructed by language that participation in a TC is privately about speech. Gale considers the place of silence in the language of TC practice and suggests that the 'full word' calls for a 'full silence'. Moreover he argues that it is only from a 'full silence' that a client can begin to respond responsibly. This response can be aided by a style of interpretation which disrupts meaning rather than just uncovering meaning.

In Chapter 2 Clare Saxon develops the connection between dialogue and community by looking at the various ways in which we use time in our work with clients to create intersubjective meaning and thereby dialogue between people. She emphasizes the way in which we work with time in our communities to enable clients to speak about their true desires for themselves and in relation to others. Saxon carefully illustrates how two aspects of time can be used to create meaning between people. First, she explains how structuring time provides punctuation in our lives. This punctuation is essential if we are to begin to make sense of ourselves: just as a text without punctuation is either meaningless or ambiguous in meaning, so too spending time without any structure involves living a life which has either no meaning or an ambiguous one which we cannot grasp. With illustrations of fixed ending times for groups, individual sessions and assessment periods, the overall educational programme, reviews, care plans and open-ended termination times for placements, Saxon looks at the various ways in which we use structure and time in our communities to create punctuation and thus meaning for our clients. She goes on to look at the interconnections between our experiences of past, present and future, illustrating the ways in which we work with clients to shift from awaiting the future to anticipating it and illustrating the ways in which we work with clients to shift away from repeating the past to remembering it. She looks at the significance of learning to translate one's unconscious language into a conscious spoken language in making these shifts. She explains how both these shifts create a space for clients to initiate dialogue in relation to others as active agents in their own lives.

In Chapter 3 Kirsty Handover introduces the connection between being able to dwell in physical place and being able to engage in dialogue in a way which is fundamental to creating the kind of meaning which inspires and motivates us to want to engage with our lives. Handover argues that the ability to truly dwell in one's physical environment, and the ability to care about it and engage with it in detail, is an ability which goes a long way towards providing responses to some of the underlying existential questions – about the point of existing – that clients implicitly or explicitly ask staff and each other in our communities. Handover also explores the idea that the ability to ask and respond to questions is central to active citizenship and dialogue. With case studies of task-orientated work groups such as cleaning groups, gardening groups and maintenance groups, as well as ongoing informal work with clients in relation to their environment, Handover illustrates how therapists at CHT work with clients to teach them to dwell in their physical environment. She explains how through practical work with clients in relation to the physical environment therapists help clients to find responses to their existential questions and thus engage in dialogue.

In Chapter 4 Anne Salway develops the theme of the significance of physical dwelling by concentrating on a particular aspect of the relationship between it and community. She unfolds the sense in which physical place stands for self in relation to others. She argues that the physical TC represents a non-static place between solitude and communion, and this she calls the hyphen ground. This, she suggests, is a place where clients are able to begin to confront their spiritual dimension. Salway provides a rich illustration of her ideas with descriptions of her drama therapy sessions in one of our communities.

In Chapter 5 Emma Smith introduces the theme of care in relation to dialogue in the sense of active participation. Smith explores what is meant by care in the context of our communities. She explains that at CHT care is not something that staff do to passive clients but rather, for us, care is an ability to be engaged and involved actively and in detail with oneself, others and one's environment. This active participation is shown to be connected with dialogue between people. Care is something which staff teach clients to do for themselves. Smith goes on to explore the sense in which care, in this active and involved sense, is an essential part of living a fully human life and illustrates her contribution with a case study of a community meeting in one of our communities.

In Chapter 6 Kirsty Handover develops the theme of care in relation to dwelling, this time in a community of other people. She explores the sense in which helping our clients to care is in a sense a cure and goes on to look at the way in which by learning to care, clients find their social dwelling amongst others. She suggests that for a person to find their true desires they must penetrate the disguises they have constructed for themselves and others, and that this requires dwelling in a community of others – it is only within the context of others that these disguises have been constructed and can be brought to a person's awareness. Handover illustrates how therapists work with clients to enable them to find a place to dwell amongst others by describing her work in an art therapy group run in one of our communities.

In Chapter 7 Anne Salway develops the theme of dialogue and its connection to community by concentrating on the educational basis of dialogue. Salway gives importance to the role of music and poetry as routes towards true dialogue, and with reference to the parable of the sower she unfolds the way in which engaging in real dialogue is in essence educational. Moreover, Salway suggests that what furnishes dialogue, as a means to education, with meaning is the fact that it requires an interdependence of responses between people. She emphasizes the importance of reciprocity and responsibility between people as an integral part of creating an environment for learning in CHT's TCs, and contrasts this with the constant pull from current Care in the Community policy towards isolated 'independent living'. Salway illustrates how therapists at CHT use dialogue to create educational TCs both inside and outside our communities. She provides a case example of a discussion group after supper in one community, and case examples of a CHT 'Project Action Committee' set up to create educational dialogue between our communities and the local community beyond.

In Chapter 8 Nadia Al-Khudhairy turns to recent innovative developments in CHT's implementation of the TC approach to Care in the Community. Via an examination of both the apparently disintegrated reality of contemporary urban communities and the changing meaning of 'community', she suggests that what is central to a community is not geographical proximity but rather an openness and commitment between people, wherever they live, to struggle together. On these grounds she argues that a dispersed scheme consisting of individual flats can provide a strong complement to 'group living' provision in the implementation of a TC approach to Care in the Community. Al-Khudhairy illustrates her contribution with a description of 'Home Base', CHT's new dispersed TC for homeless ex-service men and women. While Home Base provides a model for future development of the TC approach, Al-Khudhairy is mindful of the tradition of the early military TC at Northfields.

NOTES

1   Rawlinson (1999) provides a recent discussion of Foulkes's ideas in relation to TCs.

2   The individualist view Foulkes attributes to Freud is essentially Cartesian. This particular theoretical position has been, and is, widely discussed in the contemporary philosophical literature. Putnam, from whom this definition of the view is taken, names the view 'methodological solipsism'. For a clear and detailed discussion for these issues and their relation to psychoanalysis see Cavell (1993).

3   This anti-individualist or anti-Cartesian line of thought has characterized the work of many philosophers this century. Some commentators of Wittgenstein's 'Private Language Argument' (Wittgenstein 1953) would attribute such a view to him. See Cavell (1993, pp.22–24) for a discussion of this in the context of psychoanalysis.

4   Maxwell Jones speaks about the culture where 'the doctor plays God'. He says: 'I am not attacking the medical profession, I'm attacking the way they are trained…they are trained to be dominant' (Jones 1985, p.23). I am speaking about the medical *culture.*

REFERENCES

Bion, W.R. (1961) *Experiences in Groups.* London: Tavistock.

Buber, M. (1937) *I and Thou.* Edinburgh: T & T Clark.

Buber, M. (1965) *Between Man and Man.* New York: Macmillan.

Carrier, J. and Kendall, I. (1997) 'Evolution of policy.' In J. Leff (ed) *Care in the Community: Illusion or Reality?* Chichester: John Wiley.

Cavell, M. (1993) *The Psychoanalytic Mind: From Freud to Philosophy.* Cambridge, MA, and London: Harvard University Press.

Cooper, D. (1967) *Psychiatry and Anti-Psychiatry.* London: Tavistock.

Cooper, R. Friedman, J., Gans, S., Heaton, J.M., Oakley, C., Oakley, H. and Zeal, P. (1989) 'Beginnings.' In R. Cooper (ed) *Thresholds between Philosophy and Psychoanalysis: Papers from the Philadelphia Association.* London: Free Association Books.

Foulkes, S.H. (1948) *Introduction to Group Analytic Psychotherapy.* William Heinemann Medical Books. Reprinted 1991. London: Maresfield Library.

Freud, S. (1915) 'The Unconscious.' In J. Strachey (ed) *The Standard Edition of the Complete Psychological Works of Sigmund Freud,* Vol. XIV. London: Hogarth Press and the Institute of Psychoanalysis.

Giddens, A. (1998) *The Third Way: The Renewal of Social Democracy*. Cambridge: Polity Press.

Heidegger, M. (1964) *What is Called Thinking.* (second edition) (trans. J. Glenn Gray). New York: Harper and Row..

Heidegger, M. (1962) *Being and Time* (trans. J. Macquarrie and E. Robinson). Oxford: Basil Blackwell.

Heidegger, M. (1971) *Poetry, Language, Thought* (trans. A. Hofstadter). New York: Harper and Row.

Hinshelwood, R.D. (1987) *What Happens in Groups: Psychoanalysis, the Individual and the Community*. London: Free Association Books.

Jones, M. (1985) 'Society and the therapeutic community.' In R. Terrington (ed) *Towards a Whole Society: Collected Papers on Aspects of Mental Health*. London: Richmond Fellowship Press.

Kennard, D. (1998) *An Introduction to Therapeutic Communities* (second edition). London: Jessica Kingsley Publishers.

Lacan J. (1977) 'The function and field of speech in psychoanalysis.' In *Ecrits: A Selection* (trans. A. Sheridan). London: Tavistock.

Lacan, J. (1981) *Speech and Language in Psychoanalysis* (trans. A. Wilden). Baltimore and London: The Johns Hopkins University Press.

Laing, R.D. (1967) *The Politics of Experience and the Bird of Paradise*. Harmondsworth: Penguin.

Laing, R.D. (1971) *The Politics of the Family*. Harmondsworth: Penguin.

Laing, R.D. and Esterson, A. (1964) *Sanity, Madness and the Family*. Harmondsworth: Penguin.

Leff, J. (1997) 'The future of community care.' In J. Leff (ed) *Care in the Community: Illusion or Reality?* Chichester: John Wiley.

Levinas, E. (1969) *Totality and Infinity* (trans. A. Lingis). Pittsburgh: Duquesne University Press.

Levinas, E. (1978) 'Martin Buber, Gabriel Marcel and philosophy.' In M. Smith (trans.) *Outside the Subject*. Stanford: Stanford University Press.

Levinas, E. (1982) *Ethics and Infinity* (trans. R. Cohen). Pittsburgh: Duquesne University Press.

Oakley, C. (1989a) 'Introducing an incomplete project.' In R. Cooper (ed) *Thresholds between Philosophy and Psychoanalysis: Papers from the Philadelphia Association*. London: Free Association Books.

Oakley, C. (1989b) 'Otherwise than integrity.' In R. Cooper (ed) *Thresholds between Philosophy and Psychoanalysis: Papers from the Philadelphia Association*. London: Free Association Books.

Putnam, H. (1975) *Mind, Language, Reality. Philosophical Papers 2*. New York and Cambridge: Cambridge University Press.

Rawlinson, D. (1999) 'Group analytic ideas: Extending the group matrix to TCs.' In P. Campling and R. Haigh (eds) *Therapeutic Communities: Past, Present and Future.* London: Jessica Kingsley Publishers.

Skolnick, M.R. (1999) 'Psychosis from a group perspective.' In V.L. Schermer and M. Pines (eds) *Group Psychotherapy of the Psychoses: Concepts, Interventions and Contexts.* London and Philadelphia: Jessica Kingsley Publishers.

White Paper (1999) 'Saving lives: Our healthier nation.' London: Department of Health.

Wittgenstein, L. (1953) *Philosophical Investigations.* Oxford: Basil Blackwell.

CHAPTER 1

The Dwelling Place of Meaning

John Gale

Language, like architecture, always tells a tale. It is the story of the men which inhabit it. In this chapter I discuss some of the ways in which the therapeutic community inhabits language, is constructed by language and is revealed to itself through language. In the first part, after my introduction, I will concentrate on some theoretical questions about the relationship between language, the unconscious and community, and in the second part I shall refer more directly to language in therapeutic community practice.

Writing almost ten years ago, Dr Horst Flegel noted that the thoughts of the late Catholic philosopher Jacques Maritain encourage us to try to look down on the therapeutic community 'from the "higher" level of philosophy' (Flegel 1990a, p.1; Maritain 1963, pp.96–100). With this in mind I shall start with a few introductory remarks about the place of language in contemporary philosophy and psychoanalysis. I think this has some relevance for our overall project, which is to go back to therapeutic community principles and restate them and rework them in a way which makes them appeal and seem more relevant to us today. This means not so much constructing a new edifice as digging out the foundations of the old building. The context for my remarks here is that, first, in its origins, therapeutic community theory drew profoundly on psychoanalytic theory, especially as this related to the theory of group functioning; and that, second, therapeutic community theory did, in the past, engage with wider philosophical debates in a way which has now largely been lost. Freud, of course, like Husserl, had been a student of Brentano (Cooper *et al.* 1994, p.6) and was an admirer of English philosophy. Early on in his career he had translated an essay by John Stuart Mill. Indeed, although the success of psychoanalysis in the United States has been attributed in part to the way in which it has been saturated with Anglo-American philosophy, the influence of Hegel on Freud ought not to be ignored (Skelton 1994, p.419). Bion applied Plato and Kant to psychoanalysis (Cooper *et al.* 1994, p.7). In the 1960s especially, therapeutic community theory was very much alive and was a vital part of the philosophical debate about the 'self and others', 'madness and civilization', 'existentialism and phenomenology', to coin the phrases which formed the titles of some popular books. R.D. Laing read Artaud, Hegel, Husserl, Sartre, Merleau-Ponty and Heidegger, and when in 1965 the Philadelphia Association was founded, Maxwell Jones and Tom Main were on the association's advisory panel (Cooper *et al.* 1994, pp.15–16). If this chapter contains an appeal, therefore, it is an appeal to those of us involved in therapeutic communities to look afresh at philosophy in order to renew our practice.

LANGUAGE: A CONTEMPORARY FOCUS FOR THERAPEUTICS

Unlike other periods in history, the twentieth century has seen philosophy take hold of a common interest – language. Language unites the major schools and draws together, under a single focus, analytical philosophy, the theory of science, phenomenology and hermeneutics. Yet this is not to say that philosophy, in recent times, has become limited to an interest in language or the study of linguistics. Far from it! I am not suggesting that an overview of the history of recent philosophy shows that all the myriad directions of philosophical interest have been replaced by the philosophy of language, but rather that philosophical questions, and this includes the classical or fundamental philosophical questions from the past – epistemological, metaphysical, ethical, aesthetic questions – are now almost universally discussed in linguistic terms (Bubner 1990, p.69ff). Perhaps of particular significance here is the relationship between language and ontology. I say this because of the historical connection between existentialism and phenomenology and the therapeutic community, and also because the form which this book has taken has come about, to some extent, because of the light that reading Heidegger has thrown on the dual topics of dialogue and dwelling. This light shone also on Jacques Lacan, and it could fairly be described as an ontological linguistic radiance. Heidegger's thesis that being in its truth discloses itself as language surely has implications for all who work in the therapeutic community.

> There is no doubt that any therapeutic community, whether or not put in as many words, seeks in one way or another to discover each patient's manner to *be-in-the-world*, his or her *life project*. And, as the *Dasein* has the capacity to overcome itself and is 'self determination', we can and must help the patient to restructure and to modify his or her failed manner of 'being-in-the-world. (Ylla 1990, p.10)

Ernst Turgendhat, one of Heidegger's last pupils, was especially interested in this interrelationship between ontology and linguistics, and to illustrate this he turned, curiously, to Aristotle. Maritain, Thomist philosopher *par excellence*, would have smiled. Indeed, another Catholic philosopher, this time an Englishman, would also have been amused by this appeal to Aristotle as a source for linguistic philosophy. I mean, of course, John Henry Newman, author of the *Grammar of Assent*. It was Newman who had puzzled the Thomists of his day by his anticipation of Wittgenstein.

> The example of ontology may, as Turgendhat shows, be demonstrated particularly well in the case of Aristotle, since his project, which gave rise to a whole tradition, for a 'science' of ontology rests on the foundation of an analysis of the *use of language*. In Oxford, by the way, it had been known for a long time that Aristotle could be counted as the first linguistic analyst! The celebrated introduction of ontology in the fourth book of Aristotle's *Metaphysics* is based on the following argument. Since all the special sciences confine themselves to particular aspects of reality, there is a need for a new science which will go beyond all specialist limitations to concern itself with Being in general or with Being as Being. Access to this domain of objects, which is prior to all scientific methodology, can come about only by withdrawing to a universal and primary mode of our relation to the world. Language in its manifold forms and modes of use establishes this original connection with the world. (Bubner 1990, p.98)

Language provides the foundation on which 'the separately proceeding traditions of the more recent developments in philosophy may be set in relation to one another with some prospect of success' (Bubner 1990, p.70; see Apel 1967). In essence, language is 'prior to all', the 'universal primary mode of being' – the place where all philosophical investigations cut across one another. It is 'the common meeting ground of Wittgenstein's investigations, the English linguistic philosophy, the phenomenology that stems from Husserl, Heidegger's investigations, the works of the Bultmannian school and of the other schools of New Testament exegesis, the works of the comparative history of religion and of anthropology concerning myth, ritual, and belief – and finally, psychoanalysis' (Ricoeur 1970, p.3). Hermeneutic interpretations of psychoanalysis and structuralist readings, in turn, 'reflect a growing concern with language in Western academic life' (Parker 1994, p.532). Heidegger's thought is crucial here, and it has been said that he is, without doubt, the most powerfully original and influential philosopher of the century in the continental tradition. 'Phenomenology, existentialism and deconstruction are unthinkable without him, but so are the philosophy of literature and many social-critical or neo-Marxian strands of thought' (Krell 1991, p.130). In fact, Luis Ylla has claimed, with some foundation, that 'the existential philosophy of Martin Heidegger and the philosophers of his school offers the most genuine philosophical bases for therapeutic communities' (Ylla 1990, p.10).

It should, therefore, come as no surprise that Jacques Lacan, the person whose name is most closely associated with a language based approach to psychoanalysis, was a friend of Heidegger and indeed translated some of his works. Like R.D. Laing he was fascinated by phenomenology and existentialism and was influenced by Kierkegaard, Sartre and, to a lesser extent, by Merleau-Ponty (Skelton 1994, p.419). But it is Heidegger's influence on Lacan which is most clearly discernible and we see this especially in his metaphysical discussions of being and in the distinction he makes between full speech and empty speech. Lacan is certainly one of the most original and influential thinkers since Freud, but more importantly, he applied his philosophical insights clinically (Skelton 1994, p.419). His ideas have revolutionized psychoanalysis and continue to have a major effect on all sorts of areas of thought – for example, on literary criticism, film studies, feminist theory and the philosophy of language. His achievement has been to subject psychoanalysis 'to a radical re-writing from the point of view of deeply held *philosophical assumptions*' (Skelton 1994, p.419, my italics). Jean Laplanche has discussed Lacan's project at some length and challenged, explicitly, the canonical Lacanian formula that 'the unconscious is structured like a language' (Laplanche 1981, pp.7–144). Laplanche has asked some important questions, notably, 'What linguistics?', 'What language?' He argues, persuasively, that if we identify the deepest stratum in man – namely, the unconscious – with verbal language, we adopt an explicitly anti-Freudian stance (Laplanche 1989, p.41). What Freud understood by language is well summed up in the following passage from 'The Claims of Psychoanalysis to Scientific Interest'. Let me quote it here:

> I shall no doubt be overstepping common linguistic usage in postulating an interest in psychoanalysis on the part of philologists, that is of experts in *speech* (those who are concerned with the *logos*, with discourse). For in what follows, 'speech' must be understood not merely to mean the expression of thought in words but to include the speech of gesture and every other method, such, for instance, as writing, by which mental activity can be expressed. (Freud 1913, p.176)

For Freud, then, the non-verbal is an important part of language. But this ought not to leave us with the impression that verbal language is not important to Freud. On the contrary, Freud was very sensitive to the spoken language of the patient and laid great stress on his puns, his word-plays and ambiguities in speech (Skelton 1994, p. 420). However, Laplanche argues that verbal linguistics, although important, are always secondary in Freud (Laplanche 1989, pp.41–45) in historical, chronological, topographical and economic ways. Let me try to unpack some of these complex ideas just a little.

In historical terms, perhaps it is easier to understand that verbal language is secondary, because we are familiar with talking about a pre-verbal stage. But in terms of chronology, topography and economics, it may not seem, at first, quite so transparent. Freud relied heavily on the work of the Scandinavian philologist

Hans Sperber to develop his theory about the origins of language (Sperber 1912, quoted by Laplanche 1989, p.42). His idea was that we can detect sexual origins in the original sounds of speech and language (Ricoeur 1970, pp.501–503). This implies that verbal language is secondary in terms of the chronology of collective history. According to Laplanche's reading of Freud, it is language which supplies the word-presentations which allow chains of thought to become conscious. The term 'word-presentation' refers to the mental image of a word; this means that there is an essential difference between unconscious mental processes and those which are pre-conscious or conscious and it is that the latter have been brought into connection with word-presentations (Ricoeur 1970, p.398–399 n.69). That an unconscious idea has a verbal image attached to it, one which has been learned from others, implies, of course, that word-presentations are excluded from the unconscious. Rycroft comments that this notion is only intelligible 'if one remembers that Freud believed that the human psyche starts as a structureless id, part of which differentiates to form the ego as a result of the impact of the environment' (Rycroft 1968, p.178). Lacan argued against his critics in two ways. First, by insisting that we only really grasp the unconscious when it is articulated verbally and, second, by suggesting that the distinction Freud made between word-presentations and thing- presentations was not as rigid as it had been understood in psychoanalysis. The latter as found in the unconscious are still linguistic phenomena (Lacan 1992, p.44–45). For Laplanche says that verbal language is secondary in Freud in economic terms in the sense that speech is governed by what he calls 'a mode of association and circulation which involves barriers and dams' (Laplanche 1989, p.43). If thought is to exist it needs to be stopped, at least now and then! I do not think that Laplanche's emphasis on the secondary nature of verbal language need throw us off course in our attempt to understand the therapeutic community as a community constituted by the word or of our therapeutic approach as a linguistic approach. After all, if we think that language is limited to verbal language, we run into problems about gesture. For example, when we think about greeting rituals, we might imagine a situation in which someone is greeted by a simple nod of the head and a grunt. This is certainly a means of communication, but is it part of a language? Surely what makes it a language is its social importance, for its boundary is 'constituted by language-users' (D'hert 1978, p.151). Lacan's reading of Hegel came via Alexander Kojeve, who had held a seminar in Paris in the 1930s. His audience included Sartre and Merleau-Ponty as well as Lacan. Partly, it was from Kojeve that Lacan's position took on a more sociological and less individualistic perspective than was common in the psychoanalytic community at the time. He became interested in the whole family and concentrated on family structures, rather than individual family members. This meant he could exploit the structuralist anthropology of Levi-Strauss as well as the language theory of Ferdinand de Saussure. For the latter, it was the structure of the sentence that mattered and not the meaning of individual words. It was the interrelation of its parts upon which meaning depended. Just so in the therapeutic community, it is in the interrelation of members that the meaning of individual client's acts is to be found. In the terminology of Saussure it is the signifiers *as a system* that determines meaning. For the former, the unconscious is not the place of instinct but the place where experience is structured according to the laws of kinship (Skelton 1994, pp.421–422).

LANGUAGE AND THE STRUCTURE OF COMMUNITY: IGNACE D'HERT ON WITTGENSTEIN

To speak of language-users and kinship structure is to speak of community.

> One cannot have a language – however primitive one may conceive of it – without somebody at least using and understanding it. Use and understanding however can only take place *where there is a community*, where things, gestures, sounds have a certain meaning. And use and understanding must always conform to certain criteria, otherwise one would not know one was understanding. 'Let us remember that there are certain criteria in a man's behaviour for the fact that he does not understand a word: that it means nothing to him, that he can do nothing with it. And criteria for his "thinking he understands" attaching some meaning to the word, but not the right one. And, lastly, criteria for his understanding the word right' (Wittgenstein 1967, p.269). What Wittgenstein is pointing to here is the fact that man is not simply the creator of his language and of his world, but that *he only has language*, only is able to form for himself a world, *in relation to and partial dependence on a community* from which he receives his language and in which he participates or against which he reacts by taking part in another language-game. (D'hert 1978, p.151, my italics)

Like Wittgenstein, Heidegger acknowledged that language seems to be what is most natural about human beings. Commenting on this, Ignace D'hert writes that, as a matter of fact, people always talk, even when they do not use words. Language seems to be as essential to human beings as their bodies are. People use language as naturally and unreflectively as they use their hands and feet, as they walk or eat. It looks as though language is what is most evident about human beings (D'hert 1978, p.75):

> To be sure, is it not a matter of fact for instance, that language is always prior to language-users? It always exists beforehand *in the community in which human beings become participants*. Man does not create language, he does not even learn it by himself, but *he learns it in the group in which he lives* and from which he receives it. Language constitutes some kind of pre-existing sphere into which man enters, or rather in which he is inescapably taken up, and

only in that way does he become a human being. Language is in some sense transcendent to man, in that it is the air he breathes and without which he cannot live. For he thinks, talks, feels, names, means, objects, agrees ... in language. It is only in and from language that the world, man and things can be viewed and located. (D'hert 1978, p.75, my italics)

This also indicates that the world that man forms for himself can never be entirely a private world. It will always be a shared world, in which rules, conventions, receptivity and man's creative response to what is given play a part (D'hert 1978, p.151). By world I do not mean an undifferentiated everything, not 'all that is given' (Kenny 1980, pp.72–75), but specific forms of life or communities in which each person's life is related to the world. The therapeutic community is the social and cultural texture in which both we and our clients are involved (D'hert 1978, p.54).

...Wittgenstein was pointing to the fact that man is not the prisoner of language. Language does not bind or restrict him, but opens a wide range of possibilities. And people do in fact engage in a variety of languages and forms of life, which means that man is fundamentally the possibility of encountering, receiving and creating meaning. He is fundamental openness to the variety of languages and meanings. (D'hert 1978, p.150)

For Wittgenstein, language could best be understood by comparing it with games. In order to understand a game we have to join in, for to an outsider the game seems meaningless. One has, in order to grasp it, to watch the game carefully, learn the rules, see how the players behave, learn certain tactics and in the end participate in the game the group is playing. Games can only ever be fully understood from the inside. It is only from inside the community, by participating in speech, that meaning is revealed. For meaning, essentially, dwells in the interrelation of the word and the community. This is why we can describe the therapeutic community as a community of the word.

So the analogy suggests that one can only understand language by looking at it, at the way it is actually being used, and one should not try to force it into some kind of preconceived idea of what language 'must' be (Wittgenstein 1967, p.66) ... A second point which is pretty obvious, is that there are different kinds of games...[this] suggests that in the same way as there are many different games, there are also a great many different kinds of language-use (Wittgenstein 1967, p.23), according to the situation in which one finds oneself, the people with whom or to whom one is talking, the topic one is dealing with, *the aim of the dialogue* or speech, the *social and cultural context.* (D'hert 1978, p.45, my italics)

Although each and every sign, by itself, is dead, use makes it alive (Wittgenstein 1967, pp.340, 432). And use is always use by a community according to its own rules or social conventions (D'hert 1978, p.51). Without the social rules of a specific language-community there could be no language, and without language there could be no community either. A rule is something for repeated application, to be applied in indefinite instances, not just once (Wittgenstein 1958, p.96). Following a linguistic rule, like any rule, is by necessity a practice or custom of a community, because 'it is not something which it would be possible for only one man to do' (Kenny 1980, p.173). To say that every single move in a language is defined by the rules of a specific linguistic community is to say that we do not keep changing the meaning of concepts all the time. And this means that we can say that the therapeutic community is a kind of language institution (D'hert 1978, p.51). Language is 'essentially connected with the total social and cultural context in which it functions' and can therefore 'only be understood from this total context' (D'hert 1978, p.52). It follows that the language we use in the therapeutic community reveals the form of life which is that community.

> Learning a language, participating in a language-game, means that we become *a member of a certain group*. That means that language reveals the social dimension of our being, that it makes us capable of sharing and taking part in a certain form of life. Language reveals our capacity to establish contacts with groups of people. To share a language is to share a whole world. And as it is possible to earn a new language, it is also possible to participate in different forms of life. This points to the possibility of sharing different worlds, the possibility of becoming an insider in foreign languages and forms of life, the eventual establishment of unexpected communion. (D'hert 1978, p.53, my italics)

Seen like this, we can say that language constitutes community not because it is not a collection of syntactical rules, but because primarily speech and spoken language is a human activity. It is through speech that we organize the therapeutic community by entering into verbal relationships with others, expressing our feelings and uncovering meaning. For 'language goes on holiday the moment we isolate it and consider it outside of the community which speaks it' (D'hert 1978, p.52; Wittgenstein 1967, p.38):

> [Our patients] are, perhaps, much closer at least at the beginning of therapy to the 'infans' than we perhaps sometimes realise. That is, to the infant desiring to come into speech but not yet knowing either the language or, more crucially, the intentions, desires or *rules of the culture they find themselves in*. (Bacon 1994, p.409, my italics)

LANGUAGE: THE FIRST AND LAST STRUCTURE OF MADNESS

One of the definitive aspects of our work in therapeutic communities is the language of psychosis. We cannot deny that psychosis has its discourse within our communities, for on a daily basis we are brought face to face with this fact. Lacan argued that disordered language was a necessary feature of psychosis in which 'signifier and signified' are stabilized in the delusional metaphor' (Lacan 1957, p.217 cited by Evans 1966, p.156–7). In his notable and acclaimed study of madness from 1500 to 1800, the French philosopher Michel Foucault discussed an example he found in Ysbrand van Diemerbroek's *Disputationes practicae, de morbis capitis* of a man suffering from depression. The man thought he had killed his son and that he had done so because he had been tempted by a demon (van Diemerbroek 1685, cited by Foucault 1992, p.95ff). Foucault says that, at a deeper level, we find here a rigorous organization 'dependent on the faultless armature of a discourse' (Foucault 1992, p.96). Although we could describe this as madness, nevertheless it is logical, and it advances by judgements and reasoning which 'connect together', and hence it is a discourse. This is the paradoxical truth of madness for Foucault, that the discourse is logical, organized, a faultless connection 'in the transparency of a virtual language' (Foucault 1992, p.97). This delirious *language* is the truth of madness 'insofar as it is madness's organising form, the determining principle of all its manifestations' (Foucault 1992, p.97). The depressed man's converse with the demon represents 'the sediment in the body of an infinitely repeated discourse. Body and soul bear traces and images that are merely 'stages in the syntax of delirious language.' (Foucault 1992, p.97). From this case study Foucault goes on to uncover what he calls the fundamental role of delirious discourse in the classical conception of madness by appealing to the case of Julie, a nymphomaniac described by Bienville (Bienville 1771, pp.140–153, cited by Foucault 1992, pp.97–98). Here, the progress of Julie into madness is seen as a movement from 'fundamental language' in which nature speaks, via 'seductive language' to 'delirious language'. 'Thus understood, discourse covers the entire range of madness. Madness, in the classical sense, does not designate so much a specific change in the mind or in the body, as the existence, under the body's alterations, under the oddity of conduct and conversation, of a delirious discourse' (Foucault 1992, p.99). Foucault notices that in the eighteenth century, hysteria was often not classified as madness, because it was difficult for nosographers to find in hysterical convulsions 'the unity of language' (Foucault 1992, p.100):

> *Language is the first and last structure of madness,* its constituent form; on language are based all the cycles in which madness articulates its nature. That the essence of madness can be ultimately defined in the simple

structure of a discourse does not reduce it to a purely psychological nature, but gives it a hold over the totality of soul and body. (Foucault 1992, p.100)

Madness is seen here to be a language very similar to the language of dreams. It is an 'unknown language'. For Foucault, the simple structure of the 'mad' discourse also includes 'the silent language by which the mind speaks to itself in the truth proper to it' (Foucault 1992, p.100).

THE 'FULL WORD' CALLS FOR A 'FULL SILENCE'

Anyone who has spent time in meditation or in long periods of contemplative silence will know that silence is full of sound. My own experience of living for over twelve years in a Benedictine monastery taught me a good deal about the sanity that comes from the practice of silence in community. On one occasion, when a group of young people visited and were busy making a racket, one of the older monks remarked: 'You'd think they would *hear* the silence!' Often, if we sit alone in the countryside at dusk, the sound of the wind in the trees, of birds singing, of bats and crickets, and the last mooing of the cows before they settle down for the night, can be a real cacophony. Yet it is only when we sit in silence and let the silence wrap itself around us that we reach the stillness necessary to hear all these sounds. Far from destroying it, these sounds curiously seem to underline and deepen the silence.

> In the *sodo* or *zendo*, monks' hall or meditation hall, of a Zen community there is, of course, nothing particularly distracting in the external sur-roundings. There is a long room with wide platforms down either side where the monks both sleep and meditate. The platforms are covered with *tatami*, thick floor-mats of straw, and the monks sit in two rows facing one another across the room. The silence which prevails is deepened rather than broken by occasional sounds that float up from a near-by village, by the intermittent ringing of soft-toned bells from other parts of the monastery, and by the chatter of birds in the trees. (Watts 1965, p.176)

Of course, this may be fine for Zen monks, but what has it got to do with the work of the therapeutic community? Let me try to answer that question. In my attempt to describe, in this chapter, something about the essence of our therapeutic communities, I have defined these communities as communities-of-the-word. Speech is the centre and core of the relationships which we have, and it is in speech that these relationships exist. But a vital part of the language which constitutes the community is silence. Wittgenstein has drawn attention to the meaning of silence and its relationship to articulate language. Silence exists as a part of language, for it is only by means of words that silence can be created, and it is only in language that silence can become audible. Only in language can silence be present (D'hert 1978, pp.139–141). There are two sides to this. On the one hand, silence is vital if the word is to be heard, understood, if it is to seep in, enter really inside the client. To define the therapeutic community as a community of the word and insist, as I am, that for a community to be a therapeutic community at all, it must be structured by language, we must take language seriously and mean far more than just conversation. It is not the simple fact that clients and staff talk to one another that makes the therapeutic community a community of the word. I mean much more than that. Because our words are full words they bear a *gravitas* which demands silence. Silence, in this first sense, is something that the client must try to attain. It is not easy for him and it is not something that he has when he first enters into the therapeutic arena. This deep interior silence or quietness is, at first, out of reach for him. He is attacked on all fronts by an indistinguishable multitude of conflicting sounds and voices. These are the foreign voices of their psychosis and they leave the client in a continual state of uproar. The client is taught to reach beyond the superficial noise of his distress and to seek out the region of quiet that lies hidden within. It is as if, in the disturbance of psychosis, the client is like a flask full of murky water. The water is murky because it has been shaken. When we set the flask aside for a while and leave it to stand, the dirt sinks to the bottom and the separated water is clear. Just so, the client must settle in quiet to find a degree of stillness inside himself. He is then, and only then, really able to understand the word we give him in dialogue. Here, his dialogic response is silence. It is silence-in-response to my word which is a dynamic word-to-him in his uproar. My therapeutic word speaks to his uproar and in its gentle *gravitas* demands his silence. Without this response of silence, my word would not have the power to reach the client's pain and would just evaporate and pass him by unnoticed, because it would have only have scratched the surface. The therapeutic word is not like the superficial words of everyday speech; it has a depth because it speaks to a person at the core of his or her distress. In silence the client can consume and digest my word; he can cherish it, embrace it, stick to it, toss it to and fro in his mind, consider it, reflect upon it. This deep listening allows him to penetrate it and crack its meaning for himself – a meaning that may often be unknown to the therapist.

But more must be said! Just as the therapeutic word, on which the community is founded, is more than the speech of everyday conversation, so the silence of the client is not a dead silence, not an empty silence but a silence filled with the word. Yet, in order to arrive at this interior 'full silence', an outward silence and positive withdrawal is necessary. A therapeutic community has to cultivate a climate of silence in order that this withdrawal can take place. If it achieves this, therapeutic dwelling has become what it is supposed to be, a 'forecourt of the inner self' where the client can find himself or herself and 'collect' themselves (Levinas 1980, cited by Flegel 1990b, pp.36–37). It is only when the client cultivates a degree of external silence that they will be able to begin to enter into a full silence.

> We have our own world (*Eigenwelt*), a shared world (*Mitwelt*) and a sur-
> rounding world (*Umwelt*). I am not aware of forms of treatment of psychotic
> patients which in practice attend to all these aspects as completely as in a
> therapeutic community. The physical environment of the clinic and its
> surrounding (*Umwelt*) which plays an important role (which is why thera-
> peutic community clinics are often located in quiet, attractive places)...
> (Ylla 1990, p.10)

This retreat into an external quiet within 'one's "own" closest (domestic)
environment' (Heidegger 1990, p.93 and n.1) is often overlooked, but it has to
be at the heart of the therapeutic community because it is part of what is meant
by dwelling. For when clients come to dwell in the therapeutic abode – what
Levinas calls *demeure* (Levinas 1980, cited by Flegel 1990b, p.36) – they are
returning to that intimate place where their ego and subjectivity are constructed
and reinforced. But this returning ought not to be seen in terms of a retreat into
a conflict free area, in the sense in which Jacob Voorhoeve conceives it in his
discussion of the relationship between the structure of the therapeutic setting
and the structure of personality (Voorhoeve 1993, p.27). Neither is it the kind
of silence and withdrawal which springs from the client's desire to protect
themselves (Berke 1990, p.240). Rather, clients need to be encouraged to use
periods of solitude and withdrawal into silence in order to engage more fully
with themselves and the community. This is a withdrawal into that 'silent
language in which the mind speaks to itself in truth' (Foucault 1992, p.100),
and here language itself is seen as 'the dwelling place of meaning' (D'hert 1978
p.155). Exterior silence enables the development of an interior silence, a full
silence in which presence to the self and presence to others is really possible.

> The significance of the home for the individual's ability to exist in the
> outside world becomes even more obvious when one considers that the
> home itself is at the same time both part of the world and symbol of the
> individual's inner self. This double position and function of the home shows
> to what extent the individual has the world both *in* and *around* him. (Flegel
> 1990b, p.36)

This full silence is itself a language and one in which the client needs to become
totally engrossed in patiently digesting. Full silence will reveal to the client the
void inside himself, and it is at this point that the therapist will encourage
further, deeper excavation and keep the dialogue going, even though the client
himself may well want to rush back into the seemingly happier state of empty
speech. Full silence is a way for the client to scoop out the void in order to find
the source of himself or herself and from this centre discover an ability to
respond to others and to act responsibly.

It is here that we see the value of our silence as a therapeutic intervention.
We need to learn to know when to leave things unsaid. A clue to discerning
when to remain silent may be to think of the client speaking to us either with

empty or full words. Silence as response can be difficult to handle, especially for less experienced therapists who may feel that they should have something to say because the silence of the client throws up for them anxiety about their own inner emptiness. But if a reply springs from our inability to cope with silence, our words will not be effective, no matter how profound they seem. Psychosis is an extreme state in which the client has found it unbearable to live with reality and has covered his inner emptiness with a delusion. Reality is not just that which a person may currently understand or accept about himself. Naturally, to some extent, there will always be an emptiness that the client, like the rest of us, will be desperate to fill with an illusion, rather than face. The client will try to convince us that he is whole by building a false self. If we always respond with words, it may imply that the client's words are always real, useful self-descriptions.

RESPONSIBILITY: RESPONDING TO THE CLIENT AND THE GROUP

Lacanian theory distinguishes between behaviour and acts. Whereas animals can be said to behave in certain ways, only human beings act. Acts are human behaviour because the actor can take responsibility for his actions. Thus the concept of human acts has an ethical aspect, and this means that human acts only take on meaning within a community of others (Lacan 1977a, p.50). However, this simple distinction becomes more complicated when we link it with the notion of intentionality. In addition to a person's conscious plans, there will also be their unconscious intentions. Intentionality, therefore, calls for interpretation.

A person may commit an act which he claims to be unintentional but which is an expression of unconscious desire. These apparently unintended acts can be described as bungled actions, in the sense that the actor does not consciously intend to do them, but they may, at the same time, be successful expressions of a person's unconscious desire. Consequently, in the therapeutic community, we take time to discuss with clients everything they do. For example, by discussing about continual oversleeping, a client may come to an awareness of his fear of facing others. This realization may lead him to move on from speaking about his tiredness to articulate his anxiety of meeting others. In its turn, this small step in self-understanding may become a catalyst in his integration into community life and relatedness. However small and apparently mundane and inconsequential something may seem at first, it might bear real meaning and significance, for it is a part of language and needs to be translated and articulated by being spoken. No matter how the therapeutic community is framed, we cannot deny that it shares, with psychoanalysis, a technique which moves entirely within the element of language.

The analyst operates with what the subject tells him, he views the subject in the discourses that the latter makes, he examines him in his locutory and 'story making' behaviour, and through these discourses there is slowly shaped for him another discourse that he must make explicit, that of the complex buried within the unconscious. The analyst, therefore, will take the discourse as a stand-in for another 'language' which has its own rules, symbols, and syntax and which refers back to underlying structures of the psychism. (Emile Benventiste: see Ricoeur 1970, p.396)

It is because it is only possible to recognize unconscious desire fully, when it is articulated in speech, that discussion and dialogue are so vital if community living is to have a therapeutic function for its members. In this we have the role of therapeutic tutors, in that we aim to teach clients to name, articulate and bring their desire into existence. This is not just an expressionist theory of language, not a question of finding a new way of saying what a person wants; it is more a question of creating desire by speaking it, in a form which is fuller and more real than it previously could ever have had (Lacan 1988a, p.183; Lacan 1988b, p.228). Desire is neither need nor demand. At its most basic, a need has at its root a biological instinct or appetite and can be satisfied. A child may, in its helplessness, demand that another fulfils its need. Desire, however, can never be fully satisfied because it is always directed towards something else and points to the future (Lacan 1977b, p.167).

...the ability to use language – both in the narrow sense of communicating and decoding intention and in the wider sense of entering into, interpreting and regulating a culture – could not happen without the presence of some such drive or desire. Talking, whether with the pre-verbal infant through systematic and repeated formats of interaction, or later with the child through increasingly elaborated grammatical speech, is the key medium in which these joint desires are articulated and negotiated. Talking is, in this sense, the place of the unconscious. (Bacon 1994, p.409)

Feelings of frustration on the part of the client are to be expected. It is not just the fact that the client will feel frustrated if we are silent; even when we respond they will get frustrated. There is a frustration which stems from the fact that, a lot of the time, the client is constructing a false self and trying to convince us that it is real, trying to seduce us into believing that this is the real him. If we manage to avoid being drawn into this mirage, the client will gradually realize that he is creating a construct, a home-made self, destined to be exposed by contact with others in the community. Take, for example, the extreme case of the habitual liar who comes into therapy.

The psychoanalyst differs from the philosopher in that he usually encounters language as a mode of misunderstanding rather than understanding, and of miscommunication rather than communication. The habitual liar may maintain his system of mendacity as a defense against a catastrophic change in his personality. The lie functions here both as a symptom and as a cure. Had he known beforehand, Bion observes, it is unlikely that the psychoanalyst would treat such a case by choice, and might well hesitate before the prospect of a 'cure' that precipitates a breakdown. But as the most effective lies are the lies one tells to oneself, the patient too may undertake analysis unwittingly. (Cantlie 1993, p.229)

Deep down, each member of the client group knows this and if we engage in dialogue, at this point, they may think we have been fooled by them. Their flood of incoherent words are designed to conceal rather than reveal, for the nature of psychotic speech is that it treats words not as vehicles of communication but as things-in-themselves (Cantlie 1993, p.230). Our apparent participation in the client's mistake will be experienced by him as something negative. Despite protestations, the client, deep down, does not want us to be fooled by him, but to see through him. Silence, when it is used therapeutically, will be a relief, and it is at this point that the client's words stop being empty words but become full with meaning.

At times we encourage clients to remember the past. At other times we focus on our relationship with the client. When we emphasize remembering, we focus our therapeutic interventions on overcoming resistance. When we stress the here and now, he will be more likely to value interpretation. These two aspects are really closely related and ought not to be seen as if they were separate. Verbalization is the key to understanding the connection between these two aspects. Verbalization is not just speaking. It means the process of putting things into words. It is by verbalization that the client links their memory of past events with the present, in relationship to others in the community. It is making this connection which often brings the client into awareness.

The unconscious can be understood as a censored part of the client, and in a sense it is the more truthful part, or it can, at least, be described as one of the core parts of the client. This is why we cannot ignore it if the dialogic relationship is to make any real impact on the client. The censoring that has taken place is really just another way of talking about how the client has ordered, sorted out and tried to make sense of his history and experience. So too, in a way, it is their history and their ordering of that history that we see in their body – the way they look and move; in their memories; in their own personal vocabularies; in the legends and traditions in which they make sense of themselves and in their dreams. All of these things are metaphors through which our clients speak to others, face the world and come into contact with us. Every fixation reveals an historical scar. It is as if the client can only read the text they have been given, which is their life. The dialogue a client has with us is a chance for them to re-write their story and simultaneously re-read it.

Access to the unconscious is gained through a process in which we interpret the meaning of unconscious phenomena. Just as we can translate the structural parts of the pictorial Egyptian hieroglyphics by reading the picture of an eye as 'eye', so we can translate the structural parts of the unconscious language as it appears in actions, dreams, jokes, transference and so on. Furthermore, the very process of this translation may in itself relieve some of the client's emotional distress.

INTERPRETATION AS THE DISRUPTION OF MEANING

In the therapeutic community, above all else, our task as therapists is to interpret unconscious processes in individuals and groups and at times to draw other clients into the process of making sense of some particular behaviour by one of their peers:

> The activities and roles within a therapeutic community provide a framework within which patients' emotional difficulties often emerge through their behaviour. For example, failure to carry out an agreed task may express a patient's difficulty in relating to others. Enabling the patient to acknowledge and explore this is one of *the key therapeutic tasks of the community*. At moments of crisis, a special meeting may be called so that those involved can share their feelings and give feedback to one another. Often the work of interpreting the meaning of a particular piece of behaviour can be undertaken by the patients themselves. At other times this may need to be done by staff members. (Kennard 1988, pp.169–170, my italics)

The process of translating and interpreting unconscious processes can, very often, have an immediate effect on clients and change group dynamics powerfully.

> Staff think of individual clients and groups as speaking to us in their particular unconscious language which we do not immediately understand. By translating this language we gain access into a new level of dialogue with them. The work in the projects takes place in our conversations and dialogues with clients because what is being said to us by the clients is already in a language. It is just that this language needs careful, often laborious, translation. Further, by pursuing this process of translation with our clients, by uncovering their own unconscious language, staff can begin to free clients from the psychological burden they carry. (CHT 1997)

The acts of clients need always to be understood and unravelled in the context of their past as well as their present life within the community. This notion of interpretation of the unconscious, whether of the individual client's process or the group process, is something that everyone who works in a therapeutic community will be conversant with, for it is, we could say, our bread and butter. It is perhaps the central part of the psychoanalytic inheritance of the therapeutic community approach. It was almost from the very beginning that psychoanalysis came to see interpretation as the key task of the analyst, but it also created some very real problems in psychoanalysis. Despite a good start, from around 1910 analysts began to find their interpretations less effective and that symptoms would often continue afterwards (Evans 1996, p.88). As a result the concept of resistance was developed. It was now seen as necessary, not just to make an interpretation based on the patient's free association, but also to enable the patient to overcome his resistance to consciously grasping the meaning of the interpretation (Strachey 1934). Lacan argued that the reason why interpretations were less effective was that analysts in this period had closed down the unconscious by making interpretations which were based more on symbolism than on association. That is to say, interpretation based on standard universal images, rather as we find it in the literature of oneirocriticism in antiquity (for a summary and list of texts see Foucault 1990, pp.4, 257–265). Freud had been well aware of this danger and had warned against it. Also, as psychoanalytic ideas became better known, patients were able to guess the interpretation the analyst would give! This led to analysts developing 'ever more complex theories in order to stay one step ahead of the patient' (Evans 1996, p.88). Lacan proposed a different approach, and it is his call for a new technique of interpretation which, more than anything else, has been taking up such a lot of time and attention in our therapeutic communities in CHT over the last few years and, I believe, stimulating our practice to such an extent that we feel a renewed commitment to the therapeutic community project. This project, which a decade ago seemed to be withering into insignificance, is finding its feet again, and, for us at least, this is due principally to taking up the Lacanian challenge so seriously in the clinical context.

Until we read Lacan and heard him speak up, as it were, our interpretations were almost always limited to unmasking hidden meanings, the truth of which would be confirmed by more associations (Evans 1996, p.88). In this, therapeutic communities operated along similar lines to classical psychoanalysis. The Lacanian project suggested that the aim of interpretation ought not to be geared so much towards uncovering meaning as disrupting meaning:

> Interpretation is directed not so much at 'making sense' as towards reducing the signifiers to their 'non-sense' in order to thereby find the determinants of all the subject's conduct (Lacan 1977a, p.212). Interpretation thus inverts the relationship between signifier and signified: instead of the normal production of meaning (signifier produces signified), interpretation works at the level of s [in Lacanian algebra s corresponds to the signified] to generate S [the symbolic order]: interpretation causes 'irreducible signifiers' to arise, which are 'non-sensical' (Lacan 1977a, p.250). Hence it is not a question, for Lacan, of fitting the analysand's discourse into a preconceived interpretive matrix or theory (as in the 'decoding' method), but of dis-

rupting all such theories. Far from offering the analysand a new message, the interpretation should serve merely to enable the analysand to hear the message he is unconsciously addressing to himself. (Evans 1996, p.89)

One of the important points here is the idea that interpretation both frees up speech, thus contributing to keeping the dialogue going in the group, and reveals the complex different meanings in the client's speech, over and above those of which they are conscious. Because this is our aim, we need to take the client's words and behaviours literally (Lacan 1988b, p.153). The image is one of reading a text rather than searching out some hidden message, and for this to be effective we need to go back to one of the basic therapeutic community notions, that of the flattened hierarchy and democratization. This means not-knowing and allowing clients to take responsibility (Kennard 1988, p.169). 'The less you understand, the better you listen' (Lacan 1988b, p.141). In order to avoid just fitting the client's words and acts into our preconceived theory, and in order to stay fresh and listen, Lacan frequently warns us of the dangers of understanding (Lacan 1977b, p.270; Lacan 1988b, p.103). This may seem strange advice at first, but the skill to put aside what we know is imperative, for we aim to take the client *literally*.

CODA

Frequently, psychoanalysis has been misrepresented as necessarily based on an asocial or antisocial model of the person (Parker 1994, pp.531–532), whereas, in fact, in the therapeutic community psychoanalytic and sociological notions meet (Hunter-Brown 1992, p.222). Foulkes had collaborated with sociologists and saw the individual 'having fluid personality boundaries and the unit as the community rather than the person' (Hunter-Brown 1992, p.223; Potter and Weatherell, 1987, p.7). Since the 1960s, social psychology has been preoccupied with a limited conception of reflexivity and Ian Parker has proposed that this calls for psychoanalytic insights to help us understand the role of reflexivity *as part of* the way social relations are structured (Parker 1994). Parker's view is important for a language approach to the therapeutic community as it links social psychology with discourse and looks at Lacan in relation to Habermas. His view is that discourse analysis gives us a more balanced picture of the individual in-relation-to-the-social and that we can identify hermeneutic and structuralist- inclined tendencies in new social psychology writing which emphasize either meaningful agency or the structure of action. By mapping on to traditions in psychoanalysis after Freud (Parker 1994, p.530), it may also reinforce a view of the therapeutic community as a dwelling inhabited by language and revealed in meaning, understanding and explanation.

REFERENCES

Apel, K.O. (1967) *Analytic Philosophy of Language and the Geitswissenschaften* (trans. H. Holstelilie).

Bacon, R. (1994) 'Stop making sense: Talking – cures and limits.' *British Journal of Psychotherapy 10*, 3, 405–417.

Berke, J.H. (1990) 'Conjoint therapy within a therapeutic milieu: The crisis team.' *International Journal of Therapeutic Communities 11*, 4, 237–248.

Bienville, J.-D.-T. (1771) *De la Nymphomanie*. Amsterdam.

Bubner, R. (1990) *Modern German Philosophy* (trans. Eric Matthews). Cambridge: Cambridge University Press.

Cantlie, A. (1993) 'The non-lover: Desire and discourse in the psychoanalytic session.' *Free Associations 4*, 2, 30, 210–240.

CHT (1997) 'Responsibility and desire: Interpretation in the therapeutic deialogue between clients and staff.' LHT Quality Assurance Manual (QA5–13).

Cooper, R. *et al.* (1994) *Thresholds between Philosophy and Psychoanalysis*. London: Free Association Books.

D'hert, I. (1978) *Wittgenstein's Relevance for Theology*. Bern: Peter Lang.

Evans, D. (1996) *An Introductory Dictionary of Lacanian Psychoanalysis*. London: Routledge.

Flegel, H. (1990a) 'Philosophical reflections on social science.' *International Journal of Therapeutic Communities 11*, 1, 1–4.

Flegel, H. (1990b) 'The individual and the psychotherapeutic community.' (Based on Levinas, E. (1980) 'Totalité et infini.') *International Journal of Therapeutic Communities 11*, 1, 33–41.

Foucault, M. (1990) *The Care of the Self: The History of Sexuality*, Vol. 3 (trans. R. Hurley). Harmondsworth: Penguin.

Foucault, M. (1992) *Madness and Civilization, A History of Insanity in the Age of Reason* (trans. R. Howard). London: Routledge.

Freud, S. (1910) 'The antithetical meaning of primal words.' *SE 11*, 155–161.

Freud, S. (1913) 'The claims of psychoanalysis to scientific interest.' In J. Strachey (ed) *The Standard Edition of the Complete Psychological Works of Sigmund Freud*, Vol. IX. London: The Hogarth Press and the Institute of Psychoanalysis.

Heidegger, M. (1990) *Being and Time* (trans. J. Macquarrie and E. Robinson). Oxford: Basil Blackwell.

Hunter-Brown, I. (1992) 'Psychoanalysis and war.' *British Journal of Psychotherapy 9*, 2, 221–227.

Jones, E. (1916) 'The theory of symbolism.' *Papers on Psychoanalysis 5*, 3, 87–144.

Kennard (1988) 'The Therapeutic Community.' In M. Aveline and W. Dryden (eds) *Group Therapy in Britain*.

Kenny, A. (1980) *Wittgenstein*. Harmondsworth: Penguin.

Krell, D.F. (1991) 'Heidegger.' In J.O. Urmson and J. Ree (eds) *The Concise Encyclopedia of Western Philosophy and Philosophers*. London: Unwin Hyman.

Lacan, J. (1957) *Ecrits: A Selection.* (trans. A. Sheridan) London: Tavistock.

Lacan, J. (1977a) *The Seminar. Book XI. The Four Fundamental Concepts of Psychoanalysis* (trans. A. Sheridan). London: Hogarth Press and Institute of Psychoanalysis.

Lacan, J. (1977b) *Ecrits: A Selection* (trans. A. Sheridan). London: Tavistock.

Lacan, J. (1988a) *The Seminar. Book I. Freud's Papers on Technique, 1953–54* (trans. J. Forrester). Cambridge: Cambridge University Press.

Lacan, J. (1988b) *The Seminar. Book II. The Ego in Freud's Theory and in the Technique of Psychoanalysis, 1954–55* (trans. S. Tomarselli). Cambridge: Cambridge University Press.

Laplanche, J. (1981) *Problematiques IV: L'Inconscient et le ca.* Paris: Presses Universitaires de France.

Laplanche, J. (1989) *New Foundations for Psychoanalysis* (trans. D. Macey). Oxford: Basil Blackwell. (Originally *Nouveaux Fondements pour la Psychanalyse.* Paris: Presses Universitaires de France, 1987.)

Maritain, J. (1963) *Distinguer pour unir ou Les Degres du savoir.* Paris: Descle Brouwer.

Parker, I. (1994) 'Reflexive social psychology: Discourse analysis and psychoanalysis.' *Free Associations 4*, 4, 32, 527–548.

Potter, J. and Wetherall, M. (1987) *Discourse and Social Psychology: Beyond Attitudes and Behaviour.* London: Routledge.

Ricoeur, P. (1970) *Freud and Philosophy, An Essay on Interpretation* (trans. D. Savage). New Haven and London: Yale University Press.

Rycroft, C. (1968) *A Critical Dictionary of Psychoanalysis.* Harmondsworth: Penguin.

Skelton, R. (1994) 'Lacan for the faint hearted.' *British Journal of Psychotherapy 10*, 3, 418–429.

Sperber, H. (1912) 'Uber deu einfus sexueller Momente auf Entstehung und Entwicklung der Sprache.' *Imago 1.*

Strachey, J. (1934) 'The nature of the therapeutic action of psychoanalysis.' *International Journal of Psychoanalysis 15*, 126–159.

van Diemerbroek, Y. (1685) *Opera omnia anatomico et medica.* Historia III. Utrecht.

Voorhoeve, J.N. (1993) 'The relationship between psychotic symptomatology and the structure of the setting.' *Therapeutic Communities 14*, 1, 19–27.

Watts, A. (1965) *The Way of Zen.* Harmondsworth: Penguin.

Wittgenstein, L. (1958) *The Blue and Brown Books* (trans. R. Rhees). Oxford: Basil Blackwell.

Wittgenstein, L. (1967) *Philosophical Investigations* (trans. and eds G.E.M. Anscombe and R. Rhees). Oxford: Basil Blackwell.

Ylla, L. (1990) 'Philosophic sources underlying diverse aspects which characterise therapeutic communities of psychodynamic orientation.' *International Journal of Therapeutic Communities 11*, 1, 7–11.

CHAPTER 2

A Time to Speak

Clare Saxon

This chapter is about how we at Community Housing and Therapy (CHT) use time as a means to helping our clients to enter into dialogue and to find a voice of their own. It is about how we use time to help clients find their true selves. In a way this chapter aims to put across how it is that our communities provide a time for clients to speak, often for the first time, in a way which is meaningful to them. It is an attempt to describe how we work with clients to create a time to speak and the way in which a placement in one of our communities *is* a time to speak.

I came to CHT after doing my degree in social studies. I wanted to gain experience in order to do a postgraduate social work course. I was offered a one-year training placement at CHT. So this chapter reflects my learning experience at CHT and my particular interest in the illusive but powerful nature of time.

There are many ways of thinking about time, but I am going to focus on two distinct ways which have direct relevance for our work with clients in creating 'a time to speak'. I shall look at time in relation to structure and the interconnections between past, present and future time.

When talking about time in relation to structure, we are talking about the familiar ways in which our time is structured into day and night and by the clock into seconds, minutes and hours. We are talking about the divisions of our time into weeks, months and years. Going on from these things, we are also talking about our relationship to these structures as they are manifested in how we spend our time. We are talking, for example, about whether we spend our time asleep at night and awake during the day, about whether we 'turn up on time', about whether we do things with our time, about whether we do nothing at all in time, about whether we take time to work, play and rest, about whether we aim whatever it is we are doing towards a given ending point in time, and so on.

When talking about the interconnections between past, present and future time, we are talking about our *experience* of time in terms of what has been, what is now and what will be. We are talking about the ways in which my experience of my past is connected to my experience of my present and future. We are talking about the ways in which these experiences of my time are interconnected in ways which override the familiar structures of time just described. For example, my experience, now in the present, of my past five minutes ago may be just as vivid as my experience of my past 15 years ago. My experience of the present minute may be of an interminable long time whereas the next one may flash by. Further, we are talking about how, for example, I may have no experience of part of my past in the present – I may have forgotten it.

In my view these two distinct ways of thinking about time are not mutually exclusive or in opposition, nor do they form a hierarchy of priority – the former, for example, being 'objective time', the latter 'subjective time'. Rather, they are two ways of being in time, or being in relation to one's own time here in the world. They are two dimensions of time that coexist. Depending on who we are and where we are in our own time, one dimension of time may be more accessible to us as a way of being in time than the other. Therapists at CHT have the task of being able to move their consciousness into the dimension of time in which the client is existing and in which the two can meet.[1]

Cooper talks of 'serial time' or 'chronological time' and contrasts it with 'my time' (Cooper 1989, pp.48–51). He talks of chronological time as being characterized by 'watching the clock', 'clocking in and out', 'filling time', 'killing time', 'going through the motions'. By contrast he describes 'my time' thus:

> It is a staying with, an abiding, rather than a mere enduring. Notions we might more readily associate with lived time are those such as spontaneity, readiness, and possibility. (Cooper 1989, p.49)

He seems to associate chronological time with those therapeutic communities which 'break the day down into…a daily round of activities' (Cooper 1989, p.48). Certainly, when we talk about time in relation to structure, we are not talking about Cooper's chronological time even though some of time in relation to structure is related to our therapeutic and educational programme. Rather than killing time, time in relation to structure is thought of in our communities as a way of precisely giving meaning to the words and actions of the people who are living in that time. As I shall illustrate presently, it is this which precisely opens out new possibilities for people in our communities.

TIME AND STRUCTURE[2]

For many clients who come to our communities, the world, other people and their place in relation to these things has become meaningless. This sense of meaninglessness may be expressed through chaotic, florid thoughts about themselves and other people, as it is with one who is in the midst of a psychotic episode; it may be expressed through withdrawal, isolation and passivity or it may be expressed through chaotic, destructive behaviour. It is not that the chaotic thoughts or behaviour have no meaning, though this may be hard to interpret; on the contrary, these thoughts and behaviours express the person's deep sense of meaninglessness *in relation* to the world and other people. They express the person's feelings of isolation and alienation from the world and other people.

One of the ways in which we work with clients in an ongoing way to help restore their sense of meaning and place in relation to the world and other people, in order to alleviate the chaos they experience, is by using time as structure. This means using a structured weekly therapeutic and educational programme of groups and individual therapy sessions to shape the days and weeks; it means having times to speak and work on one's 'issues' and times to engage in relaxing social conversation; it means having fixed time trial periods; it means having fixed starting and finishing times for groups and therapy sessions; it means having interdisciplinary reviews every three to six months; it means creating care plans for clients looking at the immediate and more distant future; and it means not having a fixed time for the placement in our community to last.

Before illustrating how we use these time structures to help clients have a sense of meaning and begin to speak and act on their true desires, I will draw on the ideas of Lacan to explain the theoretical background upon which we understand how it is that structuring time can provide meaning for a person *in relation* to the world and other people in the context of our communities. At the heart of this is the idea of time as structure and rhythm that serves to *punctuate* the client's often chaotic words, thoughts and actions, and this in turn serves to help the client create meaning out of these chaotic things in relation to the world and other people. It is this which provides the space for the client to say what they really mean, to speak authentically, to enter into a meaningful dialogue with the world and other people.

For Lacan, time can be used to punctuate a client's dialogue with his or her therapist. The time when the therapist chooses to make an intervention serves to punctuate the client's speech. The client's speech may take the form of silence or words, and the therapist may choose to make an intervention in the form of silence or with words. What is important is the time at which the therapist chooses to do this. A very clear example employed by Lacan as a technique for punctuating a client's dialogue is choosing when to end a client's session. Lacan famously did not use fixed times for ending a session, but rather would leave it open to the moment when he thought it helpful to punctuate the client's speech by ending the session. For example, he says:

> ...the adjournment of a session...plays the part of a metric beat which has the full value of an actual intervention by the analyst for hastening the concluding moments. This fact should lead us to employ it for the purposes of the technique in every useful way possible. (Lacan 1956, p.14)

For Lacan, the timing of interventions, whether this be in the form of finishing a session, choosing to remain silent or choosing to speak to the client, serves to punctuate the client's dialogue. What is so important about this is that, for Lacan, it is the punctuation that determines a particular meaning to strings of words. He says:

> It is a fact, which can be plainly seen in the study of the manuscripts of symbolic writings, whether it is a question of the Bible or of the Chinese canonicals, that the absence of punctuation in them is a source of ambiguity. The punctuation, once inserted, fixes the sense; changing the punctuation renews or upsets it; and a faulty punctuation amounts to a change for the worse. (Lacan 1956, p.78)

By analogy, without punctuation the client's words would have no meaning at all. By using time to punctuate the client's words, the therapist removes the ambiguity of the meaning of the client's words as well as helping them to see perhaps a hitherto unseen, new, meaning to the words that the client utters. A therapist can make an intervention which punctuates a client's discourse in an unexpected way, thus altering the intended meaning. This is a way of showing the client that they are saying more than they think they are. The goal of this punctuation as a form of intervention is to help the client find for himself or herself what they really desire, to help them find their Truth and to speak with a full or authentic word. For Lacan, timing of speech, silence and endings of sessions, as a form of punctuation, is an intervention designed towards this goal. It is thus that Lacan says:

> ...this technique only breaks the discourse in order to bring about the delivery of the Word. (Lacan 1956, p.80)

USING TIME AND STRUCTURE TO PROVIDE PUNCTUATION

I now turn to illustrate the ways in which, in the community in which I have been working, we use time and structure to punctuate the client's speech and actions and thus to provide a place from which they can begin to really speak.

Fixed ending times

In the community that I have been working in, all our groups, both practical and therapy groups, as well as our individual therapy sessions, have fixed starting and ending times. Unlike Lacan we do not improvise the ending times of these sessions by way of punctuating our client's speech and thus providing it with meaning. Rather, in these cases we believe that the fixed ending times of sessions precisely provide a structured framework of the time to speak which clients learn to relate to in a way that enables them to punctuate their own speech.

For example, in our Community Meeting the first forty minutes is given to an open experiential dialogue group called the 'Feelings' section. Without the limit of forty minutes, the clients may not get to the point of what it is they would like to say or talk about. Knowledge that the section will end at a fixed time helps the client to get to the real point and to speak authentically from their unconscious language. Clients over a period of time will learn to use this forty minutes constructively. Experience of meetings during which clients may have found it difficult to speak will give an impetus to speak in the next week's meeting. One week a client in the project had something that he wanted to say in the meeting. It concerned the fact that he felt under pressure because he felt he took responsibility for doing all the chores around the house which others left undone. The therapist team were aware of this as he had expressed these feelings informally during the week. We wanted to wait to see if he would bring the issue himself rather than reminding and prompting him to do so – we felt that his difficulty was in speaking to, and confronting and negotiating with, others. His difficulty was having to actually deal with the people with whom he was living, as they were not as he wanted them to be. We felt that this was what left him stuck doing other people's chores, for this was, for him, easier than speaking to and confronting others.

The forty minutes passed and the client did not speak; in fact, the meeting moved on to the next part which concerned the community business arrangements. The client acted out this unspoken issue through angry behaviour during the rest of the meeting. He sat stiffly and his face was flushed a beetroot colour. When clients and therapists approached him for his view or engagement on some matter of community business he either remained silent or replied with monosyllables.

In the post-group following this meeting, the therapists, as a team, agreed that the way to work with this client was to leave him stuck with his issue and stuck with his angry feelings which were being played out in his overt behaviour. The idea was that the client should use the punctuation in the time for speaking – provided by the structure in the fixed ending point of the 'Feelings' section – to put into words himself the meaning of his angry actions. The next week, towards the end of the forty minutes, the client finally used the time to his advantage and actually said what he had intended to say the previous week.

In this way he was able to overcome his difficulties in having to confront and deal with others as well as give his angry actions meaning. However, if the time to speak in this way in the Community Meeting had no fixed ending point, I believe that this client would not have found the impetus to put his feelings into words and to force himself to deal with others. Further, if the therapist team had not remained silent, but rather prompted him to speak, I do not think that the client would have spoken in way that really dealt with his frustrations and difficulties in dealing with others – his words would not have come from himself but rather would have been literal or metaphorical echoes of the therapist's words. Our intention is to allow the client to find what it is they mean to say and say it themselves. Our role is not to provide the answers for the clients; rather, it is to be there alongside and to gently guide whilst the client finds the answer for themselves. In my view, it was the fact that he had experienced the fixed time to speak come and go the previous week without being able to speak, and the frustration that this caused him, that propelled him into dialogue the following week. In my view, what helped him to speak was the fact that the 'Feelings' section was punctuated with a 'full stop' and the fact that therapists chose to punctuate his speech and actions with silence during this fixed time.

In addition to our groups and individual therapy sessions having fixed ending points, we also use trial periods as a way of working in structured time with clients. On arriving in the community in which I have been working, clients have a stretch of time which serves as a trial period. This is a fixed time of usually one or three months. The question of how long this period will be is decided by the staff team in conjunction with other professionals involved with the clients, such as their social worker, psychiatrist and CPN. It depends on the particular issues that the client has and the way they manifest them. Clients can and do respond to the finite nature of this trial period in different ways, and their response may change at different stages of the trial period.

One client with whom I worked was set a three-month trial period because it was felt that he would take time to settle and really feel relaxed enough to trust the community to begin for himself, and thus for him and the community, to assess whether this was a place where he could grow and benefit. During the first month to six weeks his behaviour reflected an awareness of the finite nature of the trial period in a particular way. He was, what he perceived to be, 'the model client', participating fully in each aspect of the therapeutic programme. In contrast, as the final month was drawing to a close, the pressure of the end was apparently too much for him to bear. He had a number of 'outbursts' where he was verbally aggressive whenever approached to participate in anything. He became uncooperative and withdrawn. He could no longer be 'the model client', perhaps resigned to his feelings of powerlessness and his perception that once the trial period was over, there was nothing he could do to influence whether or not he would stay on. These feelings of powerlessness were reflected in a change in his behaviour. However, during these outbursts, although we made clear the verbal aggression was not acceptable, a number of important issues and concerns were raised by the client, issues which we could work with. These were his issues of feeling out of control of his own life, of feeling controlled to behave in certain ways by others and his feeling that he had no centre from which to be a responsible agent – he was merely a reflection of other people's desires.

So although the model behaviour at the outset appeared more in line with what the client thought would be acceptable, it was the behaviour shown in relation to the pressure of the time that reflected what was really going on for the client. Although he did not go about it in a way which we would encourage, with uncontained outbursts, in the end he was able to express his true self and what he was really feeling. For this client, the fact that the trial period had a fixed ending point enabled him to really speak to us about what was going on for him, albeit in a chaotic way. It was important that his trial period was three months rather than one month as, in my view, had it been one month he would not have had time to really speak to us in this way. Again, the punctuation in time, provided by the fixed end of his trial period, really did seem to serve to give the client impetus to say what he wanted to and to begin to make meaningful contact about himself with others in the community.

Weekly therapeutic and educational programme

In each of CHT's communities there is a structured therapeutic and educational programme for clients. This consists of therapy groups, practical groups and individual therapy sessions. Groups include the Community Meeting, Morning Groups, Art Therapy Groups, Reading Groups, Experiential Dialogue Groups, Pool Groups, Cleaning Groups, Maintenance Groups, Catering Groups and Gardening Groups. Each group is organized so that it takes place at a specific time on a specific day; this then becomes a regular feature of the weekly therapeutic programme. In addition to this structured programme within the communities, we work with each client to create a plan for clients to do things outside our community in the wider community. This is particularly relevant for those clients who have benefited from the programme in the communities and are ready to venture out. This programme may include times for doing voluntary work, paid work experience, college courses, and so forth.

This overall way of structuring time for clients who come to our communities provides a rhythm of gatherings and dispersals which punctuates their speech and actions in two ways. First, at a very basic level the very fact that there are times for coming together and doing gardening, cleaning, speaking about oneself, discussing poems, voluntary work, and so forth, and times for not doing these things or anything in particular at all, in and of itself punctuates time and gives meaning to one's time. For just as a sentence with no punctuation in it has no meaning, so a day, week or year with no structure in it has no meaning. If one is active all day and all night, the meanings of one's actions are lost as well as the meaning of night and day. If one is passive or resting all day and all night, the meaning of rest is lost. Many of our clients are apparently drawn towards passivity, towards doing nothing and towards giving up making any articulation in their days by acting and then resting. We believe that providing this sort of programme for clients is not a way of imposing a regime on already alienated people, but rather a way of introducing a very basic level of meaning back in their often unarticulated time.

The other very important way in which this overall structured programme serves as a therapeutic tool for working with our clients is the way in which we use it to help clients to build a whole sense of themselves in relation to others. By this I mean that by having, for example, an experiential dialogue group, an individual therapy session and a reading group, a client has specific times where it is safe to be close to others, to reveal themselves and explore themselves with others. This time that they have is different in quality to the time they have chatting after supper or over coffee in the morning. At this time, rather, it is safe to be entertaining, laugh, explore ideas and enquire in a 'social' way how one is. This is the time to 'play' in dialogue with others; it is not really the time to 'work' on oneself and work oneself out in dialogue with others. The time for 'play', however, is equally important as a therapeutic and educational time as the time for therapy 'work'. Living a human life is not constituted by always living the life on the end of a therapist's gaze. This only breeds an institutional sense of self as one who is by definition a client in need. Further, the really important thing is that it is precisely at the point of learning when to speak in these different ways that clients learn to build a whole sense of themselves. This is best illustrated with an example.

One client in our community was a young woman in her early twenties who had been physically and emotionally abused by her father during her child-hood and teenage years as she was growing up to be a woman. When she came to us she was extremely promiscuous, and had this reputation in the local 'psychiatric' community in the hospital ward and other mental health hostels. She would literally bring back half a bus queue of men to the house and take them into her room. In addition to this she would tell strangers in the street her most personal history and feelings. This behaviour was also reflected in the way she spoke to staff and clients in the project, at any time, about her innermost self. I remember being so confused when I first came to the community, and I would in arrive in the mornings and greet her, saying: 'Hello, how are you?' She would always tell me exactly how she was. She would tell me about her bowels and about her feelings of being ripped apart inside, or about her father's abuse, all within two or three minutes as I edged towards the kitchen to make a coffee.

I soon learnt that the team was working with the community and this client to help her regain a sense of herself by the very simple act of providing times when it was all right to speak about these things and times when it was, rather, appropriate to sit and chat over coffee about 'nothing'. In this way we were working with this woman to help her regain a sense of where she ended and others began, to help contain her confused and painful desire to expose herself and contain her uncontrollable feelings of needing to be loved right now. I learnt that, however hard I found it was to do, responding with silence to scenes like the one I described in the mornings, or even with a light joke about something else, was a way of helping her regain a sense of herself. In this way we punctuated her speech with these silences and jokes in the informal periods of contact around the community, and in so doing provided a way for her to explore the meaning of her words and her promiscuous actions. This is a very literal way in which I realized our communities provide 'a time to speak' about one's insides, and that the fact of this time to speak about one's insides by definition needs a time to speak from oneself but not about one's insides. Only thus can we have a sense of ourselves in relation to others.

Reviews and care plans

Clients have a review held in our communities every three to six months and to which psychiatrists, social workers, CPNs, friends and family are invited. Just as the academic year is split into and punctuated by terms and years, so too is a client's placement in one of our communities. In conjunction with the review, therapists work with each client to devise a care plan. The care plan considers the present, the past progress since last review and the future. An important aspect of the care plans is that they help clients to think about the future, *their* future. The care plans are structured in such a way as to assist the clients to endorse their future.

Again, the way in which these reviews, in the context of the care plans, serve to punctuate the client's ongoing dialogue in our communities is best illustrated with an example. I worked with a man in his early thirties who was diagnosed with schizophrenia and had characteristically spent much of his time sitting alone talking out loud to himself. He had been in our community for about a year and half, during which time he had shifted from spending most of his time asleep during the day and awake at night (and only participating during the day on the rare occasion) to sleeping at night, being up during the day, taking charge of our maintenance group and step-by-step speaking more to others than himself.

However, during a period of about five weeks he began to behave in a different way. He missed three of our weekly individual therapy sessions, and when I spoke to him about this he said he had forgotten. However, it became clear that he was going out of the house at the time for our sessions and walking to the local pub where he would drink two or three pints. On his return he would stumble into bed. When I spoke to him about what these actions might mean and about my concern that he was not able to speak to me, he politely agreed but then kept on doing the same thing from week to week.

It happened that at the end of five weeks of this it was time for his review, to which his social worker came. This client had made his own agenda for the review and proceeded to run through it, taking command of the group. As if suddenly, he spoke about how he had been feeling that there was no point and about how he felt he had lost his direction. He spoke about how he was avoiding talking to me because this was how he felt; it was easier for him to 'drown his sorrows'. When I confirmed that I had thought something was awry with him because of the way he had not wanted to speak to me but that overall I admired him and was especially impressed with his creative work with others in the garden, he looked surprised. He admitted that he had thought that I thought he was not 'doing well'. From here, in the weeks to follow, we were able to look together at what was underlying his feelings of having lost his direction. This review served as a punctuation for the client in the development of his silent dialogue with me, as a time for taking stock, a time for really looking at what was going on in an honest way and as a time for speaking.

Three minutes at a time

Another client in our community was a fifty-year-old man who was diagnosed with schizophrenia and had spent fifteen years in one of the long-stay 'asylum' hospitals, after which he had been discharged in to the community to live in an independent flat. Here he deteriorated over about eight years. In particular, he neglected his self-care, never washing himself or his clothes and rarely eating. He heard voices constantly abusing him and at which he would outwardly swear. One of our aims with this client in our community was clearly to help him engage with himself on a very basic physical level in terms of dealing with his mess and dirt and smell. On the whole, every time we attempted to carry out any of these practical tasks with him he would swear at us, just as he swore at his voices. We thought as a team about this man, and about how painful he perhaps found it to engage with his own mess on a very basic level as well as on a psychological and emotional level. His only response was to swear, with the effect of removing himself from the possibility of dealing with his physical and emotional mess. Of course, this tactic only had a temporary result, for his physical mess remained and was still there to confront him. His voices returned to confront him too.

We used time to help him engage with his mess, as a very first step on the physical level. We would literally go and help him wash his clothes for three minutes at a time and return at hour-long intervals for another three minutes with him on the task in hand. With three minutes at a time this client could very well manage to engage with his mess. However, this was really all he could bear at a time. By punctuating his day with him, we were able to help this client begin to deal with himself, and this was something that he was then able to take pride in. In this way, perhaps, we were beginning to help him relate to himself in a meaningful way.

Open-ended placements

While we do use fixed ending times for groups, individual therapy sessions and trial periods as a way of helping clients to punctuate their own speech, the length of a placement in our communities is not fixed. On average, clients stay in our communities for between one and three years, but they may stay longer. This is because we believe that it is essentially in the client's hands as to when they have had enough time to begin to speak about their true desires. We believe that not only is this something that cannot be determined by us or them in advance, but also that it should not on the whole be determined by us during the client's placement. Of course, there are exceptions to this when we decide to terminate a placement. However, this may often follow an extreme incident which can on some occasions be interpreted as the client themselves in effect ending the dialogue with the community. The open-ended nature of our placements is based on the belief that it is up to the client to determine when they have finished, when they have begun to articulate their truth.

However, this process of the client realizing the time to finish their placement is an essentially intersubjective one which happens at the interface between the client and the community (see Lacan 1956, pp.74–75). In essence, it involves the therapists not taking charge of fixing the ending point. If we do so, in a sense the client's truth will be eternally in our hands. If we resist the temptation to take charge of the ending time, and thus of the nature of what the client really desires, we enable the client to take charge of this themselves. However, if we were not there, precisely not fixing the end point, the client would have no others, in the context of which to speak about their true desires, the client would have no one in the context of which to take charge of the ending of their placement. So while therapists do not set a time to end the placement, the eventuality of the client speaking their truth and finding an ending point precisely depends on therapists being there and not fixing the ending point. The client could not find his ending point outside the context of his dialogue with others. It is an essentially intersubjective process in which therapists punctuate the client's whole dialogue in the community during their placement with silence with regard to the ending time.

INTERCONNECTING THE PAST, PRESENT AND FUTURE

The ways in which we experience our past in the present and the ways in which we experience our future in the present have a powerful impact on the ways in which we are able to live our lives in the present. In this section, by drawing on the ideas of Lacan and Heidegger, I shall explain how learning to speak about one's future authentically and learning to speak about one's past authentically results in one being able to live one's life in the present, in a fully engaged, active and participative way. I shall explain how these things result in one being able to take responsibility for one's life in the present with the choices and possibilities for the future that go with this way of living in the present. I shall illustrate how we work with clients to enable them to speak about their past and their future, in the present, in a way which enables them to fully endorse their lives and make choices which truly reflect their desires.

What is important about this way of thinking about time, and thus this way of using time to work with our clients to enable them to speak truly from themselves, is that we are clear that here we are not always making use of a linear conception of time. We are making use of our *experiences* of the past at the present time and of our *experiences* of the future at the present time, and in this realm of experiences it is not always true that the past comes before the present and the present before the future in a linear way. For example, here, as I shall explain in much more detail, the past can be literally in the present – as when we repeat events and relationships in our past when 'acting out'. Moreover, here the past is not necessarily a fixed-objective fact that determines the present but something which can be under constant revision in the present – as when we strive to make sense of our histories. So when we are thinking about the interconnections of our experiences of past, present and future, it might be that the linear dimension is abandoned. It is to this that Heidegger refers when he says: 'Temporalising does not signify that ecstases [our experiences of past, present and future] come in a succession' (Heidegger 1962, section 68).

The future in the present

There are two experiences of, or attitudes towards, the future that one can have in the present. One can await the future or one can anticipate the future (see Heidegger 1962, sections 61–72). If we merely await our future, we remain passive victims of events that will happen to us. Our future will not be something for which we have responsibility, it will be something ready-made and determined without our choice. For Heidegger, this awaiting attitude towards our future is inauthentic. For him, what we await is determined by our alienated experiences of what we think others expect of us, what 'they' want our future to be. Awaiting the future precisely prevents us from fulfilling our own true desires and potential in the future because it is predetermined solely by what we think others expect from us. By contrast, if we have the attitude of anticipating our future, we take on an authentic openness to, and responsibility for, the possibilities, choices and creative potential of our own desire. With this anticipation of the future, we are able to project our selves on to whatever possibility best releases the capacity for our genuine selves to emerge. With anticipation, we do not wait for predetermined future events to happen to us, we create our own possibilities. This is not to say that what we truly desire for ourselves and the nature of our genuine selves is never affected by, or responsive to, the desires and expectations of others. Given the fact that we are essentially social beings, who we really are and what our possibilities are come about in the context of others. However, with anticipation of the future, we take an attitude by which we can be the authors of our choices and future possibilities rather than being the slaves of the desires and expectations of others. This experiencing of the future, in the present, with anticipation requires that we relate to our life in the present as a place where we have the possibility of making our own choices and decisions now. Thus the openness and anticipation of the future determines a comparable openness and active engagement with our present lives. By contrast, when we await the future, in the present, we are stuck in an alienated, impotent and passive relationship to our present lives. We are in the present absorbed by the dictates of others. Changing our relationship to our present lives involves shifting our experience of the future from awaiting to anticipating.

Being the authors of our own choices and possibilities means anticipating the events to come in the same sense that we construct our sentences in dialogue with each other by ordering the first words in anticipation of the words to come. The meaning of our sentences and paragraphs are not fully determined until the last words and sentences are added (see Lacan 1977a, p.303). In the present we are constantly adding to our sentences in anticipation of the words and sentences to follow in the future. We are constantly anticipating and creating the meaning of our words as they are added to our sentences and paragraphs. It is not that the meaning is already determined; rather, with anticipation, we constantly create new meanings to our words. In this sense we also create the meaning of our true selves and of our lives with anticipation.

Perhaps, on examination, many of us may realize that we are awaiting the future rather than anticipating it. Certainly this is so for many of the clients in our communities. This awaiting of the future is reflected in a pronounced way for many of our clients in a severely passive attitude towards the present and the future, an attitude which lacks any sense of self as the locus of one's actions, one which lacks any sense of agency in one's own life. This awaiting of the future is reflected in the loss of a sense of meaning in doing, feeling or thinking anything now or in the future and in a constant sense of frustration with this meaninglessness.

Part of helping the clients in our communities shift from an attitude of awaiting the future to one of anticipation involves simply providing a time for them to speak their true desire, in which time we resist their unconscious invitation for us, as others, to impose a predetermined future upon them and thus collude with their awaiting of the future. Another part of helping clients to shift their attitude towards the future involves making sense of the past in relation to the present and future. I shall turn to this presently. First, I want to illustrate the way in which one client I have worked with has awaited the future and the way in which we have worked with him to give him time to speak without colluding with his awaiting the future.

Peter was a forty-year-old man with a diagnosis of paranoid schizophrenia who came to our community after spending some months in hospital on a section. He was taken to hospital after having been found in his basement flat which he had not come out of for months. He had a neighbour who had delivered shopping for him. Apart from this he had had no contact with other people and was in a state of great fear, believing that a terrorist group were scheming to destroy him. He was thin, and he and his flat were extremely dirty. When he came to our community, he talked at length and repeatedly about how he should never have been forced to go into hospital, how he was not 'mentally ill', how he had had his life taken from him and how he could not abide this control. He had, he felt, been controlled by the mental health professionals in a damaging way. He admitted he had been going through 'a rough patch', but was adamant that he was a 'free spirit' and that this had to do with his ancestors. He was concerned about the levels of control that our community would place upon him and in particular those that the staff would place on him. During his first months, Peter spent a good amount of time in his room listening to music and reading but also developed a relationship with the rest of the group in the community. He would make impromptu snacks for himself and others when he felt like it. These evolved into quite elaborate community meals. He would also plan video-watching evenings for himself and others. He contributed to the ongoing running of the house and attended the Community Meeting and individual therapy sessions. He began to comment that he liked our community because people were treated 'as adults' there.

However, as the months went by he repeatedly declined and then insistently refused to take the role of chair of the Community Meeting. During one Community Meeting, many members of the client group attempted to persuade Peter to take this role. They reasoned that they understood that he might find it difficult to take control of the meeting but that everyone had to take it in turns and everyone else did it anyway. They went on to say that, really, he had to do it if he was to contribute as part of our community, and anyway he did contribute to the group in many other ways, so why couldn't he do this? During this conversation, Peter replied with excuses, saying that he was terrible at doing such things, and moving on in desperation to saying that if he had to wash up on Tuesday evening then that ruined his evening and he certainly could not take on chairing the meeting the next day. He needed time to rest. He said there were others who had not chaired the meeting for a while anyway. Finally, a therapist joined in, saying that like the others he wondered why Peter seemed so insistent not to take on this role when he was such a valued member of the community in so many other ways. He wondered what it was about this chore which Peter found so difficult to bear. At this point, Peter said to the therapist in a resigned way that since this was being demanded of him, he had no choice but to do it.

Peter was awaiting his future rather than anticipating it. Paradoxically, he allowed himself to be controlled by the member of staff precisely to take control of the Community Meeting by taking the role of chair. It was not until the therapist spoke that Peter was able to allow himself to experience being forced and controlled to take this role. Despite the open discussion from his peers in the group which preceded the therapist's contribution, Peter agreed to take the chair on the grounds that the member of staff was relinquishing his freedom of choice. It is a difficult and open question, as it always is, as to how damaging his having been sectioned and thus controlled to be in hospital was. However, what struck us in our team was Peter's fear of being controlled by us, together with his perception that being involved as part of our community was a demand from the team which served to control him, and this seemed to lie deeper than his recent experiences in hospital. Indeed, Peter had taken this to the extreme of feeling controlled to take control of the meeting. Peter was in a position of awaiting his future, of acting towards the future only on the demands of those controlling others, the staff. Peter's insistence that he would not take this role was also a response to his experience of others making him do it. Whether he took the role of chair or not, his experience was one of not being able to make his own choices with respect to his future, and this he manifested in a particularly vivid way in this meeting.

Our task was to attempt to work with Peter in order to help him shift away from awaiting his future, in the form of experiencing being controlled, towards an anticipation of his future in which he had full agency. For us, this might be reflected in one small way by Peter being able to desire to be the chair of our Community Meeting, by Peter being able to desire to be a full agent in our meetings through this role. Of course, this would only be a reflection of a much deeper change which would hopefully be manifested in many other, perhaps more colourful, ways.

The problem for us was that what seemed to lie so deep for Peter was precisely that he felt so unable to be an agent, unable to take control and make his own choices and thus to take an open, anticipatory attitude towards his future. This, we felt, had partly to do with his bringing his past into the present, and I shall turn to a discussion of this presently to describe how getting to grips with this was an integral part of Peter getting to grips with anticipating the future. However, what we were able to do in helping Peter shift from awaiting to anticipation, even without examining how his experience of the past related to his experience of the present and future, was work on giving Peter a time to really speak about his desires without colluding with his unconscious desire to be controlled, which was at the heart of his awaiting the future in this alienated way. This meant creating a delicate balance between Peter's experience of what was indeed expected by the team and the rest of the group in our community and Peter's evident desire to be in some way part of the community. In particular, we encouraged Peter to speak openly about what it was that he meant when he said that he liked this community because people were treated like adults and to speak about what this desire to be an adult was. In this way we attempted to create an environment in which Peter could begin to anticipate his future as an adult rather than merely awaiting his future as controlled by his experience of our expectations.

The past in the present

There are two ways of experiencing the past in the present. One can repeat the past in the present or one can remember the past in the present (see, for example, Freud 1920). When we repeat the past in the present, we 'act out' events and relationships occurring in the past in our present lives. When we 'act out' the past in the present, we are usually not aware that we are doing so, although we may be aware of what we are doing but still be unable to stop ourselves from doing it. When we are not aware that we are 'acting out', the *experience* of the past in the present takes the form of, for example, repeatedly experiencing relationships with authority figures as alienating, whatever the real nature of the authority figure, or repeatedly experiencing intimate relationships as disappointing, whether or not there has been a possibility of a successful relationship.

'Acting out' involves literally repeating the past in the present. It indicates that we have forgotten the past. The past remains in the unconscious, and because of this we are left stuck in the present, unable to make our own lives and choices now because we are somehow determined to repeat the past from a time when we were, more often than not, so young that we really did not have the capacity to change the course of events. Our experience of, and relationship with, the past is one which we now, in the present, do not have any integral choice about. The past determines us now, and we have the experience of not being able to do anything about it.

The forgetting resulting in 'acting out' is connected with our failure to have been able to communicate in conscious words with the person to whom we have wished to communicate. Our words have been ignored or have gone unheard. Thus we are forced to attempt to communicate our message in actions. 'Acting out' is a ciphered message from the foreign unconscious language which we address to others and leave for them to decode in our attempt to make contact with them (see Lacan 1977b, pp.238–239). However, because this message is usually so hard to interpret, it goes unheard again and again, and so we continually repeat it in the effort to make ourselves understood by others.

By contrast, when we are able to remember our past we are able to bring events and relationships from the past fully into our consciousness. This means translating into conscious language the message ciphered in the actions that manifested our repeating the past in 'acting out' (see Lacan 1977b, pp.238–239). These messages may or may not reflect the objective facts of the past. What is important is the way in which we remember the past and the way in which we now, in the present, synthesize the past (see Lacan 1988, p.36). Once we have remembered our past by deciphering our unconscious messages to ourselves and others by putting into conscious words what we remember, we are able to experience our past in the present in a very different way. We are able to acknowledge the ways in which our past has determined us but not be captured by this determination in the present and future. We are able to take responsibility for creating new possibilities for events and relationships now in the present rather than being caught in an apparently pre-programmed repetition. Just as shifting from an experience of awaiting the future to one of anticipating it results in an opening up of our own agency in our lives, so too does a shift from an experience of repeating the past to remembering it. Indeed, a shift from repeating to remembering in the present is part of being able to shift from awaiting the future to anticipating it.

To illustrate this I want to go back to the example of Peter. While we felt that Peter was awaiting the future by acting on his experiences of what others expected of him, we also felt that, at the same time, Peter was bringing his past into the present by repeating it in the form of 'acting out'. We felt this was so because of his extreme insistence on not wanting to take the role of chairperson in the context of the facts that, on the one hand, this was not such a remarkable task to do and, on the other hand, Peter's relative willingness and ability to contribute to the group in other ways. We began to wonder what Peter was attempting to say to us through his action of experiencing coercion at the hands of the therapists in the context of the whole group. We wondered whether this was something that Peter was literally repeating from the past and, in so doing, communicating to us something in a coded message from his unconscious. We were particularly struck by the way in which this message was apparently presented for the therapists to decipher rather than other clients in the community, and the way in which it seemed to demand a response from us, even though we were not immediately sure how to do so. It was as if Peter had entrusted the decoding to us in particular, and this we felt was a positive sign of Peter opening up a time for dialogue with us.

Gradually, during his individual therapy sessions, Peter began to speak about himself and his family history, the details of which had not been known to us when he came to our community. Peter was the child of a Jewish survivor of the Holocaust. His mother had survived a concentration camp; his father had died in one. On the one hand, he spoke about this traumatic and tragic history and, on the other, he spent much time explaining his feelings about the idea of 'the wandering Jew'. We began to understand Peter's extreme response to being asked to chair our Community Meeting in terms of his confusion about, and complex response to, the perpetrators of the Holocaust. Very gradually, we began to articulate in conscious language the connections we found in Peter's actions and responses to us in the present, to those of his family ancestry. Thus, very gradually, we began to enable Peter to remember not only his past but that which had in some way been transmitted to him via his parents. As Peter began to be able to articulate these things for himself in speech, his relationship with us changed in small but, we felt, significant ways. Peter continued to refuse to chair the Community Meeting, but he began to be able to speak about this in terms of his feeling about taking control himself and what unsustainable damaging effect this might have on others. He spoke about how he feared destroying others and how this connected with his family history of being victims of the Holocaust. Through remembering and acknowledging his feelings about his family history rather than repeating them in distorted ways, Peter gradually made small moves towards shifting away from experiencing staff as offering him no choice for his own future, away from awaiting his future.

I think that Peter's example goes some way towards illustrating the way in which moving from repeating one's past in the present towards remembering it, by having the courage to begin to speak about it, can at the same time provoke a shift from awaiting one's future to beginning to anticipate one's agency and choices for the future. In this way it illustrates the interconnections between past, present and future that are so important as a frame of reference for initiating dialogue about our true desires in our communities.

NOTES

1   There is some discussion of the therapeutic use of time in music therapy, a discussion of which falls beyond the scope of this chapter. However, it is of note that Aigen discusses four dimensions of time in music therapy with children – physical/concrete time, growth time, emotional time and creative time – and stresses the importance of the therapist being able to meet the child in the dimension of time in which he or she is functioning (Aigen 1998, pp.146–148).

2   The theoretical material in this section is based on an unpublished paper by Sarah Tucker.

REFERENCES

Aigen, K. (1998) *Paths of Development in Nordoff–Robbins Music Therapy.* Gilsum, New Haven: Barcelona Publishers.

Cooper, R. (1989) 'Dwelling and the "Therapeutic Community".' In R. Cooper (ed) *Thresholds between Philosophy and Psychoanalysis: Papers from the Philadelphia Association.* London: Free Association Books.

Freud, S. (1920) 'Beyond the pleasure principle.' In J. Strachey (ed) *The Standard Edition of the Complete Psychological Works of Sigmund Freud,* Vol.XVII, 7. London: Hogarth Press and Institute of Psychoanalysis.

Heidegger, M. (1962) *Being and Time* (trans. J. Macquarrie and E. Robinson). Oxford: Basil Blackwell.

Lacan, J. (1956) *Speech and Language in Psychoanalysis* (trans. A. Wilden). Baltimore and London: The Johns Hopkins University Press, 1981. (Originally published as 'Fonction et champ de la parole et du langage en psychanalyse.' *La Psychanalyse 1*, Paris, 1956.)

Lacan, J. (1977a) 'On the subject at last in question.' In *Ecrits: A Selection* (trans. A. Sheridan). London: Tavistock.

Lacan, J. (1977b) 'The direction of treatment and principles of its power.' In *Ecrits: A Selection* (trans. A. Sheridan). London: Tavistock.

Lacan, J. (1988) *The Seminar. Book I. Freud's Papers on Technique, 1953–54* (trans. J. Forrester). New York: Norton; Cambridge: Cambridge University Press.

CHAPTER 3

Building a Home of One's Own

Kirsty Handover

DWELLING INVOLVES FINDING ONE'S PLACE
IN RELATION TO THE WORLD

> The way in which you are and I am, the manner in which we humans are on earth is...dwelling. (Heidegger 1971, p.147)

For Heidegger, dwelling is the 'basic character of Being' (Heidegger 1971, p.160). It is a way of being on earth. However, it is not any old way of being in relation to people and our physical environments. For him, authentic dwelling is something we need to continually learn to do and involves an open attitude of involvement and concern towards other people and our physical environment. Through this 'being-towards' our social and physical environments, the people and things in those environments can become real and meaningful to us at a deep level. It is thus that Heidegger says of an everyday hammer:

> [T]he less we just stare at the hammer-Thing, and the more we seize hold of it and use it, the more primordial does our relationship to it become, and the more unveiledly is it encountered... (Heidegger 1962, section 15)

Not only does the open involvement, the 'being-towards' implicit in authentic dwelling, provide us with a meaningful relationship with our environment, but further and importantly, authentic dwelling is what goes towards providing meaning to our own beings, to ourselves. Without really dwelling in the world, without finding our place, we ourselves cannot give full meaning to our lives. It is thus that Heidegger says:

> With the 'towards-which'...there can be an involvement: with this thing ...which we call...a hammer, there is an involvement which is hammering; with hammering there is an involvement in making something fast; with making something fast there is an involvement in protecting against bad weather; and this protection 'is' for the sake of providing shelter for Dasein – that is to say, for the sake of Dasein's Being. (Heidegger 1962, section 18)

Here, Heidegger explains one way in which our dealings with the physical environment are done in relation to our own lives and being. They are done, as it were, in the context of making room for our lives. Without these dealings with the physical environment there would be no room for our lives to meaningfully exist. Conversely, without our lives, these dealings would have no point or meaning either.

In order to find our place in the world we need to form a meaningful relationship with our physical and social environments. This happens at the *interface between* ourselves and our physical and social environments. Who we really are emerges in the context of our relation to our environment, and if, as many of our clients do, we suffer, we have the task of building a new and changed relation to our environment. It is to this which Heidegger refers when he talks about learning to dwell as learning to be-towards-the-world.

In this chapter I concentrate on the work we do with clients in our communities at Community Housing and Therapy (CHT), which focuses on building a meaningful relationship to the physical environment and in particular to the place where clients live, their home. In our view, building a relationship with our physical environment is important in and of itself in the sense that who I am, my identity, is partially constituted and created by this relationship. It was in this spirit that Jeff Bishop emphasized the following:

> ...it is essential that anybody involved in therapy understands the ways in which man consciously and unconsciously uses space, in order to bring in the environment as a contribution to therapy.' (Bishop 1979, p.59)

However, building a relationship with our physical environment is also important as a starting point towards developing the ability to build a new relationship with one's social environment. Finding one's place in the context of one's physical home serves as a way of creating one's identity and also as a stepping stone towards finding one's home among others.[1] This work at the interface between our clients and their physical environment is so vital precisely because so many of our clients have in one way or another retreated away from any creative contact with anyone. For many of our clients, beginning to be able to make a positive relationship with their physical environment is a first step out of an alienated isolation from others.

A central forum for the work that we do in helping our clients learn to dwell in their physical environments is our task-groups. These include cleaning groups, gardening groups, maintenance groups and leisure groups. The other place where this work takes place is in an ongoing informal way; for example, thinking and speaking with clients about their relationships with their rooms and about their relationship with their beds! As I have already indicated, the therapeutic aim of these task-groups and informal interactions is more than teaching clients practical skills. These are useful for people who have not had a forum in which to learn them or have somehow forgotten them during, for example, a long stay in hospital. However, our task-groups aim to do much more than this. They aim to help clients understand themselves in relation to their physical environments and thereby to enable them to dwell in their physical environments in a creative way. We take as central to therapy with our clients a working through of their responses to their physical environment. These responses, we believe, are often unconscious manifestations of their relation to themselves and others. Voorhoeve reflects in a clear way on the importance of this kind of sensitivity to the physical environment, in this case in the context of a hospital setting, saying:

> ...before and during intake the patient creates illusions and expectations about the setting on the basis of his/her fusion need, having in this way an imaginary fusion with the setting. Thus the patient transfers aspects of his/her infantile object-relation fantasies to the hospital. (Voorhoeve 1993, p.23)

Very often our clients approach practical engagement with their physical environments with a very low level of motivation. Sometimes this is expressed by direct questions to staff, such as 'Why do I have to clean the kitchen?', 'Why bother planting these bulbs?' or just, 'Why should I do this?' At other times these questions are expressed through actions, such as not turning up to a cleaning group, wandering off after the first three minutes of the gardening group or attending the group but sitting on the edge doing nothing. In our view these questions which clients ask staff, explicitly through language and implicitly through actions, are questions which we need to translate. They are all indirect ways of asking about the point of being here in the world and our relationship to the world. They are deep existential questions which precisely reflect the position of so many of our clients of not having a meaningful place in the world, of not having a meaningful relationship to the world. Beginning to search for, and find answers to, these underlying questions, answers which speak meaningfully to each of us, provides us with foundations upon which to build the rest of our lives. This is precisely what is involved in finding a place for oneself. However, when our clients ask us these questions they manifest their inability to dwell in the world, they manifest an alienated turning away from the world and a fractured relationship with it. In asking us these questions, our clients manifest their emotional homelessness.[2]

Alexandra Fanning speaks about the importance of creating a 'psychic space' for *therapists* in therapeutic communities, a space in which one can have inner dialogues (Fanning 1990, p.218). Our practical work with *clients* in task-groups provides a physical place in relation to which clients can begin to articulate to others some of the deep and troubling questions that have consciously or unconsciously filled their 'psychic space'.

In this chapter I aim to explore how therapists work with clients to begin to respond to, and help find a response to, the underlying existential questions that clients ask us by helping them learn to dwell in their physical environment, by building a home with them in our communities and thereby beginning to show them how to find meaning in relation to the physical environment. In the following two sections, by drawing further on the ideas of Heidegger, I explore in more detail the grounds for treating our practical task-groups as forums for providing so much more than the acquisition of new skills. First, I explore the way in which dwelling in relation to one's physical environment is the craft of caring. I look at the sense in which this craft provides a context for remembering that one can think and speak and thus the first step to re-creating a meaningful relationship with one's physical environment. Second, I explore the way in which dwelling in relation to one's physical environment is the craft of asking meaningful questions. In the final section I illustrate the ways in which we use these ideas in our work with clients in our task-groups and informal interactions in order to help them to build a meaningful relationship to their physical environment and thereby open the way to deeper self-understanding and meaningful relationships with others.

DWELLING AND THE CRAFT OF CARE[3]

As I have described, for Heidegger, dwelling requires learning to be-towards-the-world. In this and the next section I explore what is meant by this in more detail. Part of what he means is that in order to build meaningful relationships with our physical environment we must learn the craft of caring for that environment. He says:

> The old word *bauen*, which says that man *is* in so far as he *dwells*, this word *bauen* however also means at the same time to cherish and protect, to preserve and care for... (Heidegger 1971, p.147)

For Heidegger, care is a craft (Heidegger 1962, p.225). It is the craft of involvement. It is the craft of being able to be alongside and involved with people and things in the world. What this means is that care is not doing things for others so that they remain passive and unable to do things for themselves. In the context of our communities it means that care is not about doing the cleaning, washing up, gardening, and so forth, for our clients. Caring in this sense keeps clients in their isolated state of being uninvolved with their environments. Rather, caring for our clients means helping them to learn to care for themselves and their environments in the sense of teaching them to be involved with those tasks. Therapists care for clients by teaching clients to care themselves. Teaching clients to do this means teaching them to see their environments as meaningful in a way that they can be motivated to engage with them.

Actively caring is being able to have a fully involved and detailed relationship with one's environment. We can begin to help clients to find meaning in their environments by helping them to perceive it in more detail, with precision, in a more articulated way. In so doing we are teaching clients to care in the sense of seeing the environment not as an uninteresting amorphous blur which has nothing to do with them, but rather as a detailed, interesting, articulated place. They can begin to care in the sense of *doing things with* care, with precision and in detail.[4]

Thus, learning to be-towards our physical environment requires us to care for it in the sense of becoming involved with it and paying attention to detail so that one can do things in it with precision. However, it requires more than this, for it requires that we learn to do this as a *craft*. What this means is that we learn to do these practical things in such a way that they become meaningful in the context of the rest of our lives. Learning to do these things as a craft means that through doing these things we learn to articulate ourselves in a meaningful way. Heidegger says:

> 'Craft' literally means the strength and skill of our hand... Only a being who can also speak, that is, think, can have hands, can be handy in achieving works of handicraft... The hand is infinitely different from all grasping organs – paws, claws, or fangs – different by an abyss of essence. (Heidegger 1968, p.16)

Here, Heidegger expresses the view that it is the human hand only that can properly engage in a craft, as opposed to the paws and so forth of animals. We might add that animals can engage in and learn practical skills but cannot learn a craft. Certainly, animals can use their paws to perform practical tasks in their physical environments, and they learn to do so with great expertise, in relation to hunting, eating, grooming, and so forth. However, in so doing, animals do not have the capability that humans have, of learning a craft in relation to their physical environments. When humans use their hands in any handicraft they enter into an intentional and meaningful relationship with the environment, and this relationship transcends merely the 'empty busy work' and 'business concerns' of performing a skill (see Heidegger 1968, p.15). Heidegger illustrates this relationship involved in the craft of the hand which transcends a skill thus:

> A cabinetmaker's apprentice, someone who is learning to build cabinets and the like... His learning is not mere practice, to gain facility in the use of the tools. Nor does he merely gain knowledge about the customary forms of things he is to build... he makes himself answer and respond above all to the different kinds of wood and to the shapes slumbering within the wood – to wood as it enters into man's dwelling with all the hidden riches of its nature. In fact, this relatedness to wood is what maintains the whole craft. (Heidegger 1968, p.14)

For Heidegger, this relatedness to the wood that a true craftsman achieves is bound up with meaning because it is precisely finding meaning in the piece of wood in relation to oneself, other people and the rest of the physical environment. Rather than leave the wood as a tree trunk, the cabinetmaker makes it into a cabinet and in so doing he creates a meaning for the piece of wood, in relation both to its natural qualities and to the people who will use it; that is, in the context of the culture of his locality. In our communities, as I shall illustrate, we use engagement in practical tasks with precisely this in mind. We work with clients to engage in gardening, cleaning, making meals, mending furniture, and so forth, not just so that they may gain the skills-based 'customary knowledge' about these things but, further, so that they can relate to these tasks and the physical environment to provide it, themselves and the context of other people with some meaning.

'But the hand's gestures run everywhere in language…and only when man speaks, does he think' (Heidegger 1968, p.16). That is, another way to express the difference between a skill and a craft is the underlying potential capacity to speak and think which informs the meaningfulness of the relatedness that defines a craft. Our potential ability to be 'craftsmen' lies at root in our potential ability to think and speak about the world in a meaningful way. It is because we are potentially able to do this that we are able to make meaningful relationships with our physical environments as 'craftsmen'. In our communities, as I shall illustrate, clients have often withdrawn from any meaningful thinking and speaking, from any meaningful relationship with the environment or other people. This does not mean they have lost the capacity to form meaningful relationships, the potential capacity to speak. We work with clients on practical tasks often as a means to, as it were, remind them that they do have this capacity to think and speak. For example, in simply making a meal but having done so as a 'craftsman' by thinking about how to chop, what ingredient to put with what, how to present it, how to lay the table, what people might talk about, and so forth, one has created meaning in relation to the world. This can act as a tremendously significant reminder of an underlying capacity to speak, to make some meaning in the world.

In summary, part of what characterizes someone who is able to truly dwell in relation to their physical environment is that they are able to engage in the craft of care in relation to this environment. Caring for one's environment means being able to become involved with it in a detailed, precise and articulated way. Engaging in a craft means being able to speak, as it were, with one's hands. That is, being able to use the precision of care to form relationships with materials, and so forth, which bring those things into the meaningful context of oneself and others, and, in so doing, one finds one is able to do meaningful things.

DWELLING AS THE CRAFT OF ASKING QUESTIONS

As I have described, what underlies the ability to be a 'craftsman' in relation to one's physical environment is the potential ability to think and speak, the ability to give things meaning. It is this ability which our clients are put back in touch with in practical task-groups and informal practical sessions. What lies at the heart of thinking and speaking is the ability to ask and engage with questions. It is thus that Heidegger says:

> It is important above all that on the way on which we set out when we learn to think, we do not deceive ourselves and rashly bypass the pressing questions; on the contrary, we must allow ourselves to become involved in questions that seek what no inventiveness can find. (Heidegger 1968, p.8)

Thus, what underlies the 'craftsman's' relatedness to the world is an implicit or explicit ability to engage with questions about their environment and about themselves in relationship to it. It is this ability to engage with difficult questions which may not have ready-to-hand answers that characterizes the other part of learning to be-towards-the-world and thus of learning to dwell in one's physical environment.

In the opening section I described how often our clients ask questions such as 'Why should I do this?' in our task-groups. I also described how some clients show their lack of motivation by not turning up to such groups or leaving after a very short time. I suggested that implicit in these questions and passive actions lie deep existential questions about what place the client has in relation to the world and what meaning they have in relation to it; these questions and passive actions express an attitude of not being able to see the point.

On the one hand, in our communities there is a sense in which we place a very high value on these implicit questions. Indeed, despite the manifestation of complete withdrawal and isolation that goes with them, once the question is understood for what it is and not bypassed, it provides a point of engagement and contact with the withdrawn person. At least one can attempt to understand their question and the thinking and feelings that have led to the question. However, on the other hand, the trouble with these questions is that they are questions that very rarely provide the possibility of opening a new door, of asking a further question. They are questions which close down further questions, they are questions which close down thought and dialogue. For example, the question 'What is the point?' seems to be *the* final question however one attempts to respond to it.

As I shall illustrate, in our practical task-groups and in other ways, we attempt to help our clients ask their questions in a way that begins to help them open out new questions and thus in a way which brings more and more meaning to their voice each time they engage in asking a question. Rather than asking a question, as it were of the world, such as 'What is the point?', a question which results in one withdrawing from the world and closing down further engagement, we try to help our clients ask questions which implicitly or explicitly carry the same weight, being about what their meaningful place is in the world, but which draw them further into the world rather than away from it. Once one is able to ask a question which does open out a new further question, one is drawn towards the world and perhaps, because each question leads to a new one whose answer we must go on to search for, it is as if the world is withdrawing from us just at the point where we are able to be drawn towards it. It is thus that Heidegger says:

> Once we are so related and drawn to what withdraws, we are drawing in to what withdraws, into the enigmatic and therefore the mutable nearness of its appeal. (Heidegger 1968, p.16)

We aim to help our clients find the beginnings of meaning for themselves in relation to the physical environment by being able to ask questions which open out further creative enigmas, puzzles and riddles.

New apprentice therapists who co-facilitate task-orientated groups with more experienced therapists often find it difficult to engage with the underlying dialogue that takes place in these groups. That is, they need to learn to listen to the underlying significance of the questions and passive actions. A dialogue within a task-orientated group will give clients an opportunity to express themselves in any number of ways, and therapists must learn to look for these, often unconscious, forms of self-expression in order to be able to respond to the questions in a meaningful and creative way.

For a new therapist, a reasonable answer to a 'Why should I?' type of question or to the person who keeps wandering away from their task might be to try and persuade the client of all the reasons why it is helpful for them to do the task. For example, 'You need to clean the fridge or you will get food poisoning' or, 'You might want to keep the garden looking nice and watch the plants grow because this is a pleasurable part of life.' In this way the therapist may try to motivate the client in some way to see the point of the task. However, because at the underlying level the client's questions are so basic, fundamental and often existential, sometimes therapists simply need to answer the question by *showing* the client, by helping them to start *doing*. In this way therapists can begin to go some way to answering the clients' questions and to helping the clients to answer them for themselves.

Task-orientated groups are so important when clients come with these fundamental questions and where at first rational words seem limp and unpowerful. They are so important when the client is not ready to enter into a verbal dialogue but needs something more emotionally basic. Further, in task-orientated groups the dialogue, the questioning and responding can be a physical experience of engaging a practical apprenticeship. Through this apprenticeship in task-orientated groups, clients can begin to find their roots and build a relationship with their physical environment. They can begin to find a place to dwell.

In task-orientated groups, therapists also work to encourage clients to begin to be able to articulate their questions verbally and from there to ask more and detailed questions about their environment and themselves, as a means to helping them to engage, become involved and care about it. This means helping them to change and develop the kind of questions they are asking, or to ask the same questions in a different way. Both of these developments will help the client come closer to finding a response either in themselves or from others to their fundamental questions.

In most cases where someone does not want to do something, or cannot see the point of it, exploring the underlying meanings hidden in the particular person's relationship with that task will bring meaning back into the doing of the task. Instead of asking the general unarticulated question 'Why should I?', therapists teach clients to ask smaller, more manageable, and perhaps more containable, questions which help them engage. Being able to respond to more manageable questions and thus engage in a more detailed way is the first step towards actively caring oneself and also, importantly, it is a first step to building answers to the bigger, more fundamental, questions such as 'Why should I?'

ASKING AND RESPONDING TO QUESTIONS BY LEARNING TO DWELL IN THE PHYSICAL ENVIRONMENT: ILLUSTRATIONS

Cleaning groups

Gregory was a 55-year-old divorcee in our project. His wife used to look after him completely, and this included doing the cooking and cleaning for him. In our community, as part of the therapeutic programme, he was asked to participate in the cleaning group, and his chore was to vacuum the stairs. He was incredibly resistant, adamantly refusing to do so, saying he had never done it before in his life and why should he do it now. I felt like screaming at him, 'Just do it!' Gregory went on to say that his wife had always looked after him and someone should be looking after him now. What was important was that I entered into a dialogue with him about his resistance. I began to talk to Gregory about the fact that his wife has now separated from him since he started living in our community and how he feels about this, how he may feel abandoned and unloved. After some discussion Gregory reluctantly did the vacuuming. In this example, Gregory's not wanting to engage with this practical task seems to have been directly about his feelings of loss of his wife and the anger that lay beneath this. By talking about it, perhaps Gregory was able to begin to go some way towards living with this loss and thus get on with his life at a practical level, to engage with his life without his wife as was symbolized by his getting on with the vacuuming. This is an example of how much deeper questions about oneself can be addressed through building a simple relationship with the physical environment. It is an example of how one's identity is created at a very basic level by one's relation to the physical environment. Here, by reluctantly doing the vacuuming, Gregory's identity was re-created as one living without his wife.

Gardening groups

Often I sense the fear that clients have of a seemingly menial task. It seems to represent the fear of problems and emotional difficulties they face in other parts of their lives, not just one of a present physical task. Take, for example, a client in a gardening group who was set the task of digging a hole in which to plant a shrub. The client seemed to have difficulty in getting started. Every time he had all his tools ready he wandered off back into the house and had to be fetched by someone else. Therapists used dialogue to explore what was going on for this person. It became apparent that the underlying significance of digging this hole was far more complex than the mere practical task and skills involved in just doing it. It became clear that this hole was, for the client, one without a bottom. It was a place where the client could get lost and could not grab hold of the sides, a place where there was nothing to stop him falling. For the client, the emptiness of the hole was too unbearable to even comprehend. It became clear that for this client to engage with this task was to engage with a mass of emotions that could become out of control. In the post-group after this gardening group, therapists explored the meaning, for this client, of the task of digging this hole as it had begun to emerge during the group. One of the ideas that was put forward was that, for this client, digging the hole presented him with the fear of his own meaninglessness, his own sense of being lost, with nothing to say and no meaningful mark to make in the world. The therapists agreed to continue to talk with the client the next week with this in mind. During the next gardening group, staff worked with this client by talking to him, both about his fears of not being able to speak but also about how the planting of the shrub in the hole would make a mark in the garden, how the group had decided together that this was the place for it and how it would make a difference to the feeling in the garden. Slowly, the client came round to engaging in the task, working very slowly and apparently enjoying the feeling of getting muddy.

This is an example of how engaging with the earthy physical environment in the garden is about much more than engaging in a skill and knowing how to do it. For this client, engaging in digging the hole involved him in realizing that he once again could make meaningful contact with the world. The meaning he made was in the context of the garden and the rest of the group by adding the shrub. Because of this, he was able to engage in a craftsmanship with the soil rather than just a skill of digging a hole. That he was able to make this mark in the garden was a reminder for him that he, rather than someone else, could have a place from which to speak and act. It was a reminder for him that his voice need not get lost and that he need not fear the bottomless-pit feeling of being unheard and unable to speak. This practical gardening group provided a safe place in which this client could express his underlying feelings and a place in which he could begin to work with them. In subsequent individual sessions the underlying sexual nature of these issues were explored with the client.

Unpacking, my room and my bed

When clients arrive at one of our therapeutic communities they are usually placed on a trial period. During this period some clients create their new place in their room, making it their own. Others do not engage with their surroundings. This is an important feature in the development and success of this trial period. It is an important part of supporting the client to stay with our community, however difficult their feelings about this might be at this early point. Therapists work with clients to help them to create a place to which they have some sense of belonging and meaning. Therapists work with clients to use the process of unpacking to allow them to show staff, for possibly the first time, a sense of their self-identity as they gradually become surrounded by more and more of their possessions and the memories that go with them. Supporting clients at this time creates an opportunity for the development of the beginning of a therapeutic relationship. Many clients may find this close contact difficult at first. However, these interactions provide a vital opportunity for them to be able to discuss their past in the safety of their surroundings. At this point in the journey it appears that most important relationships are formed, both with the physical environment and with others, via, literally and metaphorically, unpacking and settling *into the physical environment.*

Therapists work to include the process of creating a link with individuals' rooms in care plans. Here clients look at the meaning of their environment in more detail. In so doing we encourage the personal stamp on each of their rooms. Initially the process might include keeping a room tidy, but then clients might start to care for it in more detail. This may include moving furniture for a practical purpose of organization, but it also gives space for personal preference and choice in choosing the arrangements and the decoration.

One client with whom I worked did settle in our community, but even after one year his room looked as though he had moved into it yesterday. He had not put anything on the walls. He had no personal possessions out, except for a small radio by his bed. This was so despite our attempts to encourage him to go out with us to buy some pictures to put up, to help him get some local authority money to buy a basic stereo and CDs as he liked to listen to music. He was a 30-year-old man diagnosed with schizophrenia. He spent much of his free time on his own talking to himself, but when he was with others he was very personable and joined in the community activities with apparent pleasure. However, his general demeanour was that of fading into the background. He was never involved in any of the more fractious moments of community life, and it was easy for everyone to take him for granted and almost forget about him. When we discussed his room with him in an ongoing way, he would become quietly defensive, simply saying he liked it how it was and he did not want to bother with fussy things in it.

It seemed that this client's difficulty in making himself seen and heard was precisely replicated in his relationship to his room. He could not make himself seen and heard to himself in his room. His identity remained private and unexpressed inside him, unavailable to himself and others beyond. Our task was to work in an ongoing way to help him find a way of taking up a position in relation to himself and others in a variety of ways in our community. At the time of writing this, we continue to do so, and he has become the facilitator of our leisure group – a position in which he has begun to speak out. However, his room remains bare. We continue to work on this with him as a means to helping him create his identity.

Sometimes clients retreat and spend much of their time in bed. It is possibly here that the first connection is made. It is often a point of safety. However, frequently, I see that not even here is it truly safe and they can find peace. Clients have a tendency to sleep in their clothes or not to have sheets on their bed, as they do not care for it or still have a destructive relationship with it. When therapists take the time to work with clients on changing their sheets, you can often sense a challenging atmosphere. However, as a rule, on the night after, most have a better night's sleep. This may be because they have given it thought and created some sense of belonging. This, in turn, has created a more secure feeling. They have taken some care over the physical environment in which they sleep.

Maintenance groups

The maintenance group I want to describe ran weekly toward termly goals. At this time the community house, although comfortable, lacked a feeling of personal attachment for the group. It appeared that clients felt little or no relation to the environment in which they lived. Through a series of questions and responses given by clients, they provided insight into the fact that they did not care for their house and had no sense of belonging to the walls in which they lived. So within the maintenance group, we obviously had a big job ahead of us. In speaking to the clients about their house, we saw that they could not identify with it. So how were we to encourage clients to look at the process in close detail so it therefore can find meaning?

The group decided that they would work on buying small items, which they would choose, to develop a personal meaning to the space. The items bought were not so much about the practical need for them but about the aesthetic effect that they would create. They went out and bought items such as place mats to have the table look nicer at dinner, and jars for storage in the kitchen. However, these carefully chosen objects seemed possibly irrelevant when put into a space that had no sense of belonging to them. The mats almost faded into the table when laid out at the following meal, and few commented. The items bought were anonymous at this stage, for they were without any central grounding of the dwelling experience. Therapists noted that this may be the first part of a journey for the clients in working to find a meaningful relationship with their environment and that the demands that it presented were greater than first realized.

What of the walls around them? The foundations on which they stood and the land on which the foundations were laid – it appeared that their sense of belonging might be rooted this deep. Many said that they did not have a sense that the house was their home and did not care what it looked like. What did seem important was that they agreed this as a group and wanted possible change to be taken on as a group. The idea of getting to grips with this sense of their surroundings felt huge. The clients seemed to be suggesting that if any one of them was to do anything to enter into this daunting task then everyone would have to pull their weight and it needed to be worked at as a team. This was their house, and as a group they had to stamp their mark.

All agreed that we were looking at a total revamp and change in decoration. Out came the colour charts. Everyone had something to say and a preference. But all agreed eventually. This process of choice seemed vital. As in the choice of items, they were given some control. So with the planning done, the group needed to go ahead. From the start, all contributed something. However, very soon the clients were asking the same old questions, both explicitly and through their passive actions, which we understood and translated as: 'What is the point of holding the brush?', 'What is the point of putting colour on the wall?' Clients used all kinds of avoidance techniques not to engage with the task. We translated these actions and questions as clients asking questions about their own lives at a deep level, as clients asking whether they could have any meaning in any context.

Gradually, by starting to show the clients what to do with the brushes and the paint, and by doing the physical work with the clients and then by discussing the details of the painting task as it progressed, we began to involve people in this task. Once the first few clients had engaged then others came to join, having seen that it was okay and that others actually seemed to be enjoying it. The physical movement and gestures between us and our environ-ment, if not for long, seemed concentrated and with care and detail. The clients were then able to work in smaller sub-groups in organizing the task, for once seemingly able to forget the way they initially formulated their questions. The initial demands of their environment had been swept over by one of 'being', a sense of belonging within the four walls. By showing the clients how to be with the paint and the brushes, and by discussing the details of the task as it progressed, we were able to break down the client's initial questions of 'What is the point?' into smaller, more manageable, pieces such as, 'Shall I use this colour or that one?', 'Where shall I begin to paint?' The very doing of the task, together in the group, provided the beginning of a response to their initial question of 'What is the point?' Indeed, people began to feel they belonged and began to feel that their contribution made a difference. Not only that, but the questions they began to ask once they were doing the task led to further questions in a way that their initial questions did not. Some people began to talk about how they would decorate their own flats when they moved on, others talked about decorating their rooms in the house, others about when to take a break and start work again, and so forth.

After the task was complete, therapists were astounded at the response. One very withdrawn client even said: 'I want to come down to groups now because of this room.' This response spoke of a relationship with the room and consequently with a sense of 'being' that had changed. By breaking down barriers which had stopped clients caring and facing up to demands, they could once again find peace. Also, their response showed that this experience was not in isolation but was a shared experience amongst the members of the group. The group therefore found something in common which gave them a purpose on which to develop further. On a basic level of engagement with the world, they had entered the dwelling experience through the contact of their environment, therefore starting once again to care and start living a fully human life.

NOTES

1   It is in this spirit that Stuart Whiteley refers to Winnicott's term 'potential space' as a central focus of the work in a therapeutic community. He says that the term 'was used by Winnicott…to describe the metaphorical space between mother and child in which both experimented in an interactive way with closeness and distance, separation and togetherness… Thus the therapeutic community similarly recreates a learning experience for both patients and staff' (Whiteley 1998, p.270).

2   For a description of the theory and practice of Community Housing and Therapy's Homelessness Project for ex-service men with emotional difficulties, see Chapter 8 of this volume. This project recognizes the significance of homelessness as consisting in more than not having four walls and a ceiling.

3   Parts of this section and the next are based on an unpublished paper by Sarah Tucker.

4   For more on the nature of care see Chapter 5 and Chapter 6 of this volume; also see
     Tucker (1999).

REFERENCES

Bishop, J. (1979) 'The environment of the therapeutic community.' In R.D.
    Hinshelwood and N. Manning (eds) *Therapeutic Communities: Reflections and
    Progress.* London, Boston and Henley: Routledge and Kegan Paul.
Fanning, A. (1990) 'The placement: My training ground.' *Therapeutic Communities
    11*, 4, 215–226.
Heidegger, M. (1962) *Being and Time* (trans. J. Macquarrie and E. Robinson).
    Oxford: Basil Blackwell.
Heidegger, M. (1968) *What is Called Thinking.* (second edition) (trans. J. Glenn
    Gray) New York: Harper and Row.
Heidegger, M. (1971) *Poetry, Language, Thought* (trans. A. Hofstadter). New York:
    Harper and Row.
Tucker, S. (1999) 'Community Care: The therapeutic approach and learning to
    care.' In P. Campling and R. Haigh (eds) *Therapeutic Communities: Past, Present and
    Future.* London: Jessica Kingsley Publishers.
Voorhoeve, J.N. (1993) 'The relationship between psychotic symptomatology and
    the structure of the setting.' *Therapeutic Communities 14*, 4, 19–27.
Whiteley, S. (1998) 'Community as playground: Some thoughts on the function of
    play in the therapeutic community.' *Therapeutic Communities 19*, 4, 269–280.

CHAPTER 4

The Meaning of Place
The Hyphen Ground between Solitude and Communion

Anne Salway

In this chapter I shall explore the connection between place and self-identity and endeavour to show that this is of particular relevance in a therapeutic community.

Finding one's place involves a search for meaning, a search which always takes place within the context of interpersonal relationships and one's relationship with the environment. One of the problems for most of us today is our isolation and dislocation from the natural world. Few of us live any longer in small, traditional rural communities. Industrialization and urbanization have contributed to an existential malaise in which people remain isolated and feel that they have no real place (Hinshelwood 1993, p.202). The search for meaning and purpose in life is at the heart of this modern malaise: 'Who am I and why am I here?'.[1] For some, this question has taken them along the road of philosophy; for others, however, it has been the rugged path to depression and despair. Is there a link between the difficulties facing people who have mental health problems and the search for identity and meaning?[2] It is this search for meaning which lies at the centre of religious experience, and this cannot but fail to include the psychological aspects of a person. For this reason it is often unhelpful in clinical practice to emphasize the difference between theological and psychological concerns, as they share the same territory.[3]

MAN ALWAYS MEASURES HIMSELF IN RELATION TO OTHERS AND THE WORLD

'Place', from a therapeutic perspective, means more than real estate! We are referring, essentially, to identity and meaning; and from this angle, we can say that one of the aims of a therapeutic community is to relocate 'homeless' people and help them find a place in the world. In fact, it may not be an exaggeration to say that the only way in which the mentally damaged can be resorted to a more healthy life is by enabling them to dwell in the world in relation to others (Hartnup 1993, p.215).

Heidegger described man's need to find his place in the world as the taking of measure:

> The nature of the dimension is the meeting out – which is lightened and so can be spanned – of the between: the upward to the sky as well as the downward to the earth. According to Holderlin's words, man spans the dimension by measuring himself against the heavenly... Man measures himself against the godhead. The godhead is the 'measure' with which man measures out his dwelling, his stay on the earth beneath the sky. (Heidegger 1971, p.221)

In order for man to make sense of his existence, he has to take measure, to try to understand where he stands in relation to the world around him. Dwelling is not just about building or cultivating (although it is also about these things); it is about a sense of belonging. Simply by the fact that human beings dwell in the world they are, in a fundamental sense, part of the world and are bound together with the planet as well as with each other. In the words of Holderlin's poem, 'poetically, man dwells'.[4] In this sense man lives in oneness with creation and can only be understood within the context of a dwelling relationship with the environment. 'By a primal one-ness the four: earth and sky, divinities and mortals – belong together in one... [They are] in the fourfold *by dwelling*' (Heidegger 1971, p.149).

Taking measure in finding a place to dwell implies a relationship with the world around us. When we enter into a relationship with the world and others in which we do not see ourselves as outsiders, but in a dwelling-with relationship, we initiate a spiritual dialogue. That is to say, a responding-to the environment, a relationship which is spiritual because it recognizes that there is something that cannot be named or fully explained in the world, a sacred element which colours our dialogue with the world. Seen in this way, man's dialogue with the world is one which should be marked by reverence and humility. By dwelling, man belongs-together-in-one with the world, not as a master but in relationship.

This spiritual dialogue in relation to the world has largely been lost, but we are beginning to see its re-emergence and today even psychologists and psychotherapists are beginning to realize that questions of ecology and the environment are intimately linked with our mental health and sanity (Ward 1993, p.179). Originally, man lived in communities, in tribes, each member knowing his or her place and role and having a great respect for the earth which provided their daily sustenance. The community occupied an area of land, or moved across land. But essentially community meant dwelling together on the land within a territory. Over the years man's relationship with the earth has changed dramatically. We are no longer so dependent on the land for our sustenance, at least not so directly, and many of us have little, if any, involvement in its upkeep. The industrial revolution changed society, dislocating many people from the land. Small village communities were broken up and family ties weakened as people moved across the country to the cities in search of work. Nowadays people tend to have smaller family units and it is common for neighbours not to speak to one another. The feeling of anonymity and aloneness is most evident in large cities. These changes which have taken place in society over the years, in terms of economics and family structures, have had an effect on the mental health of society at large, and some psychological problems may be linked with the problems of modern society. Many people feel desperately alone and feel a lack of meaningful relationships:

> ...the insane person is the one who has completely failed to establish any
> kind of union, and is imprisoned, even if he is not behind barred windows.
> The necessity to unite with other living beings, to be related to them, is an
> imperative need on the fulfilment of which man's sanity depends. (Fromm
> 1956, p.30)

How can we initiate a spiritual dialogue with our damaged clients in order to help them in their search for a place? Our therapeutic dialogical/educational approach seeks to unlock a client from their prison by teaching them to speak to others. When a person is in their own world, in psychosis, they are imprisoned, dwelling in their mind, so to speak, locked up in the imaginary. Teaching our clients to speak in dialogue is not an easy task, for it involves us facing the problem of the symbolic, which is, of course, at the heart of both language and psychosis.[5]

Dialogue is being in relation to the Other in speech, for it is speech which continually recreates the aloneness–togetherness which has been described as the ideal state of relationship (Hobson 1979, p.238). Dialogue cannot exist when people are in isolation, for dialogue implies involvement with the Other. There are two ways of relating to the world and others. We can either respond to the wholeness of the Other which includes them as a subject of experiences or we can treat the Other as an object. We can either enter into a full and mutual relationship with the world and others or we can exploit the world and others:

> The man who experiences has no part in the world. For it is 'in him' and not
> between him and the world that the experience arises... I do not experience
> the man to whom I say Thou. But I take my stand in relation to him, in the
> sanctity of the primary word. (Buber 1937, pp.18–22)[6]

In therapeutic dialogue with others, we stand by this sanctity of the primary word. When we speak of dwelling, we mean being in relation to others through the oneness of belonging. Dwelling is the ground upon which we connect with others. It is the true meeting of I and thou. When we write about the I-thou relationship, the hyphen is an image of the fragile ground upon which true meeting takes place. It is the hyphen ground. The therapeutic community is a sacred territory, a place set apart, within which dialogue takes place. Clients of one particular community expressed it thus:

> I am someone here
> I am heard
> I am not alone.
>
> Here I have substance
> I matter
> I mean something.
>
> I feel more at home
> here in this place
> than I ever feel at home.
>
> I have a share in the world.
>
> I am not odd
> I am even here.
>
> I am not assailed.
>
> (Wolf forthcoming)

These simple evocative words cannot fail to move us. Robin Cooper described eloquently the change that took place in a client at Kingsley Hall. The client had a wish to withdraw, which led him to spend, more or less, the next two years in bed. Cooper wondered how his community could help the man:

> Not at any rate by 'helping' – having to be seen to be engaged in some sort of proprietary activity such that the possibilities of attentive non-intervention are unquestionably pre-empted. Rather, the response of the house is to gesture the opening of a conversation. It is to open or extend a conversation which is abiding, going on, being lived. It gestures the hospitality of dwelling. (Cooper 1989, p.53)

Despite the client's wish to withdraw into himself, the placement worked out well because while the man was withdrawing, life around him was carrying on, and it was this ordinary rhythm of life which eventually had an effect on him. 'Beyond what is going on, there is nothing' (Cooper 1989, p.55). This normal, everyday community life was founded on speech, and it was the abiding conversation which signalled dwelling. The hospitality of dwelling is always opened or extended by dialogue.

I would now like to turn and look in a little more detail at what else is involved in dwelling. I shall spend some time discussing the sense in which each of us needs to settle in our own place, to find ourselves, before we can begin to find others and extend to them our hospitality.

SPATIALITY AND TEMPORALITY[7]

According to Xenophon, the reason why the gods created the human couple was because all human beings needed a *stegos*, a shelter, so that they need not 'live in the open air, like beasts' (Xenophon, *Oeconomicus*, VII 19–35). Here, in their shelter, a person can bring in, preserve and store that which they have collected. This is for the future. So a shelter, a place, always implies a future, and in this fundamental sense it is always related to hope, and hope-in-the-future lies at the centre of the human experience (see Vernant 1966, pp.124–170). Two aspects feature here. There is the aspect of bringing in from the outside and the aspect of preserving for the future that I would like to try to tease out a little more. Before doing so, however, it needs to be said that having a place means marking a boundary between inside and outside. A shelter marks the limit of one's domain and gives spatial organization to that area. In this, man is seen imitating nature, for the world is not just a void – it is a space with regions:

> [The] celestial regions, which need not have any geographical meaning as yet, provide the 'whither' beforehand for every special way of giving form to the regions which places can occupy. The house has its sunny side and its shady side; the way it is divided up into 'rooms' ['*Raume*'] is orientated towards these, and so is the 'arrangement' ['*Einrichtung*'] within them, according to their character as equipment. Churches and graves, for instance, are laid out in accordance to the rising and the setting of the sun – the regions of life and death, which are determinative for Dasein itself with regard to its ownmost possibilities of Being in the world. (Heidegger 1962, section 103)

These two aspects, bringing in from the outside and preserving for the future, are complementary and without the one the other would make no sense. The first, the bringing in from the outside, implies going outside, relating to the outside and being in relationship with the outside. And so the shelter, although marked off from the outside as my place, is necessarily connected to that outside, and that outside will include the shelters of others. So, to speak of my place and to assert the importance of having a place is not to be isolationist in the world but rather the opposite. It is only by having a place that is separate from others, set apart, a place that I call my own which is by implication no one else's, a place where I belong, that I can become fully involved in the world. For if I do not have my own place, I have nowhere from which to make contact with others. 'Belonging-somewhere has an essential relationship to involvement' (Heidegger 1962, section 368). The second aspect, that of preserving, of sorting out, is obviously dependent on going out into the world, for otherwise there would be nothing to preserve. And so the shelter is always a store-house. It is the place where I keep my things, the things that connect me to the world because they have come from the world and because I have claimed them and named them as my own. Again, these things, these objects from the world, may be something like plums that I then preserve for the winter, but they may equally be ideas or even other people with whom I have made a bond and a connection. These people may enter my dwelling for life, as in the case of marriage, or for visits, as in the case of friendships. And in this case my shelter stands as a metaphor, for these other people are let into my dwelling because they have been let into my heart. So dwelling and heart are made transparent as if they were one and the same, as if the shelter was really just me, all along. But the aspect of preservation, of keeping things secure, is important, for without it the object which is brought back would not last and would not, therefore, be-for-the-future.

This mention of things being-for-the-future is an important one and one which roots dwelling with time. First of all, the two aspects of going outside and returning to the inside denotes time for a person. We cannot, after all, be inside and outside at the same time! And so what seemed at first to be a discussion or reflection on spatial organization is seen to hinge on temporal organization. This should not surprise us:

> Temporality is the meaning of the Being of care. Dasein's constitution and its ways to be are possible ontologically only on the basis of temporality, regardless of whether this entity occurs 'in time' or not. Hence Dasein's specific spatiality must be grounded in temporality. (Heidegger 1962, section 367)

And because there is a link between preservation of things and time, there is an aspect of memory and recollection, *anamnesis*, of putting things away and remembering where some are stored and forgetting about others. In essence, organizing, owning and ordering the world. In the shelter we see man organizing space, splitting up space into places, ordering his relationships with the world and with others, externalizing the interior world of his affections and psychological processes (the heart, desire, forgetting), and organizing his time within the context of himself as a project-for-the-future (see Heidegger 1962, section 104). This self-definition of man as a project-for-the-future is paradoxical, for it means that man is someone with hope, someone with anticipation, yet at the same time someone who must, if he is to be authentic, take death seriously. This is because death in our earthly dwelling is man's ultimate future (see Heidegger 1962, sections 325–326).

Memory of the past is not about the forgotten-past but about the still-held past – whereas in recollection we recall the forgotten. Both memory and recollection are vital to man. Memory is that symbolic history of the person, a chain of signifiers linked up together, 'a signifying articulation' (Lacan 1992, p.223). Something is memorable and memorized only when it is 'registered in the signifying chain' (Lacan 1992, p.212). In this sense the unconscious is a sort of memory, since 'what we teach the subject to recognise as his unconscious is his history' (Lacan 1977, p.52). Sometimes we forget – what an interesting idea!

Hope is always hope-in-the-future. Hope always includes both conscious wishes and unconscious desire, and because unconscious desire is always present in man's hopes we cannot really speak about man in relation to the future without reference to his sexuality (Lacan 1977, p.142). There is something about desire which means that it can never be fully satisfied and thus it is always present. It is always a desire for that which is not yet present. Man cannot live without hope if he lives between solitude and communion with others. But hope – authentic hope – is not an illusion. It is the opposite of despair, and springs from that middle place where a man knows his own place in the world, marked out and delineated by the shack, hut, tent or cave which he calls home. It is from this place which he knows as his own place that he can reach out and link with others. The vagrant, conversely, has no place, and without his own shelter he is not solitary and cannot therefore make communion with others.

Death is man's ultimate future, and an authentic life cannot avoid facing death. Directly, everyone knows of death and that their death is a certainty. However, this everyday acceptance of death is ambiguous, and while it is true that everyone knows they will die, death remains hidden from us and is only dealt with indirectly:

> Nobody doubts that one dies. On the one hand this 'not doubting' need not imply that kind of Being-certain which corresponds to the way death – in the sense of the distinctive possibility characterised above – enters into Dasein. Everydayness confines itself to conceding the 'certainty' of death in this ambiguous manner just in order to weaken that certainty by covering up dying still more and to alleviate its own thrownness into death. By its very meaning, this evasive concealment in the face of death can not be authentically 'certain' of death, and yet it is certain of it. (Heidegger 1962, sections 255–256)

Often this indirect coping with our own death is founded on the principle that life and death are intrinsically linked. For this reason, we can say with confidence that death, like that other aspect of the future (namely, hope as it is felt in the form of desire), is always in relation to sex. For it is through the very principle of reproduction that man passes life on into the future which lies beyond him. Reproduction is the way in which man cheats death and the march of time. Here in sex we see man's desire for immortality and self-perpetuation. In the *Symposium* we find Diotima pointing out that a longing exists in all animals which, seized by the urge to procreate, fall prey to a violent love-sickness, and they are ready to die if need be in order to secure the survival of their progeny (Plato, *Symposium*, 207ab).

Dwelling and being amongst others also involves something inward for each individual:

> Familiarity is an accomplishment, an energy of separation. With it separation is constituted as dwelling and inhabitation… To dwell is a recollection, a coming to oneself, a retreat home with oneself as in a land of refuge… With dwelling the separated being breaks with natural existence…but this suspension does not reduce to nothing the relationship of the I with the elements. The dwelling remains in its own way open upon the elements from which it separates. (Levinas 1961, p.156)

Without a refuge from the natural elements we are not able to be ourselves. However, this refuge does not isolate us or cut us off from the natural elements completely. On the contrary, it is precisely from our dwelling, our *refugium*, that we are able to cultivate and build with the elements. Building a dwelling involves building something for ourselves away from the world. In a similar way, being able to settle amongst others involves being able to take refuge within oneself, being able to be apart. This separation need not leave one outside dialogue but, on the contrary, provides the basis from which to cultivate and build links with real Others.

A HIDING-PLACE FOR THE SELF

> But the Self, which the appeal has robbed of this lodgement and hiding-place, gets brought to itself by the call. (Heidegger 1962, section 273)

We live in two worlds, in two places. Both worlds, the conscious and the unconscious world, are not unconnected zones of existence but related, interconnected areas of discourse. Yet they remain apart. In the therapeutic community we know this only too well, and each day and each moment we focus on the disjoined, seemingly unconnected stuttering in which these worlds are linked together and thus begin to take on meaning. This therapeutic dialogue is not just between isolated people but between these two worlds in which we all live, between the solitary self and the self in community; not just between me and others, but between me and me with others. All speech includes others, even when, at first glance, it seems to be a soliloquy. And the things spoken of are always spoken to someone. We often include the idea of conscience in our wider understanding of speech, and this links speech with morality.

We say that we hear the voice of conscience. If conscience is present in speech as a voice, we can rightly think about conscience as something that speaks to someone – namely, to the self. The voice of conscience speaks to us and we are called by it. Conscience is a call, a form of utterance. It can be heard and understood by us, the hearers. Yet while the call of conscience is addressed to us, to our deepest self, its structure as discourse means that it speaks about us as we exist in relation to others. It is more than an analogy to call conscience a part of speech (Heidegger 1962, section 27). But while our conscience speaks to us about others, it speaks not in public but in the hiding-place of our inner world. The hiding-place is a necessity, a place we all need to find, and it is built into the nature of the human person. Total transparency and communality are impossible as well as unwanted. There is some justification, therefore, for speaking about the self in relation to dwelling.

In his study of dreams, Freud spoke of the process whereby the energy (cathexis) or emotional charge is separated from its real object and transferred to another object (Freud 1988, pp.414–420). Hence, trivial things are accompanied by strong feelings or vice versa: important things appear in dreams but with little emotion attached to them. This process is known as displacement. Hence, the manifest content of the dream is more like a coded message conveying a secret meaning. Translating the seemingly meaningless code reveals meaning and significance. Displacement is designed to evade censorship, to get the message across in code, while seeming to conform (Stafford-Clark 1987, pp.65–67). This is important. Displacement is one of the primary processes. Freud distinguished between two types of mental functioning – primary processes (unconscious) and secondary processes (conscious). Symbolization and sublimation depend on serial displacements. Transference is also a form of displacement. Here we find the client displacing their feelings about previous figures in their life on to us, the therapists (Rycroft 1986, pp.35, 168).

Taking stock of these two points has deep significance in our dealings with clients in the therapeutic community. By speaking of the necessity of a hiding-place within ourselves, within our own minds and within our relationships with others, I do not mean that we hide from the Other in the sense in which that is often meant in everyday speech. What I mean is that interrelationship is constructed around an ambiguity, the desire to reveal oneself and the need to hide – not just the need to hide from the Other but the need to hide from oneself in relation to the Other. In our relationships, even the most healthy relationships, we do not want to see ourselves naked, but disguised. In general, this is neither understood nor valued by practitioners within therapeutic communities, who avoid serious reflection on the implications of an analysis of the structure of relationships and the way this links back to the individual in their existential solitude. It is as if, to assert the therapeutic value of community, the self is forgotten. However, the self always emerges and cannot be held down. Indeed, we may go so far as to say that at the core of much of the difficulties experienced in therapeutic communities is the neglect of the self:

> Aloneness and togetherness are interdependent. I can only be alone in so far as I can be together with others. I can only be together with others if I am able to be alone. That is what it means to become an individual with an identity and to be a member of a community. In the lifelong quest (conscious and unconscious) for a personal identity, I continually seek to make new sense of new inner and outer experience, at the same time maintaining a

stable sense of continuity. I have a basic 'need' for relations with others – to maintain the stability of important bonds and yet to remain alone… (Hobson 1979, p.238)

The client in the therapeutic community is often seen as one who has withdrawn from others and divorced themselves from reality and the world. In response, the treatment offered often centres around confronting this crass avoidance, challenging it and practically press-ganging the individual into communalism, joining-in and belonging. We think that this fellow needs to become part of the community, part of the world, a citizen taking his part in the decisions which the community makes for itself. He needs, we say, to communicate directly with others. And probably all this is perfectly true. However, it is also naïve and over-simplistic and, as such, frequently unsuccessful and frustrating for staff. In essence, we are built to evade. We are constructed in a far more subtle way than might at first be imagined, and at our centre is the need to hide from ourselves, not to process everything today, not to relate with complete openness, to see significant others in the faces, gestures and words of those around us and to take our time and be sceptical with so-called reality. We need the store-room of our minds to hide things away for tomorrow, to sort them out at leisure. The unconscious and the unconscious process of displacement is vital for us. Transference, that oh-so-common form of displacement with which we struggle on a daily basis, is not just an error, it is part of the structure of relationships.

PHYSICAL PLACE AND THE INNER WORLD OF RELATIONSHIPS

Our place is always more than just a *locus*, more than just accommodation. It bears the metaphorical sense of the Greek word for place, *topos*; it is an occasion, an opportunity. In it we have the opportunity to show ourselves to others and the world and in it we reveal our past. Our inner chaos and our desire for control proclaim themselves here, and it is here that we strive to create our own identity. Yet it is through the struggle to separate ourselves off from others that we find the key to relationships.

Whether we have our own house or live in a bedsit or a room in someone else's house, the healthy individual needs some personal space. By creating our personal space we are able to create a sense of personal identity; our place, one could say, is a physical expression of our inner self. You can tell a lot about a person by looking at where they live, and it can be fascinating to see how the personality of that individual is reflected in their environment. Their cultural and spiritual identity, their passions and interests, and their taste in music and art as well as their history often shine through the place. At a very basic level, for example, family photographs, or the lack of them, displayed in a person's room may express not just whether a person has a family but also the way the person identifies with their family – where the individual sees themselves fitting into the family grouping. In our community, some years ago, I was struck by the difference between the photographs in two halves of a shared room. Both clients were from very similar backgrounds and both had two siblings. But although one of them had photographs of both of his siblings, he had none of his parents and he did not feature in any of them. The two siblings (both brothers) appeared in each photograph. The other client, however, had about six photographs of himself with his mother, none of his siblings (a brother and a sister) and one very small photograph of his father alone, separated from the other photographs which he had grouped together. Gradually, as the story of each client unfolded, it became clear to me that these photographs were a kind of map of the relationships each had within their families.

At a slightly deeper level, our house or our room can reflect our state of mind and how we respond to our environment. It can tell us of something about the way we feel in relation to the world around us and our place in it. Hence, our personal place can express inner processes; for example, order and structure in our environment may indicate our desire to control our life. Complete lack of structure can imply chaos; one might say that madness implies a complete lack of structure – perhaps as a response to some over-demanding and controlling structures in society or in the family. The environment of a person who is not coping is often messy and dirty. They are overwhelmed by their environment and feel they have no control over it. The structure of the therapeutic community is able to contain this kind of chaos whilst the individual is coming to terms with the interior uproar they are confronting. Sometimes, meticulous order in an individual is an attempt to cope with the chaos they are experiencing around themselves and within themselves (Hartnup 1993, pp.218–220, 225).

So our personal space can give many clues about our inner psychological processes, for place gives us a sense of identity. When we have not got our own personal space it will affect our relationships with others, for it is always in a setting that relationships *take place*. When we invite people into our space, we are opening up something of our world to them. We are saying, 'I want to show you some more of who I am, where I come from', and so forth. We could say that we know a person better when we have seen them in their own home, for seeing them in the environment they have made their own by putting their stamp on to it usually means that things about them start to make more sense. The things which we have on display, in our homes, are pointers to the people we are. We are saying to those who enter that these things are important to me, this is what matters to me. It is important for us to feel that we have created our environment, put our mark on the space in some way. If we were to move into a ready furnished apartment where we are not allowed to put pictures on the wall, how much more difficult it is to make the place our own!

This is why it is so important for clients who are resident in our therapeutic communities to create their own room environment:

> Many of our clients come to us either without or having lost a sense of identity, of who they are. Clients come to us with their modes of self expression undeveloped or blunted. They often come to us unable to speak about themselves and unable to express themselves creatively. Staff are taught that their role is to provide an environment in which clients can gain or re-gain a sense of being a whole person with potential by nurturing their individual creativity. One example of a practical way of doing this is encouraging clients to express and create a sense of themselves by making their room their own. That is by encouraging them to choose how to arrange it, how to decorate it and to choose what furniture and objects to have in it. We learn that we can educate clients in this way by nurturing their unique creativity and thus restoring their sense of self. (Tucker 1998, p.45)

The relationship we have with our environment reflects the way we relate to others. When we are involved with our environment, we are looking outside ourselves. Many clients who come to therapeutic communities have no involvement or interest in their environment. They do not notice the beauty of a sunset or the smell of the flowers, they are desensitized to their environment. Part of the therapeutic process is to help them to learn or re-learn how to appreciate the things they see around them. Thus we find it is important to concentrate on physical activities – getting their hands in the earth during a gardening group, walking in the rain, feeling the rain on their skin, eating food which activates their taste buds rather than bland, unseasoned food. Allowing dwelling to open out into cultivating, as Heidegger puts it: 'Dwelling as…cherishing, protecting and caring for, especially to till the soil, to cultivate the vine…such dwelling tends to growth… Building as dwelling unfolds into the building that cultivates growing things' (Heidegger 1971, p.147).

More than this, it is important for clients to have a sense of involvement with their environment in order for them to fully engage with the Other. What Heidegger says about staying with things applies to relationships as well. Building responses requires a staying-with the Other. When others fail to speak to us, fail to concern us any longer when we lose rapport with them, this is possible only in the context of a kind of staying-with those others over time. So settling amongst others, finding a place in a community of others, involves cultivating and constructing responses between oneself and others and, importantly, being able to stay with others even when those relations of response are temporarily broken. This is building outwards from oneself, towards others. This building and cultivating between oneself and others requires care and precision and cannot happen quickly. It requires time. Finding this dwelling amongst others involves a staying-with, a staying-amongst people. This is of the essence for the therapeutic community:

> Even when mortals turn 'inward', taking stock of themselves…and [when we] reflect on ourselves, we come back to ourselves from things without ever abandoning our stay among things. Instead, the loss of rapport with things that occurs in states of depression would be wholly impossible if even such a state were not still what it is as a human state: that is a staying with things. Only if this stay already characterises human being can the things among which we are also fail to speak to us, fail to concern us any longer. (Heidegger 1971, p.157)

At the heart of our search for the Other lies the question of separation. Everyone wants a place they can call home; as children we may have played at being mummies and daddies, and so on, rehearsing a time when we will have our own house and family. This is what growing up involves, leaving one's parents and going to live somewhere else, often with a partner. In this sense building one's own environment is part of the process of separation from one's parents, and it is one of the most basic principles of life. The need to separate from one's parents and to start the process of autonomy begins as an infant. It is a physical, psychological journey towards autonomy, but it is one in which place features actually and symbolically. For our clients, the therapeutic community is often a transitional place, halfway between the childhood home and a home of their own. In this case home is, first of all, the place where the client's parents are. Leaving home involves a physical separation, a wrenching apart, of parent and child. Home is the symbol of security and nourishment, and leaving this haven provokes much anxiety and fear. Growing up involves the progressive achievement of a capacity to be alone as well as a capacity to be together with others (Hobson 1979, p.238). Separation anxiety is something that affects all children as they develop. The well-known fairy tale of Hansel and Gretel is a romantic story which expresses many of the issues involved in leaving home. A woodcutter and his wife are extremely poor, and when famine hits the land they are unable to feed themselves and their two children. The stepmother suggests they leave the two children in the forest so they will have fewer mouths to feed. The story expresses a basic anxiety about being provided for. However, rather than dying in the forest, the two children come across a cottage made of sweets. The gingerbread house symbolizes the children's fixation with food and survival (Bettleheim 1991, p.60). The house stands for the good mother, provider of nourishment, and the children in the story literally eat the mother figure. The witch represents the bad mother who does not protect or provide for the children and who literally wants to eat them! When the witch is overcome and the children return home, they are laden down with the treasures they found at the witch's house. In the forest, the children learn to become independent and to gain autonomy, and in order to gain this autonomy the story describes how a child must be able to separate from its parents. After learning the danger of devouring the mother represented by the gingerbread cottage, the children learn to look after themselves.

This fairy tale recognizes the importance of the home as a symbol of nourishment, but the gingerbread house is also a symbolic representation of the struggles involved in the process of separation. The message of the story is that it is necessary to achieve autonomy from our parents and that we can conquer separation anxiety and achieve independence in our own lives.

RELATIONSHIPS AND TRANSFERENCE WITHIN THE THERAPEUTIC COMMUNITY

Finding a place to speak from, a dwelling amongst others, involves translating the unconscious. This is a way of responding to others which builds relationships of responsibility between oneself and others and is the characteristic of therapeutic dialogue.

When a new client comes to one of our communities, they begin to try to forge relationships according to old familiar patterns. Much of this is unconscious and quite out of their awareness. Their forgotten past is transferred on to the whole group, and their efforts are hindered by the fact that the unconscious past which they bring to the community is of attempts to respond to others that have gone wrong. Transference may also occur, not just towards the other in the place, but towards the place itself. These dwelling-transferences or place-transferences may be directed towards the house, garden, district, the therapeutic regime or the organization (Denford and Griffiths 1993, p.237). In order for the new client to settle into the community, they need to be helped by the community to understand how the way in which they are acting connects with their past. This process marks the beginning of a new way of responding, in which the past is sorted out, ordered and given meaning. Once a client is able to begin to do this, they will have begun to dwell in the therapeutic community and to find a new base from which to speak. 'To dwell is a recollection, a coming to oneself, a retreat home with oneself as in a land of refuge...' (Levinas 1961, p.156).

Part of this recollection, then, in the context of settling into a therapeutic community, is recalling conscious memories and unconscious recollections of past relationships. For a new client, one of our communities can begin to become a retreat home only when he or she begins the process of remembering, recollecting and translating the forgotten, for this always marks a change from which they can stop acting out in the group. I will try to illustrate the way in which beginning to dwell in the community involves remembering, recollecting and gaining insight into acting out in the group, by describing the arrival of a new client in one of our communities.

A COMMUNITY TRYING TO UNDERSTAND

Jane was a middle-aged woman who was referred with little known social or psychiatric history, except that she was originally from Calcutta and that she came to London about 25 years ago. Her exact age was also unknown and she had no known family. She had recently been evicted from her flat by the landlord because it smelt so bad that her neighbours had complained. When a social worker went in, she found hoards of decaying food and the whole flat in a terrible mess. Jane had become extremely thin and had not been eating properly for some time. She had lost most of her hair due to malnutrition, and it was clear that she had not washed herself or her clothes for months.

When Jane arrived at our community, we were informed that while she needed support with personal hygiene and eating, her one pleasure was going to the Royal Festival Hall. The social worker had to inform us of this as Jane was mute. She neither spoke nor appeared to hear anything anyone said. There was some concern that she may be deaf, and we were asked to arrange for her to see a specialist to investigate this possibility. However, this puzzled us as we had been told that Jane enjoyed going to concerts!

Over the first four weeks of her stay Jane appeared extremely dazed and withdrawn and outside everything that happened in the community. She seemed to be stuck in unconsciously re-enacting her arrival in this country. Gradually, staff and clients began to be able to communicate with her by writing things down, which she responded to well, writing long and fluent responses. She began to attend the weekly community meeting and to join in the cooking, shopping and cleaning responsibilities, and she agreed with staff a weekly plan for washing and self-care. About a month later Jane began to stop and listen when we called her name. She began to speak to us. She told us that she came to London to avoid an arranged marriage. First in individual counselling sessions and later in therapy groups, Jane spoke of the trauma of arriving in this country all those years ago. It seems that she knew no one, felt dazed and confused, and was subjected to some very harsh, most probably racist, treatment. She began to sense that people found her repulsive. We felt that Jane was beginning to build a place to speak from, a place to respond and be responded to, by having been allowed to act out her forgotten past when she had felt dazed, excluded and outside everything. Soon after Jane began to speak and respond to vocal communication in the community, a dreadful smell began to emerge from the kitchen. After some time a member of staff discovered about 15 pints of milk in cardboard cartons, stored in one of the cupboards. The milk must have been there for some time as it had gone off and smelt repulsive. In the next community meeting this was discussed, and Jane admitted that this was her milk. She explained that she used it as 'medicine' to help her hair grow back. The community listened, and there was much discussion as to what to do; however, many members of the group were emphatic that the milk must be removed and that Jane could not be allowed to store milk in the house, outside the fridge, because the smell was 'repulsive and intolerable'. A few days after this meeting Jane retreated to her room and would not come out. She stopped attending the community meeting, cooking, cleaning or shopping. However, when staff or clients went to talk to her, she was still able to communicate verbally. Nothing needed to be written down. She said she wanted to move away from the community, that it was a silly place where she was treated like a child. She said she knew how to look after herself and became adamant about this, although the staff confronted her about the fact that her room was now becoming very smelly and, indeed, that she herself was beginning to smell.

The community discussed how to respond to Jane at the next community meeting. It was decided that every member of the group, apart from one who refused, would visit Jane on a daily basis, taking her food and drink and letting her know that they would like her to come down and join in. It was decided that while non-participation like this was usually not acceptable in the group, Jane's strange behaviour would be tolerated for a while as she was new and she was not harming anyone.

One way of understanding Jane's retreat to her room, after having been rejected on the basis of producing a repulsive smell in the kitchen, was as a re-enactment of her feelings of being rejected, of not being accepted and of being responded to as repulsive on arrival to London. Jane did not retreat right back into not responding verbally but continued to hear what staff and clients said to her, even though she stayed in her room. Jane did not pack up her bags and leave the house despite her stated intention to do so. Rather, she was beginning to find a place from which to speak and to be responded to by the community inside the house, from the vantage point of her private room, by enacting some, but not all, of her feelings towards people in the past. The fact that she was able to begin to unpack these memories, while tremendously frustrating for the community, showed them that she might be able to begin to find her place there, to dwell there, to be in relationship with them.

Jane was also discussed at length in the community meetings which she missed. The whole group was involved in debating how to respond to her, how to understand her, how long we should tolerate her, and so forth. Really finding her place would of course depend on whether she was able to move on from acting out her forgotten past to being able to understand it, to sort it out, in relation to the others. However, all felt that this was, a least, a beginning for Jane. At the time of writing, the situation with Jane remains unresolved.

DRAMA THERAPY IN A THERAPEUTIC COMMUNITY AS A MEANS TO CREATING A POWERFUL DYNAMIC FOR CHANGE

Spatiality and temporality

Space in drama therapy is extremely important. It is within the 'sacred space' that anything becomes possible and change can take place. The therapeutic community itself is a transitional space, a place where change is encouraged; the nature of therapeutic communities allows a place which is perhaps more permissive and more accepting than the 'outside' world. The drama therapeutic space takes this one step further and creates a space which is free from all restrictions (apart from agreed boundaries of containment) and allows the participants to experience situations which seem or are impossible in their everyday lives. This space can be whatever the group wants it to be, with the poetic licence of the imagination.

Many people are stuck in the roles they play, and are bound by meaningless routine. In the drama therapeutic space they are able to re-create themselves and their relationships with others and their environment. Drama therapy may give a group the opportunity to experience places, stories, action and relationships far beyond their everyday experiences. Therefore, the exploration of their environments and relationships within the therapeutic community setting can act as a rehearsal for their own life changes.

It is important for a group to create a space in which they feel comfortable. This may mean transforming the room from its usual state at the beginning of the session. Once a group feels comfortable in its environment, it will facilitate relationships which take place within. I encourage a group to explore the space. An exercise which is quite useful is to get individuals to give objects in the room a name or a sound and an action, then gradually to share these and to find a group phrase and action for several of the objects. This takes the individual members from their individual connection to the room to a group awareness of it. The members of the group are able to find their place together in their space.

A creative exercise I have used with one group was to get them to divide into two and for each group to create their own community. This can be as imaginative and wacky as they choose. They have to give themselves a name and to create an environment, customs and a language (four or five words – not recognizable in their own language) which are important to their culture. Through this exercise the groups are able to define and express their relationship to each other within the context of the culture and environment. On a particular occasion, one woman, in a community which had taken on the identity of creatures from outer space, took on the role of servant to the others. When she fed back at the end of the session, she realized that this was a role she played consistently in her life with her family and friends. This realization made her determined to seek to create change in her own life and the way in which she related to others. The world of the imaginary community reflected her own relationship to her environment and others, and created a powerful dynamic to motivate change.

In another drama therapy group a running theme was 'journeys'. The fifteen weeks of the group was a journey: to explore their aims for being in the group; to discover their place within the group; to understand from where they came; and to motivate themselves for change. In one session I facilitated a guided fantasy of a journey in which individuals had to leave something or someone behind and travel to a new place. What would they need on their journey, what would they take with them? What would the terrain of the journey be like and would it be easy or difficult to walk? In the guided fantasy itself they come to a clearing with a water place and there they meet other travellers. They share their stories in small groups. What have they left behind? What was their hope for the journey? What do they need from this new community?

Through this exercise of imagination, of leaving behind and moving on to a different place, the group were able to explore what they might need to do in order to create change in their lives. They were able to see where others fitted into this and what they needed from others for sustenance. A placement in a therapeutic community implies a future, for it is within this setting that the individual is able to explore their hopes and needs for the future. In the session, the members of the group had a chance to give something to the group and to receive something they needed from the group. They were able to explore what they wanted from others in the setting of their fantasy resting place. It was acceptable to want to be alone and to seek the company of others. They were able to recognize their present position as a step along their life journey and to explore their hopes for the future.

A hiding place for the self

Community implies relationships. Groups often make people think of commonality and conformity; that is, for example, 'We are in a group because we share something in common...' Group therapy encourages people to be able to talk to each other and open up, to have group revelations. However, the group, like the therapeutic community, is made up of individuals, and just as it is necessary for people living together to have their own private space, so too it is necessary for members of a group to have a hiding place for the self.

A uniqueness about drama therapy is the way in which clients are able to take on the role of characters from stories, plays and myths. Within the containment of the session, clients have the opportunity to act out their deepest and most secret desires, fantasies and fears. This may mean expression of anger, hatred, murder, passion or greed. Feelings which are not 'acceptable' in society usually must be kept locked up in the unconscious until they are displaced on to others. The magic of drama therapy is that one can not only project those feelings on to someone else, but also one can freely express them in the safety of the knowledge that they are the character's feelings.

As well as this embodied displacement, it is important to have space for private expression. A particularly powerful way of working is with mythical characters, as they tend to embody such extreme emotions. I have used the exercise of asking a group to take a paper and pen into a space and to write down the wants and needs of the character with which they are working. Six revealing starting points are: 'I am...', 'I want...', 'I have...', 'I am afraid of...', 'I need...', 'In my secret self I know...' The clients need to know they will not need to share this information. When one client read back sentences they had written, they were surprised to recognize many of their own needs and fears. However, it is not always necessary for these truths to be revealed to the group. What can be helpful, though, is to offer the client an opportunity to mark the revelation or desire to change with a public symbolic ritual. This will satisfy both the need for communal revelation and private reflection.

Physical place and the inner world of relationships

We all have imagined our 'ideal home'. This ideal has become institutionalized in the 'Ideal Home Exhibition'. Some people may achieve this ideal more easily than others. A person's image of their ideal home says much about the person they are, how they relate to others and what they need for their sanity. Many of our clients come to us with little or no sense of personal identity and a difficulty in thinking about what they want for themselves in the future. The ideal home exercise gives an opportunity for the group to explore their fantasy home, however unrealistic this may be to them at this point, and to think about what is important to them. In turn, a member of the group asks the rest of the group to create their ideal home, as they describe it to them. The group will use their bodies and voices and any props which may be available to re-create the image which is described to them. This exercise is empowering, as the individual is supported by the group to get what they want and it gives an opportunity to experience how it might feel to actually live in this home. It is also interesting to note where the home is – is it alone in a forest or on a cliff, where are the nearest neighbours and what kind of atmosphere is generated in the home?

The ideal home will give the individual ideas about what they want for the future and may be a first step to aiming for this. Again, the drama therapeutic space is free from the limitations of everyday life. What may seem an impossibility to achieve becomes, for five minutes, a reality. This may spark motivation to work towards this goal whilst in a supported environment.

Finding a place from which to speak

Dialogue implies a sense of response and responsibility between people and a 'staying-with' others in order to work through conflict and difficulties. In order to do this it is necessary to find your own voice. The climax of one group's work together was to enact a scene from a play which took place around a family dining table. Each of the characters were talking over each other and were not listening to what others were saying. The group improvised the scene in character, then a neighbour had to enter into the scene making a complaint. Although the neighbour's entrance interrupted the scene, everyone continued to argue and talk over each other. We realized that person was having a monologue, so that the scene could not go anywhere. At the next session we continued to work on the scene and started by getting into character. As a warm-up exercise, I asked the group to think of one thing that they would like someone else in the family to hear and then to get into pairs with that person. We then tried the scene again, and each person took it in turns to get everyone's attention and to say what they wanted to be heard. The rule was that everyone had to stop and give undivided attention so that each person experienced being heard. This exercise was extremely powerful as many of the group would not usually get the chance to get people to listen to them and to be heard. It also gave an opportunity, during feedback, to understand how each character felt and the effect they had had on others. From being a 'dysfunctional' family made up of individuals leading lives of monologue, the group was able to experience a shift which came from entering into dialogue.

CONCLUSION

In this chapter I have tried to open out some of the complex issues surrounding the notion of place and point to the way in which these issues relate to dwelling in a therapeutic community. I have suggested that place always carries a resonance of time – past, present and future – and that it is not just a physical entity but that it stands for the self and especially the self in relation to others. It is in this therapeutic place that clients work through past relationships and forge new identities in interrelationship. For this process to be truly therapeutic, there needs to be a recognition on the part of therapeutic community practitioners that the self is formed in the non-static space between solitude and communion and that to work within this hyphen ground is to confront the spiritual dimension of the client.

I am aware that I have only touched on these issues here, but I hope that my stutterings and stumblings may inspire others, more able, to explore these ideas in greater depth.

NOTES

1   It is interesting to notice the way in which key twentieth century writers, as disparate as André Gide, Francois Mauriac and Jean Genet, have been preoccupied with meaning. Robert Kanters has discussed the way in which this preoccupation appears to characterize our century (Kanters 1952). This may be a mark of the thinkers of our time because we live in a situation of transition, an 'axial time', to paraphrase Karl Jaspers (Jaspers 1966).

2   It may be worth reminding readers that Michel Foucault's (1961) *Madness and Civilisation* was published in R.D. Laing's series *Studies in Existentialism and Phenomenology* with an introduction by David Cooper, inventor of the term 'anti-psychiatry'. Foucault's book had first appeared in 1961, an important year for existential psychiatry and other alternatives to traditional psychiatric approaches. Both Thomas Szasz's *The Myth of Mental Illness* and Laing's *Self and Others* were published in 1961. In the same year, the *Review of Existential Psychology and Psychiatry* published its first volume and included essays by Viktor Frankl, Paul Tillich, Rolo May and Carl Rogers (Foucault and Biswanger 1993, p.7–8). Given this fertile climate, it is not surprising to find Cooper in his introduction to Foucault writing that people do not in fact go mad, but are driven mad by others who are driven into the position of driving them mad by a peculiar convergence of social pressures!

3   The common ground between psychology and spirituality has been increasingly acknowledged by the leaders of the mainstream Christian churches and the psychiatric establishment in recent years. For example, the Archbishop of Canterbury, Dr George Carey, in a recent address to the joint conference of the Royal College of Psychiatrists and the Association of European Psychiatrists, described religion and psychiatry as occupying the same country, sharing many basic concerns, including significance, guilt, belief, values, vision, suffering and healing. Dr Carey also went on to quote sociologist Paul Hamos's view that *agape* was a central aspect of psychiatry (Carey 1996, p.971).

4   Heidegger used this phrase of Holderlin's poem as the title of his essay.

5   Lacan's notion of the symbolic owes much to Levi-Strauss. He takes the social anthropologist's view that the world is structured by the symbolic exchange of gifts and sees language as the most basic form of exchange. By focusing on the symbolic, Lacan points to the basic element in determining psychosis; namely, the hole in the symbolic order caused by foreclosure and the consequent imprisonment of the client in the imaginary. This leads Lacan to value, above all, the importance given to language phenomena in psychosis as the most fruitful lesson of all (Lacan 1993, p.144).

6   For Buber, 'Thou' and 'It' can only be spoken in relation to 'I'. Whenever 'It' is spoken, this immediately presumes that the 'I' is experiencing, rather than relating to the other.

7   For this section I am indebted to my colleague, John Gale, who has kindly allowed me to use his unpublished paper 'Speech and Place'.

REFERENCES

Bettleheim, B. (1991) *The Uses of Enlightenment.* Harmondsworth: Penguin.

Buber, M. (1937) *I and Thou.* Edinburgh: T & T Clark, 20 July, p.971..

Carey, G. (1996) 'Address.' In *The Tablet,* 20 July, p.971.

Cooper, R. (1989) 'Dwelling and the therapeutic community.' In R. Cooper (ed) *Thresholds between Philosophy and Psychoanalysis: Papers from the Philadelphia Association.* London: Free Association Books.

Denford, J. and Griffiths, P. (1993) '"Transferences to the Institution" and their effect on inpatient treatment at the Cassel Hospital.' *Therapeutic Communities 14,* 4, 237–248.

Foucault, M. (1961) *Madness and Civilisation* (trans. R. Howard). London: Routledge.

Foucault, M. and Binswanger, L. (1993) *Dream and Existence* (ed. K. Hoeller). New Jersey: Humanities Press.

Freud, S. (1988) *The Interpretation of Dreams.* Harmondsworth: Penguin.

Fromm, E. (1956) *The Sane Society.* London: Routledge.

Hartnup, T. (1993) 'To boldly go: Space and safety for children at the Cassel Hospital.' *Therapeutic Communities 14,* 4, 213–226.

Heidegger, M. (1962) *Being and Time* (trans. J. Macquarrie and E. Robinson). Oxford: Basil Blackwell.

Heidegger, M. (1971) *Poetry, Language, Thought* (trans. A. Hofstadter). New York: Harper and Row.

Hinshelwood, R.D. (1993) 'The countryside.' *British Journal of Psychotherapy 10,* 2, 202–210.

Hobson, R.F. (1979) 'The messianic community.' In R.D. Hinshelwood and N. Manning (eds) *Therapeutic Communities: Reflections and Progress.* London: Routledge and Kegan Paul.

Jaspers, K. (1966) *Los Grandes Filosofos I: Los Hombres Decisivos.* Buenos Aires: SUR.

Kanters, R. (1952) *Des Ecrivains et des Hommes.* Paris: Rene Julliard.

Lacan, J. (1977) *Ecrits: A Selection* (trans. A. Sheridan). London: Tavistock.

Lacan, J. (1992) *The Seminar. Book VII. The Ethics of Psychoanalysis, 1959–60* (trans. D. Potter). London: Routledge.

Lacan, J. (1993) *The Seminar. Book III. The Psychoses, 1955–56* (trans. R. Grigg). London: Routledge.

Levinas, E. (1961) *Totality and Infinity* (trans. A. Lingis). The Hague: Martinus Nijhoff.

Plato (1961) *The Symposium, The Collected Dialogues of Plato* (trans. E. Hamilton and H. Cairns). New Jersey: Princeton University Press.

Rycroft, C. (1986) *A Critical Dictionary of Psychoanalysis.* Harmondsworth: Penguin.

Stafford-Clark, D. (1987) *What Freud Really Said.* Harmondsworth: Penguin.

Tucker, S. (1998) 'Dialogue: Training for active citizenship.' *Therapeutic Communities 19*, 1, 41–53.

Vernant, J.-P. (1966) 'Hestia-Hermes: Sur l'expression religieuse de l'espace chez les Grecs.' *Mythe et pensée chez les Grecs I.* Paris: Maspero.

Ward, I. (1993) 'Ecological madness: A Freud Museum Conference, December 1992. Introducing Thoughts.' *British Journal of Psychotherapy 10*, 2, 178–187.

Wolf, R. (forthcoming) *Poems from a Poetry Workshop.*

Xenophon, *Memorabilia and Oeconomicus* (trans. E.C. Marchant), Loeb Classical Library. London: Heinemann.

CHAPTER 5

Care and the Source of Being

Emma Smith

This chapter is primarily about care. What is care and how do we, who work with people who have mental health and emotional difficulties, go about putting care into practice? At the time of writing this chapter I am nearing the end of my one year's placement at Community Housing and Therapy (CHT) as an 'Apprentice Therapist', and these questions about care have preoccupied me during the year. I came to CHT after doing my A-levels and having had a few temporary jobs. I decided I wanted to become a social worker and so set about gaining experience and exploring whether this was what I really wanted to do by joining the year's training placement with CHT. One of the first ideas I was introduced to when I joined CHT was that we have an educational approach to working with clients and that this approach stands in sharp contrast to an approach which treats clients as irreversibly ill and unable to change. In a way, this chapter collects together my responses to this idea with particular reference to care. Perhaps it is as much about what I have learnt as about a certain aspect of the educational approach to working with clients in the culture at CHT.

I start by describing the active, involved concept of care employed in CHT's communities and contrast it with a passive concept of care. In the second section I explore CHT's concept of care in more detail, with reference to the ideas of Heidegger. I then go on to explore two aspects of the care implemented at CHT: practical care and cognitive care. Finally, I illustrate the central points about the nature of care by means of a case study of the Community Meeting in the community in which I have been doing my placement.

HOW CAN WE CARE?

The word 'care' can bring up a number of different images and can be employed in many different ways. Some people may regard 'care' in what I think of as a nursing sense of the word. For me, this conjures up an image of doing whatever is necessary for a person, such as bringing them meals and helping them to wash and dress. It means meeting all of the person's needs by doing things *for* them. Perhaps it is this type of care that is generally employed in a nursing home for the elderly. Some of the people in these homes are not capable of doing things for themselves or even thinking for themselves. Therefore, the nurse cares for the person by meeting their various needs, such as helping them to the lavatory, bringing them food and helping them to eat it, washing and dressing them, and so on. Although the elderly person remains largely passive through this type of care and, as a result, is perhaps encouraged to see themselves as ill, it seems to me that in this setting, given the needs of the clients, this kind of care is probably appropriate.

There are other settings where this kind of care seems appropriate too. In intensive care units in hospitals this model is used. In this setting, patients are so physically vulnerable that it does not seem to make any sense to consider an alternative approach to care. These patients literally could not physically survive unless they had every need attended to by nurses doing it for them. Often this even takes the form of machines doing the tasks that the patient's body is unable to perform; for example, when someone is put on a ventilator machine. Again, if somebody is terminally ill, then it seems fit for nurses to make their last days as comfortable as possible. Alternatively, if somebody suffers from diabetes, this model of care also seems appropriate, as the person needs to be 'maintained' in order to live as normal a life as possible. It seems to me that nurses in nursing care homes for the elderly and nurses in hospitals dealing with these kinds of patients need to work on the basis of this model of care in order to give these people the type of care most suited to their needs.

The therapeutic community I have been working in during my placement is registered by the local authority as a 'Residential Care Home', as are the other therapeutic communities run by CHT. However, the model of care just described does not apply to the people that we work with. However much suffering our clients have endured, however disturbed they may feel and however passive some of our clients may have become, by contrast to the elderly in nursing homes, the intensive care patients and the terminally ill patients just described, we do not believe that our clients are irreversibly incapacitated to do things – be they practical, emotional or cognitive. More-over, we do not believe that our clients *simply* need to be maintained to live as 'normal' a life as possible given some malfunctioning for their bodies, in the sense that a diabetes patient may need to be maintained. For this reason we do not perform care on our clients as passive recipients. Care is not something we do *to* or *for* our clients.

This is so even though most of the people who have come to live in the therapeutic community where I have been working have spent some periods living in hospital. In many of these hospital wards the day-to-day tasks of cooking and cleaning have been performed for them. Although they have occupational therapy of various kinds on offer, when I visited our local hospital ward my impression was that patients had little to stimulate them. They seemed to be so many people sitting, smoking or staring aimlessly at the daytime TV. None of the patients seemed to be talking to each other.

Maxwell Jones has discussed a distinction between 'treatment' and 'care'. In this distinction, 'treatment' is given largely by medical professionals in hospitals and 'care' happens outside hospitals making 'relatively less demand on [any] mental health professionals' (Jones 1979, p.6). I think that what is referred to as 'treatment' here is similar to what I have been referring to as the nursing model of care. Jones rejects both the distinction between what goes on inside and outside a hospital but also the very concept of 'treatment'. He says:

> My objection to the use of the word 'treatment' in relation to what is 'done' for the patients in therapeutic communities is that it implies a relatively subservient role for the 'patient'. This cuts across what to me is the most important lesson that therapeutic communities have shown, i.e. the importance of the 'patient's' own peer group. (Jones 1979, p.6)

By endorsing an alternative to the nursing model of care, we echo Jones's spirit of pulling away from the idea of subservient clients having things done for them as part of being a member of one of our communities.

Because we do not believe our clients have become irreversibly debilitated, the care on offer at CHT is different from the nursing model outlined above. At CHT, caring is more a process of education which enables clients to take more responsibility for their own lives. We are not there to simply do everything *for* the client, such as bringing them cups of tea or cooking their dinner for them. Rather, we work alongside clients through practical task-groups, therapy groups, individual therapy and helping to find training and employment to enable them to learn to care for *themselves*. We facilitate these processes but allow clients to come to their own conclusions. Because we work alongside clients to help them to learn to care for themselves and others, clients become actively involved in a process of change rather than remaining passive and entrenched with a sense of themselves as helpless and ill.

This process of educating clients to care for themselves is at the heart of our approach, and has grown out of the therapeutic community approach. In essence, it involves active participation. Rex Haigh has recently defined involvement and participation as 'quintessential' to a therapeutic community environment (Haigh 1999, pp.252–254). In the therapeutic community in which I have been working, clients have an active role in making decisions about how the community is run. In weekly meetings, issues are being raised and addressed. I think this would never happen within the nursing home model of care, where all these decisions would just be made by staff and management and the clients would probably not be consulted. This enforces the belief that the clients are ill and therefore not able to make such decisions using their own initiative. Clients within CHT have the opportunity to discuss decisions, such as whether the living room should be painted and what colour, to look at how much money is there in the budget and how this could be spent, where a community outing should take place, what issues should be placed on the agenda of the catering group, and so on.

In all groups that take place in our therapeutic community, clients have the chance to be active and treated as human beings with their own opinions and thoughts. Therapy groups particularly give this opportunity, as the clients create the direction the group progresses in. For example, in a dialogue group which is an experiential therapy group, clients can talk about whatever they want to. This could be: 'Why are we in this group and what is it for?' This type of thinking is positive, as the client is beginning to question what is happening in his or her life and not simply accepting it as an unchangeable given. The group could also become a debate about a particular item in the news that week. This group does not have a set direction and allows the clients to take responsibility over the course of the group, with the staff as facilitators but not leaders. The ultimate aim of the group is for the clients to be able to engage in dialogue and have a better understanding of themselves and others. They alone can make this happen, as the therapist is just there to facilitate and assist. The client has in effect been given responsibility for a small part of their life and this can then spill into other matters of their existence.

As I have said, the nursing model of care views the client as completely dependent on the staff, as extremely passive, and it encourages them to see themselves as ill and in need of somebody to look after them. Through this type of caring from others, the client is unable to learn to care themselves because they cannot engage with others or their environment as this is all done for them by staff. This model of care promotes a hierarchy of staff over clients, for it promotes the belief that staff always know what is best for the client and the client therefore gives up their basic human rights to be free and have opinions or make decisions for themselves about what is best for them. This nursing model of care is not in accordance with Rapoport's four principles:

> [I]t is undemocratic in that it promotes hierarchy, it is prone to non-permissiveness in that the staff take control, it is prone to smooth over and avoid reality rather than confront it and it keeps a sharp barrier between staff and clients thereby preventing significant communalism. (Tucker 1999, p.153)

CHT take a different approach to care, because at the heart of our approach is educating clients through dialogue. At CHT, clients learn how to interact with others through speaking about how they feel and they also learn about what they are thinking and how to listen to others. It is through this learning process that clients can become part of the world again and begin to shift away from being detached from everything, as they often are when they come to us.

Implementing this active model of care is not always easy. The fact that therapists at CHT are there to educate clients to care for themselves and others, rather than being there to do things to or for clients, can sometimes be difficult for therapists. This is something I struggled with in the first months of my placement. It was not that I did not intellectually understand what my role was or that I thought that this role was in some way something I did not want to engage with. It was more the emotional and dynamic situations I found myself in which I found so difficult. On so many occasions I found that in the role of attempting to help clients to care for themselves, I came up against enormous resistance from them, and this resistance evoked such strong negative feelings in the clients that they seemed to completely reject me. I found this rejection so painful because it made me begin to believe that perhaps I was the ogre that the clients told me I was.[1] In supervision and staff dynamics I had to work through these difficult feelings in the light of my overriding desire to be perceived as a good, kind person by the clients with whom I had come to work.

I want to illustrate this kind of difficulty that can come up for therapists working with clients with an example. Adam came to our therapeutic community in order to learn practical skills and work towards his goal of having his own flat and a full-time job. He had a very troubled upbringing, and due to events that had occurred in his life he found it extremely difficult to converse with others. Whenever he was asked a question he would either remain silent or respond with a 'Yes' or 'No'. Adam did not find it easy to trust other people and could not understand why they cared and wanted to help him. The staff team seemed to me to be very patient with Adam and did not get annoyed when he found it difficult to hold a conversation. In groups, he was confronted by other clients as well as by therapists as to why he found it so difficult to speak. In individual sessions with another member of the team, reading, writing and drawing were used to encourage Adam to express his thoughts and views. After some time, Adam began to re-learn how to communicate what he wanted to say to others and also became far more self-confident about himself.

However, this process was not as easy as it may at first appear. At the beginning, Adam used to become very defensive with me when I confronted him. He would tell me I was useless and not doing my job properly. He would tell me to leave him alone. I think this was because I was not colluding with him or comforting him in his mute silence. Instead, I was gently challenging him. I think part of him wanted to remain as a passive person and wanted me as a therapist to reinforce the fact that he was ill and in so doing avoid confronting the reality of his problems. He became angry or defensive with me because I appeared to him as uncaring and unhelpful at that particular time when the situation was, I think, just the opposite. In reality, I, with the rest of the team and some other clients, was not leaving him in his isolated silent position but attempting to get him to speak about the issues which made him feel like behaving in this way. We were trying to respond to the underlying meaning of his silence rather than taking his silence and his protests against speaking at face value.

Although I began to understand the dynamics which made Adam flare up at me when I tried to get him to speak, I still found the situation very difficult to deal with, as I really felt that Adam was trying to force me to believe that I was cruel and uncaring. However, I began to realize that the fact that Adam felt like this towards me, and was able to express it to me, was probably a positive step for him. That is, it meant that he was beginning to enter into a struggle with me. This takes some courage, and the fact that Adam had the strength to enter into having negative feelings about me meant that he may have the courage and strength to enter into a struggle with himself. I think that this engagement with himself through a struggle with himself is what lies at the heart of his beginning to learn how to care for himself and his existence in the world.

It is important to be clear about the nature of the distinction I have drawn between the nursing model of care and the model of care employed at CHT. What lies at the heart of the distinction is that on the nursing model of care, those cared for are passive, while on the model employed by CHT no one is passive. Rather, caring is an active practice that we must each learn. However, it might be thought that the distinction between the two models of care is that CHT's model of care simply involves actively caring for *oneself*, in contrast to the nursing model in which someone else cares for one and thus one remains passive. Further, it might be thought that actively caring for oneself rather than letting others care for us presupposes a selfish and individualistic basis for thinking about our relationships to ourselves and others. Indeed, it might be thought that active caring requires that we must do everything for ourselves independently of our relationships to others, and that being active excludes the possibility of caring in relation to another person. In this way it might be thought that the model of care employed by CHT rests on an individualistic notion of a person.

Foucault discusses the issue of whether active 'cultivation of the self' or 'taking care of oneself' presupposes an individualistic model of a person in his book *The Care of the Self* (Foucault 1986, see especially pp.39–68). In his view it does not, for according to him, taking care of oneself is much more than simply attending to one's own needs rather than those of another. It involves the whole 'art of existence' and this:

> ...came to constitute a social practice, giving rise to relationships between individuals, to exchanges and communications... (Foucault 1986, p.45)

> ...it constituted, not an exercise in solitude, but a true social practice. (Foucault 1986, p.51)

> ...it found a ready support in the whole bundle of customary relations of kinship, friendship and obligation. (Foucault 1986, p.52)

[It is a] practice which is at once personal and social... (Foucault 1986, p.58)

In a similar way, I would argue that the active model of care employed by CHT does not presuppose an individualistic notion of a person simply because it is based on activity and this activity includes caring for oneself. This is because the model we employ goes beyond simply taking responsibility for caring for oneself; it includes this but it encompasses much more than this. Our model of care involves learning a whole way of being, not only in relation to oneself but also in relation to other people and the physical context in which one lives. This way of being which we strive to learn has at its root activity rather than passivity; but this does not necessarily mean that we cannot be on the receiving end of someone else's activity or that our activity must only be directed towards ourselves. Rather, learning to care is something which each of us has a responsibility to do, and it essentially takes place for each of us in the context of others and our physical environment.

CARE, CONCERN AND INVOLVEMENT AS INTRINSIC TO BEING HUMAN[2]

In this section I shall explore CHT's concept of care as an active way of being which we and our clients learn, with reference to the ideas of Heidegger. For Heidegger, care is at the core of being a human. He says: '...in care this entity has the "source" of its Being' (Heidegger 1962, section 198). For him, without care we cannot lead a truly human existence. Care is intrinsic to our nature. This is because humans cannot fully exist without being part of the world around them, which includes other people. Being part of the world requires that we care about the world in the sense that we have concern about it. This, in turn, means that we form an integral relationship with it, that we are responsive to it and above all take responsibility for being fully and actively involved with it.

Heidegger says:

> The...totality of Dasein's ontological structural whole must therefore be grasped in the following structure: the Being of Dasein means ahead-of-itself-Being-already-in-the-world as Being-alongside-entities-encoun-tered-in-the-world. This Being fills the signification of the term 'care' (Heidegger 1962, section 41)

What I think he is saying is that the very essence of a human being is being involved with thinking about one's future (being-ahead-of-itself), being in-volved with one's past (being-already-in-the-world) and being involved with one's environment in the present, including other people (being-alongside-entities). He is saying that being involved with these three things is what it means to care. I think his point is that intrinsic to being fully human is being able to be concerned with entities that we encounter in the world and being able to be solicitous of other human beings. His point is not that we must always be caring or concerned but that, if we are to be fully human, we cannot fail to deal with the world and be involved with the world. If we are to be fully human, the world and everything in it cannot fail to matter to us, we cannot fail to care in this sense.

These ideas can be explained further by looking at Heidegger's thoughts about death. A person may go through life doing what they think they are 'supposed' to do but never questioning what they are doing. In this way they may go through their life never caring about themselves and their life by becoming fully engaged and involved. For instance, all children go to school and then perhaps some are expected to go on to college, then university, and then work in a good, well-paid job, buy a house, get married and have children. If a person lives their life in accordance with such expectations but never questions what they are doing and in this way fails to care, then, according to Heidegger, they are living an undifferentiated life.

Further, someone who begins to question their life and changes its path as a result by, say, leaving university and joining the army instead has still not begun to care fully and still remains living an inauthentic existence. According to Heidegger, it is only when a person can allow himself or herself to feel, think about and question the inherent anxiety that pervades each of our lives and, in particular, anxiety about their own death, their future nothingness, that a person can really begin to care and live an authentic existence. When they fully face the anxiety involved in realizing that one day they are going to die, they are then freed to take responsibility for the life they are leading. A person who has faced this has become a 'being-toward-death'. It is this which allows the person to respond to the world and other people and take responsibility for their own life. It is this which allows the person to be really concerned about themselves and their relation to the world and other people in it. It is this which allows them to be actively involved with their own life. It is this which allows them to care. Indeed, Heidegger calls this transformation from an undifferentiated existence to one where a person has faced up to anxiety, and thus taken responsibility for himself, 'care'. In caring for oneself and one's world, we can live a truly authentic human existence, free from our defences. We can stop waiting for things to happen in our lives and can begin to create possibilities for ourselves. It is thus that Heidegger says:

> [I]n anxiety, there lies the possibility of a disclosure that is quite distinctive …basic possibilities of Dasein…show themselves in anxiety as they are in themselves – undisguised… (Heidegger 1962, section 40)

What characterizes care, for Heidegger, is a person's concern and involvement with himself or herself, the world around them and their relationship to it. It is learning to have this concern and active involvement, as I described in the previous section, that lies at the heart of what we promote for our clients at CHT. When new clients arrived at the community I have been working in, they were often very detached from the world, other people and themselves. They seemed to see nothing to catch their interest in the world, the world apparently seemed to them dull, they often seemed to have no motivation to become involved in anything. In my view, these clients come to our communities in a state of not being able to care.

What therapists attempt to do for such clients is to teach them to care, to gain or regain a concern for themselves and their environment, and enough sense of purpose to become involved in their own lives again. Part of what we do is helping clients to open their eyes and look at the world, to start to pay attention to things, to be able to see things in detail and to listen to what is being said in conversation so that they can become involved and respond.

Opening the eyes of clients and reawakening their thoughts may take many forms for us in our projects. It may involve appreciating a work of art, enjoying reading a book, smelling the aroma of a meal, listening to and enjoying music or enjoying the sensation of touch when giving an affectionate pat to a pet. By learning to care in this involved way, clients gain a new perspective on themselves and the world, and this happens, in particular, by coming to view the world with them *as part of it*. Two ways in which clients learn to care are by becoming actively involved in practical and cognitive ways.

TWO ASPECTS OF CARE: PRACTICAL AND COGNITIVE CARE

In this section I describe the practical and cognitive ways in which clients who come to CHT learn to care. At a very basic level, we all engage with the world on a practical level. Learning to do this is a very important part of learning to care for our clients. This involves caring about the place in which they live – the house and the garden – through cleaning, decorating and maintenance.

One client with whom I worked attended the beginning of our gardening group every week, but appeared to have absolutely no interest in the tasks that needed doing. He would wander off each week after a few minutes. He would go back to his room and sit alone or go and have a cigarette, again on his own. When I went to talk to him, he often told me he could not join in because he was 'hearing voices'. After a few weeks another therapist mentioned to me that she had noticed him sitting at his window one afternoon watching the birds in the garden. She had struck up a conversation with him about the birds and found that he knew quite a lot about them. She said that his eyes lit up when he was talking about the birds. I worked with this client in the gardening group the next week by engaging him in conversation about birds when he arrived ready for the group. This week he stayed in the garden during most of the group, sitting in a deckchair watching the others work on the flower beds. The next week I had been to buy a bird feeder and set to work with him on fixing it on a tree and filling it with seeds. From this week on, this client joined the gardening group to fill the bird feeder. In this way he began to participate in some way with the group of others working in the garden, but also he had found a way of paying attention to his environment in the garden. It was a way which he chose and for which he took responsibility.

After a few more weeks in this group, I began to work with this client, showing him around the garden and pointing out the different flowers and shrubs and talking with him about them. We spent time looking at the various details and differences between the plants. Finally, this client began to take part in the weeding. He would only do about five minutes and then go and sit in his chair, but, still, the process of being able to appreciate the detail of the garden environment, and of becoming involved with it and the others in the group, had begun. This client had moved from sitting alone in his room or smoking to engaging in this practical care of the garden. I think this was so important because he had begun to be able to enjoy doing things in which he related to the outside world. He had begun to be able to make contact with the world. He had begun to be able to find the inspiration and impulse to act in the world.

Our clients learn to care and to engage with the world and other people, not only in a practical way but also in a cognitive way, by thinking. This centrally involves engaging with oneself and the world by learning to formulate and ask one's own questions about it. At the project where I have been working, we have various forums where clients are encouraged to think, inquire and ask questions, and in this way take an active part in their contribution to the community. These include a reading group, a women's group, a discussion group, a leisure group which goes to plays, films and art galleries, and informal conversations and debates, especially after supper.

However, a vital part of clients learning to care in a cognitive way means engaging in trying to understand their feelings about themselves and others. Often clients (and therapists) need to re-learn how to understand what is happening inside of them and how their feelings and emotions have developed. For all of us, but perhaps in particular for many of our clients, our true feelings are out of our grasp and appear in unexpected ways through behaviour and particular things we say. One client I worked with, who had a diagnosis of paranoid schizophrenia, arrived at our community with many concerns and fears about being controlled too much by the community. She had been on a section, first in hospital and then for a while after she had been discharged. However, she was not on a section now. She expressed fears of having her food controlled by others if she had to eat with others in the evening. She said she wanted to lose weight. I talked to her at length about how she could arrange and negotiate in the catering group what food she wished to eat. However, this did not seem to help her get rid of her fear of the possibility of being controlled. I also noticed that during the three months that she had been in the community she had not yet offered to chair the Community Meeting. Staff and other clients had suggested that she do so on a number of occasions, but on each occasion she declined, saying that she did not feel capable of being the chair. On one occasion, when I pressed her a little to offer to chair the meeting, she became uncharacteristically angry in her refusal to do so.

I began to talk with her in individual sessions about the issue of control and her fear, both of being controlled but perhaps also of being the one 'in control' as the chair of the Community Meeting. In this way I began to help this client to engage in a deeper understanding of her feelings, both with respect to herself and others. She was able to become involved in a process of caring about why she had the feelings she did.

THE COMMUNITY MEETING: ILLUSTRATIONS OF CARE

In this section I aim to illustrate how this model of care is put into practice. A very important forum in the community I have been working in is the weekly Community Meeting, which is attended by all clients and staff. It is a group where everybody in the community has the opportunity to express their feelings about their own situation or about that of the group. It is through this group that we can really work with our clients to take responsibility for themselves and to learn to care about themselves, each other and the environment. In this section I shall look at various experiences I have had in our Community Meeting as a way of illustrating how our model of active care is put into practice.

First, every meeting has a client who is a chairperson. The position of chairperson alternates between all clients on a rota basis. The chairperson reads out the agenda and generally takes responsibility for the meeting. For example, if someone is not paying attention to the subject and is whispering to somebody else, the chairperson asks them to be quiet. This is a very important role in the Community Meeting because it means that it is a client who is active and takes responsibility for running the meeting rather than therapists. It is also important that every client takes a turn at fulfilling this role, as it can greatly assist someone who is very passive and quiet to speak in the meeting. Getting used to being the chair can give someone more confidence to converse with others outside the community and, as I have described in the previous section, it can give people an opportunity to look at some of their feelings about taking responsibility and about others taking responsibility for them.

The other important role in the Community Meeting is that of the person who takes the minutes. This works on the same principle as the chairperson, with every client taking a turn according to a rota. At the beginning of each meeting, the minutes of the previous meeting are read out so everyone is aware of any issues that may need to be followed up. If anyone has been absent at the previous meeting, they still have the chance to find out what happened and to comment on it if they wish. This role also helps clients to really listen to the meeting and think about it.

The foremost aim of the Community Meeting is to encourage dialogue between all the members. This is certainly not an easy process. Many find it far easier to sit silently and wait for others to speak. A Community Meeting is an active group about talking and listening. The role of therapists is to facilitate the group by teaching the clients how to use dialogue effectively. It also involves teaching clients to care for themselves by taking their own space and time to talk in the group and how to care for others by respecting their time and listening to what they have to say. These aims can be achieved in many different ways, but the ultimate aim is to encourage and educate clients to care and take responsibility for themselves. It is imperative to engage the clients in dialogue, so that they become involved with the issues and dynamics raised in the meeting.

In a Community Meeting it is obviously not feasible to actually carry out practical tasks, such as cleaning, cooking and gardening. However, it is a place where practical issues can be discussed. Practical care can also be incorporated into the structure of the group. Time keeping is a practical issue, and therapists can aid clients in this skill by setting an example by being on time for the meeting. It is easier to learn from example than by being told to do something by someone who then completely disregards it themselves. In such a situation the client may lose respect and confidence in the therapist.

Discussion of the practical tasks in the Community Meeting is also used as a therapeutic tool. It is important to notice how clients react to each other when discussing practical issues. This is an aid to working out the underlying dynamics of the group and to looking further than just at the content of what is being said. It is often easier for a person to engage in dialogue about practical skills than about intimate feelings or emotional issues. Therefore, it can be used as a starting point for dialogue about other, deeper, issues.

Kelly was a client who had trouble keeping her bedroom tidy. On the outside, Kelly appeared a very smartly dressed and well-groomed woman, but the state of her bedroom indicated that underneath the surface she was not as orderly and together as she appeared. This subject was broached in Community Meetings on numerous occasions, by clients and therapists, and through the practical issue of cleaning her bedroom, Kelly was able to begin to say that she was not as all right as she attempted to convey and that underlying this there were many other issues. Kelly had discovered a forum where she felt safe and comfortable enough to express her real feelings.

The Community Meeting is also a forum for learning emotional care. Carmen was a young woman who had a four-year-old daughter to whom she was denied access. Her child was being raised by her sister, but Carmen was finding it increasingly frustrating not being a part of her child's life. The father of her child was in prison, and Carmen was only allowed infrequent visits to see him. She seemed to be very frustrated about her whole situation and began to blame herself and become very angry. However, we only realized this when Carmen spoke, for she found it very hard to talk about her feelings, being used to keeping them bottled up.

In one particular Community Meeting, the issue of clients' children had been brought up, and a few of the male residents were discussing the impact it had had on them not having access to their children or only seeing them rarely or with supervision. At this point in the meeting, Carmen became openly angry, saying that she was the only woman present who had a child and that the men in the community did not really understand her situation because they had not carried a child or given birth. After some time one therapist turned to Carmen and said that it was very good to hear her speak and that she sounded very angry. Carmen's response was to throw a hot cup of tea at the staff member while shouting angrily at everyone present, saying that nobody knew how she felt and how dare they presume it. She then ran out of the house. Subsequent Community Meetings were used to help Carmen talk about her frustration, her feelings of isolation and her feelings of inadequacy. In particular, they were used to help her take the care to understand the feelings that had prompted her aggressive behaviour.

Finally, the Community Meeting is a forum for learning cognitive care, thinking and attentive self-reflection. Raymond was a reasonably new member when he asked the question: 'Why do we have to go shopping every day?' One therapist gently pointed out that he did not have to do it every day as everyone took a turn; why did he think he should not have to go shopping? Raymond then became defensive, saying that he was suffering from a psychiatric illness and did not consider himself well enough to go to the shops once a week and cook a meal. Other clients began to intervene and say that it was only fair that everyone took part, and suggested that another client may be able to go with him and the therapists would be able to help him cook. One therapist, at this point, reverted to something Raymond had said earlier about suffering from an illness; how did this make him feel when he went outside? The therapist was trying to encourage him to think about what he had said rather than simply labelling himself as ill as other people in his life may have done. Something very important had been said, and it needed to be attended and thought about carefully. It is very important that other clients made suggestions so that Raymond did not feel alone or totally dependent on the therapists.

These are just a few illustrations of the ways in which the team I have been part of during my placement have worked, via dialogue in the Community Meeting, to attempt to teach clients to care for themselves and others in an active, involved way. I have illustrated how staff care for clients by empowering them to take active responsibility, to care in a practical way, to care for each other on an emotional level by using dialogue and to learn cognitive care.

NOTES

1   Kate Hardwickie describes a similar dynamic between therapists and 'guests' at the Arbours Crisis Centre. She says: 'There is often pressure from guests for resident therapists to behave like nurses ...' (Hardwickie 1998, p.315). She goes on to give moving case examples of this dynamic.

2   This section is based on an unpublished paper by Sarah Tucker.

REFERENCES

Foucault, M. (1986) *The Care of the Self. The History of Sexuality,* Vol.3 (trans. R. Hurley). Harmondsworth: Penguin.

Haigh, R. (1999) 'The quintessence of a therapeutic environment: five universal qualities.' In P. Campling and R. Haigh (eds) *Therapeutic Communities: Past, Present and Future.* London and Philadelphia: Jessica Kingsley Publishers.

Hardwickie, K. (1998) 'Doors in the mind: Reflections of a resident therapist on the metaphor of doors in a therapeutic community.' *Therapeutic Communities 19,* 4, 315–322.

Heidegger, M. (1962) *Being and Time* (trans. J. Macquarrie and E. Robinson). Oxford: Basil Blackwell.

Jones, M. (1979) 'The therapeutic community, social learning and social change.' In R.D. Hinshelwood and N. Manning (eds) *Therapeutic Communities: Reflections and Progress.* London, Boston and Henley: Routledge and Kegan Paul.

Tucker, S. (1999) 'Community care: The therapeutic community approach and learning to care.' In P. Campling and R. Haigh (eds) *Therapeutic Communities: Past, Present and Future.* London and Philadelphia: Jessica Kingsley Publishers.

CHAPTER 6

Clearing Away Obscurities and Breaking Down Disguises[1]

Kirsty Handover

BUILDING A SOCIAL DWELLING

One important aspect of the therapy in CHT's communities is that of learning to dwell in the building, of finding one's sense of self in relation to the physical environment (see Chapter 3). However, in this chapter I concentrate, rather, on the task of learning to build a social dwelling, of finding one's home in the context of other people. I start by providing a context for the rest of the chapter with a clarification of the sense in which we at CHT understand the notion of care and its relation to cure. With reference to Lacan, here I spell out the way in which dialogue plays a central role in our conception of care and cure. By drawing on the ideas of Heidegger, I then move on to look at the theoretical underpinnings of what is involved in shifting from an alienated isolation to a community membership and thereby finding a social dwelling. With the use of examples, I pay particular attention to two aspects of the struggle involved in this shift into community membership: first, that of welcoming others into 'my space'; second, that of being able to belong amongst other people. Finally, I illustrate the way in which, through the medium of art therapy, we work in our communities to create a verbal space in which clients can find their place amongst others.

CARE AND CURE: THE CONTEXT FOR BUILDING A SOCIAL DWELLING[2]

When we, at CHT, talk about the therapeutic process, we are not thinking along medical lines at all. We are not conceiving the problem of the client as a medical problem. We are looking at this whole thing rather differently. Of course, we are not the first to do that, but it is still something that people find difficult to grasp, and because of the dominance of psychiatry in the treatment of 'mental disorders', a truly therapeutic point of view is often lost or sidelined. We believe it is usually sidelined somewhat unthinkingly and often for pragmatic reasons. Curiously, psychoanalysis itself has sometimes lost the therapeutic perspective as well, substituting a quasi-medical model involving the idea that analysis is essentially intended to cure an underlying disease. Not that the notion of 'cure' needs to be understood in that medical way, but holding on to a genuinely therapeutic rationale enables us to conceive of therapeutics rather differently, not so much in terms of a 'medical cure' or 'physiological cure' but in terms of a search for the truth about oneself. This search for truth will always involve a process leading to change, but this change may be paradoxical.

Fundamentally, the treatment, or 'therapeutic process' or 'therapeutic curriculum', as we prefer to say, within CHT, is geared towards establishing speech and maintaining dialogue.[3] The resulting change will always be a change from isolation to community membership, from the empty to the full word. This can be seen as articulating the truth about one's desire, and this cannot come about without developing concern – and as soon as we enter a dialectic of concern with an-Other, we are at once drawn into a something which can legitimately be called a curative dynamic (see Lacan 1950, p.144).

In practice, of course, psychiatry generally adopts the view that patients suffering from major mental disorders, such as schizophrenia or bipolar affective disorder, cannot be cured but can be helped, through a regime of regular medication, to maintain a level of functioning that enables them to lead a fairly normal life in society. Treatment here is seen largely as a question of the management of an ongoing illness. Perhaps, unexpectedly, it is this resistance to the notion of cure in favour of management which brings, albeit pragmatically, psychiatry and our therapeutic approach closer to one another. Our emphasis is not on cure in the sense of the removal of symptoms, but on the clearer articulation, in speech to others, of a person's truth. And here it may be important to say that this truth is not a truth waiting to be uncovered, although it is often repressed, so much as a truth that gradually evolves and endlessly unfolds and develops in dialogue with another. Our therapeutic curriculum or process might be defined as the gradual construction of the client's truth about themselves in dialogue (see Lacan 1950, p.144).

Does this emphasis which we place on getting into dialogue with clients, and keeping that dialogue going, mean that we have thrown out the idea of cure altogether? Well, yes and no! I suggest that we try to see the idea of the cure in the context of care. We are more used to thinking of care as something we give to those for whom there can be no cure: the elderly and the terminally ill being the prime examples. The psychiatric approach to the mentally ill also tends to see the mentally ill more or less within this paradigm. Local authorities, who register our communities, follow suit. They emphasize the need to look after those who cannot look after themselves. In our approach, we tackle things rather differently.

In order to find some middle ground, I want to go back to the Latin word *cura*. *Cura* is the root of both words – care and cure. Basically, *cura* meant watchfulness, solicitude and concern. *Cura* could be bestowed on anything. It meant taking pains to pay attention to more or less anything. In this very general sense it came to mean management or administration and public business in the sense of taking charge of something. In the law it became, logically, trusteeship and guardianship. There are examples of it being used to describe husbandry, the farm animals being one's charge. Authors referred to the effort (*cura*) necessary for them to write and the study (*cura*) they had to do before putting pen to paper. It could also denote anxiety, worry or concern, and in this sense it came to be seen as a goal to live a life free from care (*curae*). That special person, the one for whom one cared more than anyone else, was one's *cura*, one's love. Finally, we find Tacitus writing that the means to healing is *cura*, a cure (Smith 1968). In English we find not only the words care and cure coming from the Latin *cura* but also curator and curate. The former, curator, continues the theme of administration, taking charge of something, often a museum. The latter, curate, is related to the French word for parish priest, curé. The parish priest is described as having the 'cure of souls'.

Here we see an interesting link between the notions of care and cure. The cure of souls or spiritual charge is an old idea which encompasses the notion of having responsibility for taking care of the healthy as well as the sick and, in the case of the latter, healing them in some sense. Of course, this was not understood as the healing that the doctor might provide; this analogous healing might take the form of merely coming to accept that death was inevitable. But is it not reasonable to consider this a veritable form of cure?

While on this brief excursion into the past, I would like to make a connection between the care–cure motif and two more ideas from antiquity. The first is the notion of the cultivation of the self (see Hadot 1981). The idea that one ought to attend to oneself – care for oneself – was a very ancient theme in Greek culture and has been discussed at some length by Michel Foucault (see Foucault 1986). It was the care of himself that characterized Socrates and one which, perhaps above all else, gave rise to a particular form of relationship between people. In many of the ancient philosophical traditions, this imperative of returning to oneself – attending to oneself – is emphasized in the physical, mental and spiritual self. We find it in the Platonists, the Epicureans and in the Stoics. Seneca and Epictetus develop the idea still further – indeed, to such an extent that the latter defines man as the being destined to care for himself. This attention or care for oneself is a labour, a work, and it takes time. It is like taking a holiday, and can involve a retreat within oneself. Although this practice of turning within and caring for oneself involved a degree of solitude for reflection, it was also a communal and social thing.

The second point I wish to make here is that both in relation to the body and the mind/spirit, the care of the self involved, by necessity, acquiring the knowledge of whether one was ill or threatened by illness. In other words, a key to the care of the self was the establishment of a relationship to oneself in which one could measure one's health. This was viewed as particularly important in relation to 'diseases of the soul', for, unlike those of the body,

> not only can they go undetected for a long time, but they blind those whom they afflict… The insidious thing about the diseases of the soul is that they pass unnoticed, or even that one can mistake them for virtues (anger for courage, amorous passion for friendship, envy for emulation, cowardice for prudence). (Foucault 1986, p.58)

Both of these notions – that is, the care of the self and awareness of one's degree of health or sickness – are fundamentally linked, in my mind, to the variety of care and cure which are on offer, very generally, within the arena of counselling and psychotherapy. In this general sense, our approach in CHT is not exceptional. It is part of a wider movement. Indeed, all psychotherapists know that the client who comes to us for help has to come with some self-awareness and the commitment to look closely at himself, to look behind the mask. More specifically, in our approach the process of therapy is indeed a process of change. It has a beginning and an end, and during this process changes will occur. As Hinshelwood remarks: 'The work in therapeutic communities has a particular objective: to enable individuals to change' (Hinshelwood 1987, p.19). Yet this is not the same as saying that the process ends when disorder is replaced by a healthy psyche. Principally, within an educational therapeutic community, we will expect the client to learn to speak, to speak not just about themselves, not just to another, but about themselves to another. For us, 'truth is grasped in dialogue with another or others: it emerges *in between*' (Symington 1986, p.18). This is what we mean by therapeutic dialogue. In this process of speaking about themselves, the client develops in speech and through speech their own truth, the truth of their desire. We aim, at all costs, to keep this dialogue going, for this dialogue is a dialogue characterized by care in the sense of concern for the self, the Other and the world. Dialogue is the way in which the client finds their place in relation to the therapist, others in the community and society. As this care develops and expands, the client moves out of his or her isolation and, while they retain their basic solitude, begins to live in-relation-to. In a very real sense this can be described as a cure – not in that physiological or medical sense of the word cure, in which the problems all evaporate, but certainly in the sense that when a person learns to care for himself or herself, for others and for the world, and learns to evolve and accept their own truth, they experience themselves as whole, as valued and valuable.

FROM ALIENATION TO COMMUNITY MEMBERSHIP: DWELLING WITH OTHERS[4]

From time to time we all experience feelings of isolation. Perhaps we withdraw from others, and sometimes in moments of extreme anguish we attempt to shut down all our usual channels of communication with others. While this is something that is true of all of us from time to time, it is thus without exception with all the clients who enter into CHT's communities. Not only this, but these experiences of isolation, which are characteristic of the clients that come to our organization, involve suffering.

The clients that come to our communities are, of course, all different individuals, and their isolation is manifested in as many different ways as there are individuals. One example was a young man (with a diagnosis of paranoid schizophrenia) who had experiences where he believed he was God. He struggled with this, questioning it, and sometimes reasoned that he could not be God but rather Jesus. Again, he struggled with this and sometimes reasoned that he was a 'nice chap'. When he was like this and speaking openly in his individual therapy sessions and groups, he often said that others were 'trying to make him have feelings that humans have'. At these moments it was as if he could not bear the pain of human emotion and human contact that others attempted to make with him. While the particular web of reasons for this were complex and took some time to emerge in his dialogue with us, on a very basic level I think it is true to say that in his position as God or Jesus he was able to retreat from the glimpses of pain that he experienced in his human contact with others. At the same time, he was left frustrated with his isolation and in particular with his desire to form a close relationship with a partner.

Another example was a middle-aged man who had recently arrived for a month's trial in our project; he had a diagnosis of depression and a history of drug and alcohol abuse. He had had a family and a good job but became homeless a few years ago. When he felt bad he said he liked to walk, and often walked for days on end. The phrase he said repeatedly during his trial period was, 'I want to be part of this family.' However, much of his behaviour was and had been (perhaps) 'antisocial'; for example, leaving the lavatories in a mess, and when on a theatre trip organized by clients, smoking during the performance and being asked to leave the auditorium. The tension between his spoken desire and his actions, in the context of his history, speaks to me of a deep isolation, albeit manifested in a very different way from the young man just described.

The isolation that I am speaking about is not necessarily characterized by a literal and physical isolation from others. That is, it may be that the clients who come to us have physically retreated from others, but this is not necessarily the case. The kind of isolation I am referring to may occur for someone who is physically amongst others; for example, in the context of a family home. Further, physical isolation may not involve the psychological and emotional isolation that I am speaking about. A monk on retreat may not experience the suffering of being alone that I believe the two men I have just described do.

As I have described in the previous section, the dialogue we wish to create and sustain with each client is fundamentally aimed at helping the client *change* their degree and experience of isolation. In this section I shall briefly outline the theoretical underpinnings of our way of understanding how this change occurs. It essentially involves the client finding his own desire. However, the first step to grasping why this is so is understanding that it is inconceivable for one to exist outside the context of other people; that is, that we are constitutively social beings.

Perhaps paradoxically, this is because, while it is true that we can become psychologically and emotionally isolated, we could not make sense of these ways of being isolated if we were not capable of being with others in an un-isolated way. As Bion has said:

> You cannot understand a recluse living in isolation unless you inform yourself about the group of which he is a member. (Bion 1961, p.131)

Isolation is a lack of contact with others, and thus its very possibility has, built into it, the means of being able to have contact with others. The very fact that we can become isolated means that we must have been capable of being with others first in order to become isolated. If we are capable of being with others in this way, we cannot be essentially solipsistic beings. Solipsism does not make room for the existence of other beings, and thus on such a picture it does not make sense to talk of being isolated *from* other beings. The suffering involved in experiencing isolation is about a lack of contact and could not be experienced if we were not capable of having that contact as in the solipsist's world. If our very constitution as the beings we are is capable of really being with others, then our very constitution is a social one. It is thus that Heidegger says: 'The Other can be missing only *in* and *for* a Being-with' (Heidegger 1962, section 26).

In our view, psychological and emotional isolation is a response to other people in our worlds with whom we are essentially capable of having satisfying contact. The isolation is a response to our fantasy of, or the reality of, the overwhelming power of other people's desires. The isolation is a response to our fantasy of, or the real, pressure to conform to one's experience of others, be it one's parents, friends, teachers or religious and moral cultures in society at large. The response to this sensation of pressure to become like others – to lose one's individuality and this feeling of not being able to be oneself – is to become alienated and isolated from the others which we correctly or incorrectly experience as threatening our individuality, our essence as human beings. It is thus that Heidegger says: 'Dasein, as everyday Being-with-one-another, stands in subjection to Others. It itself *is* not' (Heidegger 1962, section 27).

We believe that the route out of this isolated alienation from the perceived or real desire of others is to begin the struggle to articulate what we truly desire in dialogue with those others to whom we have these alienated feelings and from whom we feel so isolated. It is this which Heidegger describes as an authentic being. For him, the everyday and alienated relationship we have with others is inauthentic precisely because, in it, we are subjected to the desires of other people, to conform to the group at the expense of our own subjectivity. However, for him, the path out of inauthentic existence is not therefore to remain in isolated alienation from the others who seem to make these untenable demands on us; rather, it is to form an authentic relationship to those others, without whom we cannot conceive ourselves as existing at all anyway. We believe this authentic relationship with others involves being able to truly speak from ourselves to others, as opposed to having ourselves created by the desires and influence of others. It is thus that Heidegger says:

> If Dasein discovers the world in its own way and brings it close, if it discloses to itself its own authentic Being, then this discovery of the 'world' and this disclosure of Dasein are always accomplished as a clearing-away of concealments and obscurities, as breaking down the disguises with which Dasein bars its own way. (Heidegger 1962, section 27)

What Heidegger describes as 'the world' essentially includes other people. He speaks of a 'disclosure' of our authentic being. It is this which we believe lies at the heart of helping our clients to move from isolated alienation into community member and which lies at the heart of our dialogues with clients. Heidegger speaks of 'a clearing away of concealments and obscurities', of 'a breaking down of disguises'. It is these concealments and disguises that manifest our clients' isolated and alienated feelings: the young man's belief that he is God or Jesus; the middle-aged man's abuse of drugs and alcohol, his leaving the lavatory in a mess and being asked to leave the theatre. These beliefs and actions conceal and disguise their authentic true desires. Our role as therapists is to discover with these clients, on the one hand, what it is that they experience others as desiring of them and why they find this so objectionable and alienating – why they find it so threatening to their very existence. On the other hand, we need to discover with them what it is that they have retreated into concealing through their beliefs and actions.

WELCOMING-IN VERSUS BEING INTRUDED-UPON

A particularly striking way in which the isolation and alienation experienced by many of our clients is manifested is in their *everyday* struggle to welcome others into their space. This struggle is striking in an ongoing way in our communities, irrespective of whether the clients are currently 'exhibiting' any florid 'symptoms' or 'extreme behaviours'. In this section I shall spend some time examining this struggle to welcome others into one's space.

What does it mean to welcome someone? The Community Meeting agenda in the project where I work has, as its first item, 'Welcomes'. The idea is that if there is a visitor or a new client in the meeting, there will be some time spent formally welcoming them as a means to genuinely making them feel they have the possibility of taking up a place in the community. However, in my experience, I cannot think of a less welcoming situation than that which, more often than not, follows the chairperson's announcement of 'Welcomes'. On so many occasions when there has been a new client at their very first meeting, the rest of the group simply remain silent. They seem to find it incredibly difficult to even make a perfunctory welcome at this point, and it is often staff that initiate these early introductions. This silence in a group certainly does not feel very welcoming to me on such occasions, but why do clients seem to find it difficult to do it?

The dictionary definition of 'welcome' opens, 'to know that convening gives pleasure'. The ability to allow others into your space with pleasure is the same for all of us, but for clients who have suffered years of isolation it is a task which involves them in taking risks, in entering into a battlefield of emotions. In this isolation, many clients become alienated from others, and thus it is perhaps understandable that for them it is not always *pleasurable* to welcome a newcomer. The journey that clients enter upon in our communities towards being able to welcome others with pleasure is one that will take them through a struggle with their feelings of alienation from what they perceive others to desire from and of them. Perhaps these ghastly and decidedly unpleasurable silences in our Community Meetings are an initial step on this journey. We recognize that this first point of engagement with another, illustrated by having to welcome a new client into the community, rarely occurs as a pleasurable experience for our clients. We recognize that it is a potentially painful one. If we think that whenever we meet another person we will always find enjoyment, then we are immediately building a false picture of relating to others, given that the starting point for our clients is one of alienated isolation (as I described in the previous section).

I believe that for many of our clients, the 'Welcome' on the agenda of the Community Meeting represents not an active welcoming on their part but rather an intrusion in which they remain passive, on the end of someone else's actions. Indeed, many of our clients have a history of physical or emotional abuse, or both, and thus they have in fact suffered years of intrusion of some kind. They have in fact been placed in a situation where they are only passively responsive to the desires of other people – in a situation where their own desires have been stifled and ignored. While welcoming and being intruded upon both involve an 'interruption' or a change in one's relation to another person, the difference in the process is clear. An intrusion is an entry by force or thrust and without permission. Intrusion creates helplessness and lack of control, and thus fundamentally invades the rights of the individual – one's command over the boundaries between oneself and another are lost. In welcoming others into my space I am the active agent; in being intruded upon I am a passive victim. It is only when I have articulated and discovered for the first time or reclaimed what it is that I desire, in the face of the real or imagined demands made by others, that I will be able to take pleasure in welcoming others into my space. While I feel helpless and passive in the face of what other people want, be this based on a real experience of abuse or on my fantasy of the desires of others, I will always feel the presence of another as an intrusion. Without an articulation of my desires, I will have no space to actively welcome others into. Our role as therapists is to help our clients articulate their stifled and forgotten desires and thus to free them from the clearly alienating experience of other people as intruders. Whether the client's experience of other people as intruders is one which is based on a real experience of intrusion or whether it is based on a kind of fantasy about the demands that the desires of others on them are, the journey from the experience of intrusion to being able to welcome others into their space will always be a struggle. It will be the struggle of re-shaping their internal and external boundaries. As a first step, it will involve careful attention to their very feelings of being intruded upon, their feelings about having had their boundaries disrupted in the past. This reminds us of 'the idea that boundary management is about survival itself' (Campling 1999, p.91).

BEING AT HOME: BELONGING

As I have described, for many of our clients it does not always follow smoothly from the fact that we are necessarily social beings that they find it easy *to be with others*. Another aspect of the kind of isolation experienced by our clients is the experience of being displaced, of not belonging in the context of other people. It is the experience of not feeling at home amongst others. Thus the journey through a placement in one of our projects has, as a primary aim, the client's achievement of being able to belong, to be able to be at home amongst others and to be able to dwell amongst others. In this section I want to put this point across by means of an example of a client who has begun to be able to articulate her sense of being able to be at home amongst others and of being able to belong to our community.

John was a client who had been living at our community for a period of eight months. He was a young man in his early twenties with a diagnosis of personality disorder. He had a history of self-harm, usually in the form of cutting himself. Often this self-harm was life-threatening. John also had a marked, and often expressed, anxiety about having *any* physical contact with other people. John had spent the last five years of his life in and out of secure units and had been admitted to many different hospitals.

When John was placed in our community, his social worker, CPN and psychiatrist expressed serious concerns about his ability to manage without the constant security that he felt in the hospital. In order to help him move to our community away from the literal security of the hospital, John was offered weekly counselling at the hospital with his social worker. John spent the initial period of the placement travelling between buildings – the hospital and our community. What tended to happen when he was in a mild crisis was that he sought support from the day hospital, the place he knew and experienced as secure. He found it very difficult to be in a mild crisis in our community.

This, perfectly understandable, way in which John was coping with his crises created a dynamic in our community, which emerged in group meetings. Many of the staff and clients began to feel rejected and were left feeling that they could not offer John anything of real value. They began to feel that if John was spending his moments of mild crisis in the day hospital, he could not really feel that he belonged in the community. Members of the group felt that John was in effect too isolated from our group to be able to make use of it.

It was not until John was actually readmitted to hospital as an in-patient, following a more serious crisis involving self-harm, that our community began to realize the attachments and real sense of belonging that John had started to develop during his stay in the community. After two weeks of 'rest' in the hospital, John repeatedly expressed his desire to return to the community. His social worker was the first to draw this to my attention when she phoned me and said that John had expressed a wish 'to come home'. When I visited him again, in my attempt to keep some dialogue open with him, to provide some response to his most recent crisis, I was struck by his choice of the word 'home'. I began to realize that John's initial rejection of our community by spending his crisis time in the day hospital was not, as the community had experienced it, a manifestation of his ongoing isolation and inability to belong, but rather an expression of his first steps precisely *towards* relating to the members of the community and thus developing his sense of himself in it. It was true that his way of relating to the community was by rejecting us, but this was an important step in his beginning to belong to it and see it as home. The beginning of his being able to feel at home amongst others in our community was in the expression of *his* desire to return to it. What was important was that this was his desire. In so doing, he began to be able to welcome others into his space, rather than reject them. When he arrived back from hospital, one of the clients hugged him. He was able to receive this with pleasure. This example reminds us of Yalom's observation about clients who proclaim, "'I don't care what they say or think or feel about me; they're nothing to me" or words to that effect ... [In so doing] [t]hey are concerned at a very deep level about the group' (Yalom 1995, p.23).

For John, as for all of our clients, finding a home for themselves amongst others is not something that happens overnight. It is something they struggle to do over time. Not only this, but it is never clear what particular 'intervention' it is that enables this process to occur. I maintain that it was the initiation of a dialogue between John and the community (albeit one in which John took the courage to reject the community) that marked the beginning of his journey towards belonging. It marked John's entry into the vocal milieu of our community. As Cooper emphasizes:

> ...openings between people are not created by psychological techniques, but by what one might call *manners*: gestures, actions, words... These gestures do not arise out of nowhere, but out of a living context, or intentional matrix. The intentional matrix which is of interest here is that of a community of people living together. (Cooper 1989, pp.37–38)

ART THERAPY IN A TC AS A MEANS TO FINDING A SOCIAL DWELLING

Here I would like to take you through part of the process of the placement of one client in our community by a description of three art therapy workshops in which this client took part. The description illustrates how, through a creative process of dialogue in the context of art therapy, this client moved from an extreme state of isolation to a place amongst others in which she experienced a sense of belonging. The description illustrates how the change in the client was not so much a medical cure but an ability to search for the truth about herself.

Pam is a woman of thirty who has a diagnosis of personality disorder with some psychotic episodes. She has a history of many years of sexual abuse as a child. Her parents have never been able to take this on, and continue to be in denial. She has spent most of her life with feelings of extreme isolation, unable to express herself, and at times when she has done she feels she has been ignored. When she speaks, she does so extremely fast and in a very high-pitched tone so that it is difficult to follow what she is saying. She wears several layers of clothes in winter and summer, including a heavy coat. She prefers not to change her clothes. Pam moves in a very stiff way and often sits bolt upright, staring into space. She appears anxious most of the time and constantly expresses fears of being 'unsafe' in the house. At other times she herself says that she wants 'to speak the truth about myself'.

One of my first close encounters with Pam was during an art therapy workshop I was facilitating. The group was given a 'guided imagery task': participants are invited to draw images that come to their minds and then are guided by the facilitator to the next image. The members of the group were allowed to work with each other if they wished. Pam said that she would not 'join in' if she had to work with others, so she started on the exercise away from the others in the group. Pam drew a door. I asked her what was inside the door and whether it was open or closed. In response, she said that she just wanted to draw flowers, and she proceeded to do so. As she did so, she remarked that she felt safe drawing the flowers. After some time, she said to me that she now saw that the door was open but beyond the open door were more flowers. However, I noticed that in one tiny part of the picture, inside the door, there was an insect.

In the discussion with the group which followed the exercise, I used the metaphor of a door, in response to Pam's image, to open up some thoughts about the way in which we can feel about our relationships to other people. I initiated a discussion with the group about the difference between being able to 'open the door' and welcome other people and keeping 'the door tightly shut' so that other people could only be experienced as intruding. I talked about how Pam had felt so uncomfortable in the session about working with others, to such an extent that she had worked on her own, physically away from others. However, I also went on to wonder with Pam whether she had moved somewhere in this group, for she had been able to draw what lay beyond the door and indeed what was her image of safety – namely, flowers. I wondered whether Pam might begin to feel that it was not necessarily unsafe to be nearer other people. Pam talked openly about how she felt the small insect was something that was out of place amongst the flowers, and the group began to think with her about whether the insect represented her feelings of being out of place or her feelings about other people. Despite Pam's feelings of isolation and fear of being with others, and despite her overwhelming desire for safety, she was, in this workshop, able to enter into a dialogue about all of this.

Another art therapy workshop which was significant for Pam had as its theme 'home'. Each member was asked to model their home out of clay. Pam's model was not a house with four walls, doors and windows but (as another member had guessed) a water lily flower. It reminded me of the flowers that had surrounded her door – the safety that she had felt from them. The lily was without any living creature; it stood out alone as starkly different from the other model-made homes which had chimneys. The lily was extremely carefully shaped with a delicate and soft form. When the group came together at the end of the session, Pam spoke at length about the safety of the lily. She spoke about the safety, not in terms of protection, but rather in terms of the safety of a place where she could express herself.

During this group, via an exploration of the idea of home, in clay, Pam was able to engage with herself on her issues of her own identity within the group, as this was expressed in the difference between her home and that of others. She was also able to begin to explore and identify her *desire* to have a place from which to express herself to others. For me, this marked a significant shift in her feelings of isolation which had been manifested in the previous group.

This workshop on 'home' had a second, follow-up, part the next week. In this session I asked the group to put their houses together to create a street. Two members of the group had not joined in until this point. One of them was moved to bring in a number of items to add to the street scene, and he specifically gave Pam a flower for her lily-home. This member had never approached Pam before, and despite her previous anxieties about working with others in such a group, she was delighted and welcomed the addition. She was beginning to move from a struggle with herself and her own issues, to be able to include and even welcome others in the group and the community symbolized by the street of houses. She was able to begin to see that she could have her safe home *amongst others*, and thus the possibility of dialogue was beginning to be formed.

NOTES

1   From Heidegger 1962, section 27.

2   This section is based on an unpublished paper by John Gale.

3   Lacan talks about the idea of 'maintaining dialogue', rather than finding a 'cure', in his discussion of transference; see Lacan 1951, p.225.

4   This section is based on an unpublished paper by Sarah Tucker.

REFERENCES

Bion, W.R. (1961) *Experiences in Groups*. London: Tavistock.

Campling, P. (1999) 'Boundaries: Discussion of a difficult transition.' In P. Campling and R. Haigh (eds) *Therapeutic Communities: Past, Present and Future*. London and Philadelphia: Jessica Kingsley Publishers.

Cooper, R. (1989) 'Dwelling and the therapeutic community.' In R. Cooper (ed) *Thresholds between Philosophy and Psychoanalysis*. Papers from the Philadelphia Association. London: Free Association Books.

Foucault, M. (1986) *The Care of the Self. The History of Sexuality*, Vol.3 (trans. R. Hurley). Harmondsworth: Penguin.

Hadot, P. (1981) *Exercise Spirituels et Philosophie Antique*. Paris: Etude Augustiniennes.

Heidegger, M. (1962) *Being and Time* (trans. J. Macquarrie and E. Robinson). Oxford: Basil Blackwell.

Hinshelwood, R.D. (1987) *What Happens in Groups: Psychoanalysis, the Individual and the Community*. London: Free Association Books.

Lacan, J. (1950) 'A theoretical introduction to the functions of psychoanalysis in criminology.' In *Ecrits: A Selection* (trans. A. Sheridan). London: Routledge, 1977.

Lacan, J. (1951) 'An intervention of the transference.' In *Ecrits: A Selection* (trans. A. Sheridan). London: Routledge, 1977.

Smith, W. (1968) *A Smaller Latin–English Dictionary.* London: John Murray.

Symington, N. (1986) *The Analytic Experience: Lectures from the Tavistock.* London: Free Association Books.

Yalom, I.D. (1995) *The Theory and Practice of Group Psychotherapy.* New York: Basic Books.

CHAPTER 7

The Therapeutic Community as *Schola*

Anne Salway

In this chapter I shall discuss some of the ways in which therapy, in a therapeutic community setting, can be understood as a form of pedagogy.

LEARNING: THE SELF AND THE OTHER

Those of us who work with the mentally ill often assume that our primary aim is to help clients become independent. This means that our work is to help clients manage on their own, in society. Broadly speaking, this assumption is supported by community care legislation. Clients are assessed across a range, from whether they present a risk to society to whether they can cook or work the washing machine without help. One of the principal attractions of this model is that outcomes are measurable. Yet, important as these things may be, something essential is being overlooked here about the value of relationships, for healthy relationships demand not just independence, though they do demand a degree of that, but interdependence. Indeed, independence is frequently just a euphemism for isolation, and isolation is the hallmark of psychotic alienation.

In a normal early childhood, personality is gradually built up and character strengthened. I am not referring to the physical health or intellectual development of the child, or even to the child's behaviour, but rather to the emotional development of the child. Little by little, through a multitude of positive experiences, the child develops a belief in people and things. These good experiences are weighed against their experiences of anger, doubt and hatred. Life for infants is not easy. It is a difficult time in which each one constructs and organizes their world. For every child there will be tears and struggles and setbacks. Even in the most balanced family, ordinary human development is often hard and in everyone there will be symptoms. That is to say, there will be metaphors or enigmatic messages.[1] These will range from difficulty in taking the breast to bed-wetting. But in the vast majority of cases, the child gradually leaves off the symptom because it has done its job! The child learns to find other ways of asserting its individuality, discovers what to call good and what to call bad and develops likes and dislikes (Winnicott 1978, pp.125–129). Because they have confidence in their father and mother, the normal child pulls out all the stops by trying out their power to disrupt, destroy, frighten, wear down, waste, wangle and appropriate. If the family is stable and the child's relationship with their parents is good, all that the child does to disrupt the home will be contained. The child slowly becomes conscious of a framework in which they are free to be irresponsible. The love and strength of their parents allows for tolerance within a secure boundary (Winnicott 1978, pp.227–228). In this way conflict and disruption are acted out in the external reality of familial relationships as a prelude to the child finding the safe internal environment they need in order to establish self-control. The acquisition of language occupies a prominent position in this developmental process, and language is closely connected with the development of thought.[2]

In a healthy and balanced family, as the child and parents relate and respond to one another, the passage from infant to adolescent is marked by discussion and debate. Bit by bit the child learns to think, and does this in-relation-to the Other.[3] However, for most of our clients, the home has failed to provide the stability within which they can feel free and has failed as a learning forum. It has failed to provide what Lacan calls the *point de capiton* or 'anchoring point', and consequently those in psychosis are inhabited by language and possessed by it (Lacan 1993, pp.3–4).[4] Immersed, as we are, in relationships of transference with our clients, we are called to help them reassess the ready-made answers which haunt them. We are thrown into picking up their childhood learning, for it is this which imprisons them in foreclosure.[5] When a client first comes to us, they need to find their place and learn to relate to the world and to others. It is through relationships, through community, that they will learn to gain a sense of self. It is here, amongst their peers, that they will learn, for the first time, to speak the full word; that is to say, speech full of meaning. This is the speech which is at the core of what we call dialogue, for it forms that truth which is only established when one person recognizes another.[6] Here the client will create themselves, in relationship, and learn the meaning of responsibility.

If we were only to achieve independence for our clients, then I do not think that we would have achieved anything much of importance. I would say that what we are aiming to do is to help each client learn to live with a reverence and value for life. When a person is severely depressed, they are not able to enjoy the subtleties of life and can only see life as mundane and meaningless. The person in psychosis is locked in an imaginary world, disconnected from the Other because they are cut off from the symbolic function of language, which alone forms a bridge between themselves and the Other (Lacan 1994, p.189). A deep detachment is awakened in them, in which they feel so rejected that they are unable even to conceive of the Other. In this place they cannot experience the wholeness of human existence, for that wholeness or completion only comes about in relationship, and relationship is rooted in speech. It is not enough to focus on independence because it is not the mere learning of a practical task or response that is important, but being able to think about the meaning and context of that task or response. It is our relatedness to that task, and our own self in that response, which alone gives it meaning. When we talk about an educational therapeutic community approach, we are seeing education as relatedness to the Other, and this forms a primal foundation to I-thou relationships.[7] Think of the apprenticeships of years gone by. Here we see something of the kind of education which has relevance to the therapeutic community. The apprentice carpenter learns his craft from the master carpenter.[8] He watches and learns from his master, but the most important thing he learns is not which tool to use or even how to use the tools, but rather how to respond to the wood as it enters his domain, his dwelling (Heidegger 1968, p.14). It is his skill at relating to the wood that makes him a craftsman. Without this ability, this skill, this *techne*, he would be a mere labourer.

Life without relatedness has no meaning. In the therapeutic community, the therapist, as pedagogue, helps create a climate in which clients teach each other the craft of relationship. More than anything else this involves drawing out language in the group and tutoring speech, for this is the basis for thought. It is never a question of the therapist giving the answer, but rather of the therapist enabling each client to forge for themselves the skill to seek out their own solutions, finish their own sentences. In the words of an ancient proverb, 'Give a man a fish, he has food for a day; teach him how to fish, he has food for life.' In order to live fully, a person must learn how to think. If we are able to think things through, reflect, question and relate to the Other, we will be able to respond to the situations and events that life brings. Just as with each new piece of wood, every situation in life needs to be 'felt out' in order that we might respond to it. The therapist is constantly 'feeling things out', thinking about what is happening beneath the surface in any given situation, and trying to respond to it genuinely. Of course, this demands real skill, for when we refer to what is happening beneath the surface we are referring to unconscious processes. What is really happening within the therapeutic arena is often quite different from what appears to be happening superficially. In order for the therapist to discern the sub-text at each moment, they must be as open to learning as the client. Indeed, the role of the therapist, one could say, is not to teach but to 'let learn' (Heidegger 1968, p.15). A didactic therapeutic method-ology is one of questioning, rather than one of conveying fixed solutions. We need to work on the basis that the therapeutic community is a place for continual learning, a place in which therapists and clients alike are attentive and learning from each other how to live. By this I mean how to live life to the full, to have meaningful relationships with one another, to respect one another, to have a reverence for life, to value each person's uniqueness, to act freely and with dignity, to cultivate our taste buds, so to speak, in the arts and literature as well as in food, to be trustworthy and loyal to each other, to dare to take risks and to treasure the environment. In this way we will have formed a therapeutic community which can rightly be called a school or *schola*, not just in the sense of a place for learning but also in the sense of a group sharing a common ideal, approach and framework, in the way in which we speak of a 'school' of painters. Yet it is the basic sense of the Greek root (*schole*) of that Latin word that I wish to place the emphasis – first and foremost, *schole* referred to a place of leisured conversation or debate.

It is because the therapeutic *schola* is constructed on dialogue, and everything we say this can involve, that the client is able to create a sense of self, for dialogue means being in symbolic relation to others. The therapeutic community that sees itself from our perspective, as a therapeutic pedagogy, takes the symbolic as its ground and context because the community members are formed through linguistic relationships. And since the most basic form of exchange is the gift of speech, dialogue is our only therapeutic technique.[9] Our therapists are, then, practitioners in the symbolic, above all else. Through verbal exchange, our clients, who have never had a strong sense of self, find themselves in the Other. This finding of the self is never static, for the self is always being called out of itself in growth.[10] Growth occurs when something is rooted in a source of life. For a plant to grow, it must be rooted in good soil. In the same way, for a person to grow, they must be fully rooted in relationship to the world and in dialogue with others. Our therapeutic educational approach is founded on dialogue, because it is only in verbal relationship with others that the self can be formed, grow and reach out beyond itself to the future.

THE THERAPEUTIC *SCHOLA* AND THE PSYCHOSES

Our therapeutic pedagogy is rooted in dialogue. That is to say, the *schola* is constituted in the linguistic structure of our relationships with clients and in the linguistic structure of the relationships our clients have with each other. It is this linguistic structure which is the schema of the therapeutic community, for the speaker's word always exists in order to be understood:

> Thus, its meaning is not only intentional. It takes its real final form only after flowing into that mould, the other half of which is always filled by the interlocutor or, more precisely, the social group. (Levi-Strauss 1987, p.275)

If there is no speech, there is no ground on which to form relationships, for 'dia-logue' always implies relationship. It is the word (*logos*) between subjects. It is, at its most fundamental, the symbolic exchange of one person to another in reciprocity. That is, the word is the symbol, the gift which stands for the one who utters it.

I would like to turn now to a biblical image in order to try to draw out something of the relationship between therapeutic dialogue and the *schola*. The image I have in mind is the familiar one of the parable of the sower. Let me start by reminding you of the story:

> A sower went out to sow. And as he sowed, some seed fell along the path, and the birds came and devoured it. Other seed fell on rocky ground, where it had not much soil and immediately it sprang up, since it had no depth of soil; and when the sun rose it was scorched, and since it had no root it withered away. Other seed fell among thorns and the thorns grew up and choked it, and it yielded no grain. And other seeds fell into good soil and brought forth grain, growing up and increasing and yielding thirtyfold and sixtyfold and a hundredfold. (Mark 4, 3–8)

Those of us brought up with a traditional Christian education are so used to hearing stories from the New Testament that we may assume that parables like this one are just simple, vivid stories illustrative of Christ's teaching. However, biblical scholars tell us that this was certainly not what the evangelist thought. For St Mark, the parables were intended to wrap up Christ's teaching and make it obscure in order to prevent it having an impact on those not meant to be enlightened by it. Although in classical Greek the sense of the word parable is quite straightforward, in order to understand its meaning in the New Testament we need to refer to the Greek translation of the Old Testament.[11] Here it is used to translate the Hebrew *mashal*, and comes to mean something indirect, sayings which call for reflection before they can be understood.[12] In this sense we are talking about things being said obscurely, intentionally to puzzle people and provoke them into reflection and consequent enlightenment. When used like this, some would undertake the necessary reflection and be illuminated, while others would gain no insight, even though they understood the literal meaning of the words.[13] Another factor here is that by the time the evangelist wrote his collection of sayings, the early Church was faced with explaining why Jesus had not been generally recognized as the Messiah, and here the enigmatic nature of his teaching helped considerably.[14] In a very general sense, then, the parables in the New Testament bear some resemblance to the Zen koan (Watts 1965, pp.174–192). Both aim at illumination and both require learning to 'work through' the text (Merton 1976, pp.69–90):

> The master breaks the silence with anything – with a sarcastic remark, with a kick-start. That is how a buddhist master conducts his search for meaning, according to the technique of *Zen*. It behoves the students to find out for themselves the answer to their own questions. The master does not teach *ex cathedra* a ready made science; he supplies an answer when the students are on the verge of finding it. (Lacan 1987, p.1)

The genre of the parable, like that of the koan, tells us something about the technique of dialogue in the therapeutic *schola*. The key is prompting reflection, allowing and encouraging the 'working through' in order to gain insight, while also acknowledging that each different client brings their own history and this is the idio-context within which the therapy takes place. This will always have a bearing on the outcome of the course of therapy.[15] This last point is an important one and one which, as practitioners, we usually prefer to avoid. For that reason, I would like to try to explore it a little, using passages from the parable as a motif.

Some seed fell along the path, and the birds came and devoured it. The basic premise of hermeneutics is that the symbol gives rise to thought. Thought, that is, is the basis of all learning and is intimately bound up with language. The child needs to be taught how to think and given the opportunity to ground their thoughts in conversation, discussion and debate. If nobody is there to listen to their questions and noone will take the time to respond to them, the child will not have the chance to formulate their ideas. The child for whom there is no response will not fully be able to develop language and thought. Without being rooted in relationship, the child may become alienated and trapped in the imaginary. This is particularly evident with clients who suffer from narcissistic and aggressive tendencies. Their world is one of deception, and their illusions are those of wholeness and autonomy. Language, for the psychotic client, takes on the appearance of a wall in which all that the Other has to say is distorted and inverted.[16]

Many of our clients are locked in paranoia. A client may feel that there is a conspiracy against them or that other members of the community are picking on them. These strange beliefs often form complex patterns and seem to be a way for the client to fill a deep interior emptiness. In this sense, the client's delusions are often positive attempts to feel better, to restore themselves to a less fractured state. The paranoid delusion is an attempt at recovery, at the reconstruction of the self (Freud 1911, p.71). The curious details of the paranoid conception of things are always of significance, and we need to pay great attention to the details of the delusion. In a sense, it is a form of discourse, and our task is to try to make sense, in words, of what at first may seem nonsense: to make sense, verbally, of the details and patterns of the client's distorted world; to translate, we might say, the persecutory delusion, say, of the Mafia who are 'out to get me' or who are 'watching my every move' into words. This may seem an odd way of putting it, because when the client talks about their delusion, they are speaking; that is to say, they are using words! But when we say we are translating their paranoia into words, we are referring to the underlying structure of the paranoid discourse. In other words, we direct their speech away from the surface, which is the story, if you like, into the meaning and function of the structure. This is what we call dialogue, and our aim is to include the whole community in the translation or clarification of delusional phenomena into speech.

When these structures are not expressed in words, they may be expressed in unconscious acts, while the client is unaware that they are intentional. These acting-out behaviours are often linked to the refusal of the Other to listen to the client. At these moments, which are frequent and everyday events in our communities, we always insist that the client take responsibility for their acts and the group rallies round the therapist, in order to help decode the client's actions:

> The acting out is thus a ciphered message which the subject addresses to an Other, although the subject himself is neither conscious of the content of this message nor even aware that his actions express a message. It is the Other who is entrusted with deciphering the message … (Evans 1996, p.3)

Translating acting out is such a common feature in our work that it is easy to forget that the message always is a message for us. That is to say, it is part of the transference and generally implies resistance (Laplanche and Pontalis 1967, p.4).

Other seed fell on rocky ground, where it had not much soil and immediately it sprang up, since it had no depth of soil; and when the sun rose it was scorched, and since it had no root it withered away. If our therapeutic word is to be effective, it must be spoken to the client in a way which recognizes the stage the client is at in the therapeutic *schola*. It is no good giving wonderfully profound interpretations if the client is still unable to receive them. In characteristic Gallic manner, Lacan makes this point by comparing psychoanalysis to cooking! A good cook, he says, has to know how to disjoint a bird with as little resistance as possible. As therapeutic community practitioners, we do our dissecting with concepts, not a knife, and these concepts arise out of language. Let me paraphrase Lacan. At first, the language entangles us. The words are the instruments for delineating things, so while the words are poor, the subject remains in darkness. Sometimes we seem to use the wrong language. We all do this and it is not just the client; we also use the wrong words at times. We therapists need to remember that; in many ways, we are just like the client, entangled in the wrong language, hunting for the right words (Lacan 1987, pp.2–3). Many of our clients lack the confidence to express their ideas, their thoughts and their dreams because they have had experiences in the past in which they have been ridiculed. Often they were unloved, and when, in their natural childlike innocence, they spontaneously reached out in trust to the Other, they were crushed. If a person has no sense of himself or herself and does not even know what they like or want, they need help to discover their creativity. Many of our clients have not had the opportunity to develop their potential, so as therapists we must believe in our clients and the potential of the group in order to kindle the spark that can grow into a fire. This fire is therapeutic dialogue, and in it we recognize the potential and uniqueness of each person.

Other seed fell among thorns and the thorns grew up and choked it, and it yielded no grain. A child who, although heard, is not given feedback will not bring their ideas to fruition. So as soon as any obstacles come along, the child will be put off. They cannot think through a problem and so they give up. To hear but not respond genuinely to the Other is not dialogue, for dialogue implies authenticity and therefore honest and realistic feedback. The role of the therapist is to respond authentically to the client and to facilitate the group to give feedback continually. This may sometimes involve reality confrontation and other things the clients may not like, but in order for them to be able to move on and fulfil their potential, they will need to be able to learn how to work through the obstacles which will face each one at every turn in the therapeutic journey.

And other seeds fell into good soil and brought forth grain, growing up and increasing and yielding thirtyfold and sixtyfold and a hundredfold. The seed which falls on the good soil is like a child who is responded to and is given the opportunity to ask questions and debate, so that when problems arise in the future, they will be able to think for themselves and reach a gestalt, a conclusion.

MEMORY AND THE PAST: PAINTING, MUSIC AND POETRY AS TRUE SPEECH

From some aspects, our life is analogous to a journey in which death is the final destination. Indeed, to paraphrase both Heidegger and Lacan, we can say that our journey through life only assumes meaning by virtue of the finite limit set by death. In this sense man is a being-for-death, and in consequence one of the core aims of our therapeutic approach is that the client comes to clothe themselves in their own mortality (Lacan 1977, pp.104–105). When the client begins to move out of their isolation and begins to care for the others in the community, and even for the physical fabric of the place, they take on a quality that could be called anxiety. This anxiety is a form of care, in the sense of having cares or worries. While formerly our client was trapped in their psychosis, all alone, now as they take their place in relation to others, he or she notices them, cares about them or about the house. Often the first real sign of change that we see in our clients is when one of them asks how another is feeling or does some chore around the house – emptying the bins in the kitchen, for example – without being asked. These are small things, but they can mean such a lot. These are the points at which the client begins to apprehend their own finiteness and vulnerability. Suddenly the world is a place of vulnerable existence for them, and at the crucial moment of change they have started to grasp something profound, something which will be the key to the far greater changes that are about to take place in them. This is the realization that, as a creature who exists in time, they bear responsibility for their own acts and, indeed, for their own existence. Here, in anticipation, a new authenticity is being formed in the client.

On this journey towards death, pleasure is found in relationships with others. If we have people to care for and people who care for us, then life is much more bearable and enjoyable. We all need someone to share our load and to share our experiences. We could say that life is about relationships, for in our journey we are seeking the Other:

> We are all travellers in what John Bunyan calls the wilderness of this world …and the best that we can find in our travels is an honest friend. He is a fortunate voyager who finds many. We travel, indeed, to find them. They are the end and reward of life. They keep us worthy of ourselves; and when we are alone, we are only nearer to the absent. (Stevenson 1892, p.v)

The *schola* is a place for looking back. It is a place of memory, recollection and the past. This is because it is a place where repetition is avoided and acting out challenged.

We sometimes find the expression 'psychotic surrender' used to characterize a reaction in individuals who are seen as reaching a point where they throw in the towel, giving up their battle to face reality and surrendering to a psychotic withdrawal (Reber 1985, p.599; Rycroft 1968, pp.100–103). Indeed, the defining feature of psychotic disorders is often thought to be a gross impairment in reality testing, of which delusions and hallucinations are prime examples (Reber 1985, pp.616–617). However, for the ancients there were some forms of madness – some forms of throwing in the towel – which could be classified as good or, indeed, of divine origin. For example, prophecy, some ritual enactment, poetry and sexual desire demand a surrender of the self. They were considered to be expressions of a kind of madness because they took the person outside themselves and, in this sense at least, demanded that they momentarily lose control or let go, at some level. In other words, the wistful verse of the poet has the ring of sincerity when it goes beyond the poet himself or herself. Just as, in prophecy, the truth about the future could be grasped only if a person was in touch with a knowledge wider than their own, so the truth about the past, as it is found in the content of early poetry (rather than the poetic form), was considered a given element and not a chosen one. The prophecy and the poem were only partially under the control of the poet and the prophet. Like the lover, to be taken up in the creative experience demanded a deep catharsis, a deep release and letting go to the Other. In this sense poetry can be seen to be true speech, and the gift of poetry, the power of true speech. Many later writers, in their own way, have had a similar feeling; namely, that creative art is not simply the work of the ego. Shelley wrote that the mind in creation is as a fading coal, which some invisible influence, like an inconstant wind, awakens to transitory brightness (Dodds 1951, pp.64–101).

This may all seem rather fanciful at first, and far removed from our mundane work with clients, but perhaps one of the values we can take from this view, albeit expressed in forms common to an earlier age, is that it frees madness from the necessity to be perceived as something unknown and foreign to the sane, thus opening a possibility for dialogue, for true speech. I think that poetry has the ability of being the most present, honest and spiritual expression of responding to the Other and being in relatedness to the world (Powell 1992, p.185). When we read poetry, we become aware of the supple and elastic nature of words. Each word can express a variety of meanings and speak to us at different levels of our being. However, it is more than this, for in the poetic word we are shown the unfathomable nature of language. These are the unconscious depths of our speech in which the reader or listener is drenched in the word from head to foot, as it were. They are stirred and challenged by the poetic word at every level of their being. The poet is *poietes* – literally, a maker, a creator. As creator, the poet charges each word to bursting point with layers of meaning, and as a result this poetic word has the power to give new life to anyone who listens in silence and has the courage to allow the word to touch them (Louf 1980, p.51).

In creating the therapeutic *schola*, I think it is important, indeed vital, that we work with our clients at the level of painting, sculpture, music, theatre, literature and poetry because these are in some ways the nearest we get to the core of language and therefore to the centre of our own being and the heart of our relationships with the Other. The arts move us, they touch us, they transform us. We must help our clients learn to appreciate the arts, because in doing so we open to them the possibility of responding at a deeper level to the word. This is none other than a quest to find their highest and truest self-expression by teaching them to listen, to think, to feel, to be moved and to speak. The therapeutic *schola* is the environment in which the client begins to learn these things, through thinking, questioning and debating with their peers.

QUAESTIONES DISPUTATAE[17]

In one of our therapeutic communities, some years ago, a series of weekly discussions were held after supper. These discussions were informal and developed naturally, initially involving one or two clients but gradually attracting more or less the whole community (which numbered about twelve). Topics for discussion were chosen spontaneously and were often the result of someone's comment on something in the newspaper. The majority of the clients were from relatively deprived backgrounds and few had been in higher education, but the conversations were complex and dealt with issues of value and meaning, morality, religion, poetry, politics, art and literature. A key to the conversation was the presence of a member of staff who facilitated these debates, although, for the most part, clients were not very aware that there was any facilitation going on. This climate of 'facilitation incognito' was aided by the fact that the discussion was not called a discussion group and took place around the dining room table. Another indirect aid to the development of this weekly discussion after supper was that there was a gap of about an hour between the end of the meal and the beginning of the community meeting. This meant that there was both time to talk and everyone knew when the cut-off time would come. Nobody was told they had to attend, but as each conversation began to take off, others, who had, maybe, stood up to do the washing up or watch TV, were drawn back to the table, either because they were curious, having overheard something, or because they wanted to say something. Some themes would return week after week and some clients would tend to take up similar positions in the group – the sceptic, the person who always saw both sides of the argument, the Thatcherite, and so on! This is how one of the facilitators described the group:

> One evening there was a discussion about education, or at least that was where the thing started. Mostly these discussions, like the medieval *quaestiones disputatae*, started in one place and ended up bringing in a whole load of other topics, some more relevant than others, but they were always very stimulating.[18] On this occasion things took off because someone referred to something or other they had read in the paper and asked me what I thought about it. I can't remember exactly what I said but we ended up talking about the usefulness of reading the classics. Remember these were mostly a group of young people from pretty deprived backgrounds and it's probable that few, if any of them, had any knowledge of the classics. Soon, however, the table was full and everyone had a point of view or a question they wanted to ask. On another occasion there was discussion about jazz and whether Ornette Coleman was worth listening to! What I noticed about these 'disputed questions' was how, gradually, members of the group learned from one another *how to argue* – how to take up a position, for the sake of the argument – and how to enjoy the process of coming to have a point of view on something that previously they may not have thought about at all.
>
> Crucial in this, I think, was my role. I was someone that, on the one hand, they felt safe to disagree with and argue with, and didn't think I would make a fool of them or laugh at them, while on the other hand they trusted my judgement and wanted to learn from me. At times this meant that showing them that I was undecided about things and didn't know was as important as being fairly predictable, stable and certain. Of course transference was central in this learning but so was the peer element and particularly competing to win an argument. Often my role was to clarify an argument and make distinctions, much as if I had been leading a seminar on logic!

Looking back on these discussions, as well as still being able to see those individuals sitting around that table, and seeing many of them develop individual identities and mature, two things stand out. Firstly, how important, as a facilitator, it was for me to risk sharing my own experiences – being bold about my doubts and certainties. And secondly, letting clients go through periods in which they imitated me as well as periods in which they reacted against me and everything I stood for – or at least, their perception of what I stood for – dispassionately. The imitating or copying was difficult for me but I understood that for a number of them they had, precisely, lacked a role model in childhood and that what I had to offer was someone against whom they could measure themselves and the world and find out where they stood, who they were.

Here we see, in the words of the educational theorist Paulo Freire, the ability to dialogue with educatees in a mode of reciprocity. According to Freire, the ability to dialogue is the mark of the successful educator (Freire 1979, p.xiii). The dialogue that occurred in these discussions of 'disputed questions' was based on trust, not so much the trust that clients had for the facilitator but the trust or belief that the facilitator had in the clients. Dialogue of this kind is always grounded in trust. Karl Jaspers was getting at this, I think, when he wrote that

> it is only by virtue of faith, however, [that] dialogue has power and meaning: by faith in man and in his possibilities, by the faith that I can only become truly myself when other men also become themselves. (Jaspers 1953, p.45)

It is this faith in man that is the prerequisite for the therapist – the therapist must be committed to the client in the sense that the therapist believes in the client's ability not to overcome all their difficulties, but their courage to accept themselves and only find their authenticity by understanding that they are in the position of the dead (Alford 1991, p.38; Benvenuto and Kennedy 1986, p.207). It is only from the position of the dead, we could say, that we are able to live in authentic relatedness to the earth in which we dwell. In the words of E.E. Cummings, the earth's lover is none other than a deathbed:

> (but
> true
> to the incomparable
> couch of death thy
> rhythmic
> lover
> thou answerest
> them only with
> spring)
>
> (Cummings 1960, p.3)

The idea for these discussions was based on the way we use others to support our sense of ourselves. This sense always remains, to some extent, alienated in the Other and never becomes fully our own. In this, we experience a funda-mental lack in human existence. It is this lack or gulf which gives rise to desire and rage (Lacan 1988, p.223).

FROM DIALOGUE TO RESPONSIBILITY[19]

When a person becomes able to be actively involved in their own life journey, they are then able to become an agent in the world and take responsibility for their own degree of understanding, their own questions and their responses to others. We must bear this in mind in the context of our therapeutic educational approach:

> Teaching is more difficult than learning because what teaching calls for is this: to let learn... The teacher is ahead of his apprentices in this alone, that he has still far more to learn than them – he has to learn to let them learn... The teacher is far less assured of his ground than those who learn are of theirs. If the relation between teacher and the taught is genuine, therefore, there is never a place in it for the authority of the know-it-all or the authoritative sway of the official. (Heidegger 1968, p.15)

A teacher who tells their students the answers, who seems to know all the answers, and who commands the authority of official knowledge, is not a teacher who opens out the possibility of thought, questions and, above all, dialogue with their students. Rather, this kind of teacher precisely closes down the possibility of thinking, questioning and dialogue on the part of the students. Indeed, the students will passively receive the official version that the teacher ladles out. As therapists in a therapeutic community, we teach clients to think, to ask their own questions and thus to enter into a dialogue with us in which they are responsible, active agents. We do this by opening out questions with them. At the same time, we must listen hard to the underlying questions that clients ask, often indirectly, through their behaviour or defensiveness. We must strive to create an environment in which clients can begin to ask questions, so that exploration and change can begin to take place. This can involve resisting the temptation (which arises out of our own defence against the client's anxieties) to act as though we have the answers. In the face of the client's anxieties, the therapist needs to be able to stay with the idea that they know as little, or even less, than the client. It is within this context that clients will be able to begin to enter into dialogue with us, by becoming agents and taking responsibility for their own degree of understanding, their own questions and responses to others.

For us, creating, maintaining and revising this educational culture, this *schola* of open questioning, in an attempt to help clients become responsible agents, is the prerequisite for establishing dialogue. All our therapeutic interventions, however apparently insignificant, have this as their goal. These interventions may be direct, in the sense that they clearly open out an explicit question asked by a client and give it back to him or her to answer, or they may be more subtle and indirect, in the sense that both the client's question and the response created by the culture in the therapeutic community as *schola* may be only implicitly articulated. I will give an example of the first of these cases. It illustrates a client at the start of the journey towards entering into dialogue, by beginning to take a degree of responsibility for his own questions.

Peter was a 50-year-old man with a diagnosis of paranoid schizophrenia. He joined our community for an assessment period that was to be reviewed at the end of three months. He had a long history of placements in residential settings, including other therapeutic communities, which he usually managed to maintain for some time, but which eventually broke down because he became extremely passive, lying in bed all day, refusing to participate. He came to us after a long period in hospital. For the first two months of his assessment period, Peter appeared extremely anxious to please, participating in all aspects of community life and often initiating conversations with the staff about how he understood that it was an expectation of this community that people learnt to take responsibility for themselves and for the running of the place. He also commented to them on how well he thought he was doing and on how much he liked this community. He began to form relationships and often stayed up late, chatting with three or four of the other clients. At the beginning of his third month, Peter started to refuse to do his weekly cooking and shopping when the time to do it actually arrived. Repeatedly, the therapist who was on the rota to work with him on these tasks tried to speak to Peter about what was going on for him, how he was feeling and why he was refusing to participate. On each occasion Peter began to shout violently and swear at the therapist, his eyes and his whole body stiffening in a threatening posture. These outbursts were interspersed with periods when Peter stood still and rigid and stared into the therapist's eyes. The therapist would feel terrified. On one occasion Peter shouted repeatedly, with an unusual accent, 'I say no! I say no! I say no!' On another occasion he shouted repeatedly, 'I have to! I have to! I have to!' On the day after each outburst, Peter appeared cheerful and relaxed and seemed pleased to apologize to the whole staff team. The whole community was involved in a series of emergency community meetings, which occured each time Peter refused to do his cooking and shopping; these were in order both to confront him and to push the client group to come up with its own solution to the problem. Despite this, Peter was never aggressive towards other clients.

Two weeks before the end of Peter's three-month assessment period, the staff team were in the process of discussing what they thought and felt about his potential to continue in our community.[20] Most of the therapists thought that

Peter's aggressive behaviour created a threatening atmosphere, and that in consequence his position in the community was very difficult. However, no one was so totally convinced that they could not work with him that they wanted to end his placement. They left their discussion open, and decided it should be discussed with clients in the community meeting. In the meeting, Peter brought up his anxiety about whether he would be able to stay on at our community, about whether he would 'pass' his assessment period, and he asked the project manager whether he would be staying. Colin, one of the other clients, said that he did not see any reason why Peter would not be able to stay. Colin said that he thought Peter had fitted in very well, and that as far as he was concerned he could not see any problems. Peter agreed and then fell silent, staring at the project manager. The manager then asked him whether he thought that this community was the right place for him and how he had felt during the time he had been there. He started talking about his angry outbursts and saying that he knew that if he behaved like this he would not be allowed to stay. Colin said that he did not see that this was a problem, that we all get angry sometimes and that if we did not, we would turn into robots. After some time the manager asked him why he thought he had these angry outbursts, how he felt when he had them and what he thought triggered them off. He fell silent again. Then he said that he did not know the answer and that he could not help having them, that he had learnt how to have them from violent patients in hospital. The manager reminded him that he only had them with staff, and opened a question with him as to why he thought this might be so. She also fed back to him the things he actually said when he was having those outbursts, as she thought that he might have forgotten them in the heat of the moment. Peter fell silent again and the conversation shifted to another issue.

I think that there were many things going on, both at the conscious and the unconscious level, with Peter in the context of our community. However, on a very basic level, this is an example of the beginning of a direct dialogue in which the project manager clearly opened out Peter's explicit question about whether he would pass his assessment period and gave it back to him to answer by asking him what he thought about whether this community was the right place for him. At this level, the simple intervention of giving the question back reflected the culture in which she, as 'the authority', did not necessarily have the answer to his question. This reflected the desire that the staff team had to think further, to inquire further with Peter and the rest of the community, about what was going on with him and their desire, as a result, for Peter to begin to open out for himself questions about himself. In this short dialogue with Peter, he was able to begin to take responsibility for his own questions, in so far as he was able to speak openly in front of the whole community about the fact that he had these angry outbursts. In doing so, he could identify for himself the manifestation of his feelings. The project manager opened out the question for

Peter further, asking him to reflect on why and when and to whom he had these outbursts. Peter was not at this stage able to engage with these questions about himself, and they were left open for him to reflect on in the weeks that followed. This 'leaving open' of the dialogue was an important part of this intervention. It was part of giving over to the client the responsibility for keeping the dialogue going, and thus the placement open. It was part of the reminder that, despite his feelings that he could not help the way he behaved, despite his desire for 'the authorities' to give him the answers, and despite his desire to confront staff and not his peers, he was nevertheless an agent. At least, he might be an agent in deciding whether he would stay in our community.

EFFECTIVE THERAPEUTIC DIALOGUE LEADS CLIENTS TO REACH OUT TO OTHERS IN SOCIETY

An educational approach cannot operate in isolation. We may educate our clients to think for themselves, have relationships of dialogue and be responsible agents in the world, but there are social aspects to the problem of madness and sanity which also need to be addressed if our therapeutic educational approach is to be something radical and not just a quasi-medical treatment. To some extent at least, I do not think it is mere hyperbole to say that our clients demonstrate the symptoms of a world in which many people have forgotten how to dwell in relatedness in the world. Dialogue is always to be seen in the context of relatedness to the Other. A therapeutic educational approach cannot remain in isolation to the rest of the world, and this means that part of our responsibility is to help our clients enter into debate about their experiences and behaviour and forge links with ordinary local people through opening out these 'unspeakable' things. I am not talking here about clients who have been 'cured' now being able to join in normal life, but rather about the way in which clients-still-struggling can find common ground with ordinary citizens by helping those citizens speak from their own struggles and difficulties.

It is in this context that I would like to say something about the work of our project action committees. At their most naïve, these committees exist, quite simply, in order to create better links between our clients and the local community. This is no easy task, and the committees are, of their nature, very difficult beasts to keep alive. But at a deeper level, they aim to involve the local lay community in an examination of what has been called the 'disease peculiar to our civilization' – namely, the invention of madness as a disease (Oakley 1993, p.292). From this angle, they try to use the client–local resident relationship as a *locus* from which to look critically at the way all of us tend to fend off and avoid aspects of ourselves and lodge all disturbance in others. '[O]thers are elected to live out the chaos that we refuse to confront in ourselves. By this means we escape a certain anxiety, but only at a price that is as immense as it is unrecognised' (Foucault 1961, p.viii). This is not to say that we adopt some dated anti-psychiatry view, but rather that we take seriously the critique that suggests that the opposition between psychiatry and anti-psychiatry is ultimately flawed and futile (Oakley 1993, p.292). Our committees usually meet quarterly at each of our therapeutic communities. They are made up of clients, staff and local people. These latter tend to be teachers, clergy, shopkeepers, members of local churches and other mental health workers. The idea is that as many people as possible, who are representative of the local community, meet and plan strategies for developing debate about mental illness. The following account, by one of our staff, describes an initiative in which clients took the lead in helping the wider community to question itself:

> For world mental health day last year, our committee decided to do something a bit different. On average our clients do not like being involved with events which simply highlight their problems and we wanted to arrange an event which would have no stigma attached to it, something which anyone might want to come to as a good evening out. We also wanted to highlight the need for people to take time out of their stressful lives to relax. The group decided on a jazz evening. It was felt that the venue was crucial, that it had to be somewhere away from anything to do with mental health services, somewhere easily accessible and in the heart of the community. We decided on the bar of our local YMCA. This would also help with the problem of publicity, as the YMCA has regular customers who either live there or live locally. This would mean that we would get a good number of the general public as well as people invited by the group. I suppose we could assume that these people would not be the most defended because a place like the YMCA had a long and venerable tradition of supporting isolated people in our society. Then there was the matter of the programme. We did not want there to be big speeches or anything long and drawn out. The idea was for the evening to be a relaxing night out and the music the main focus. At the same time, however, we did not want to lose an opportunity to promote some awareness of the difficulties experienced by people with mental illness and we wanted non-mentally ill people to be encouraged to seek support and to talk about *their* problems. So we decided to have a slot near the beginning of the evening, while the band took a rest, which would include a small talk, some poetry and some drama, and an exhibition area where some of the clients' art work could be exhibited, together with different stands with information from other organisations about how and where to get counselling and psychotherapy. The event was a success. The great thing about the evening was that there were so many different people involved. The jazz group were a professional group who had done some charity gigs and seemed sympathetic to our cause. A poet, a friend of mine, who is also passionate about Buber's idea of I-thou relationships, read some of his poems. These highlighted the value of relationships. The medium of poetry is extremely powerful and people

afterwards said how it had made an impact on them. I spoke a bit about the masks people wear and how difficult it often is for all of us – not just clients – to be real and to tell others about the difficulties we are having. Unfortunately, my back was bad and I wasn't able to do the mime with masks, but I spoke about it instead! The overall atmosphere of the evening was as I had hoped – the jazz band were really mellow and people went away feeling they had had a good night out, not that they had been to a world mental health day event! The great thing for me to see was one of the clients from the project, who, seeing the band with all their instruments, decided to go back to the project and fetch his own bongos, and he sat with them and played along! Also, a good number of the other clients came along, overcoming their fears of being in a social context. They were able to relax and enjoy themselves. I felt that some kind of dialogue was taking place in the sense that people were simply being together.

Another example of clients being active in educating the community is through the committees' schools education programme. As part of their work, our committees aim to visit as many local sixth forms as possible to facilitate discussion. I was involved with another project in planning and taking part in a schools visit. The programme consisted of three parts. First, the pupils were encouraged to take part in a brainstorm exercise entitled 'What is mental illness?'. We discussed some of the images and associations the pupils had with mental illness and, in particular, schizophrenia. A client from the project worked together with his therapist to create 'spontaneous art', painting images in response to the ideas that the pupils called out. This added a visual stimulus and encouraged the pupils to feel that it was safe to name some of the words which conjure up the stigma associated with mental illness; for example, 'loony', 'nutcase', and so forth. Second, we presented a play called 'Teddy Boy'. One of the clients involved in the committee offered to have his own story dramatized for this purpose, and I worked with him, listening to his story and giving it a voice through a play. I wanted the play to be an accurate account of his story and not to embellish it for dramatic purposes. As it worked out, his story provided a very dramatic structure in itself and he was pleased with the result. The wonderful thing about working on this play was that it involved so many people in a creative and therapeutic exercise. The actors were made up of clients, staff and other members of the committee. Clients were also involved in making and finding costumes and in providing music, photographs and pictures for the set. We all participated equally with the aim of sharing our group effort with a group from the sixth form, in order to provide a vehicle for debate. It proved to be an inspiring project.

The third section of the programme involved discussion in small groups, using the play as a springboard. We discussed how one's mental health is affected by stress and where people can go to find support. These groups were facilitated by the members of the committee, which included the clients themselves. Here clients had an opportunity to share more about their own history and how they had learned to work through their difficulties. Also, the students had an opportunity to speak about some of the difficulties they had experienced and to think about whether they had been able to get support. They also discussed their experiences of meeting people with mental health problems and whether or not they had been able to respond to the person and not just the symptoms.

CONCLUSION

I have tried to show here, in this chapter, that the therapeutic community approach is essentially an educational process. Unlike other Care in the Community approaches, it is not primarily aimed at helping clients achieve independence, so much as helping them learn how to construct relationships of mutual interdependence. It is a pedagogy in which authentic dialogue with peers retraces developmental stages for clients and helps them find their *point de capiton*. From this stability point, clients gradually learn to take more responsibility for their own questions and for their own struggle to work through psychological conflicts. Staff endeavour to assist them in this process of self-learning and self-understanding by creating a non-hierarchical climate or therapeutic *schola* in which peer-dialogue leads clients naturally to dialogue with others outside the project.

NOTES

1   I am using the notion of symptom here in the way in which the early Lacan used it. This corresponds, more or less, to a medical usage except that it is understood linguistically. Later Lacanian writings distinguish this sense from that of *synthome*.

2   For an overview see, for example, Bloom 1973; Braine 1976; Condon and Sander 1974; de Villiers and de Villiers 1978; Nelson 1976; Rosch 1973.

3   Lacan distinguishes between *Autre*, the big Other, and *autre*, the little other. The latter is not really other but a projection of the ego, whereas the former indicates another subject.

4   Lacan was especially interested in the way in which language is used by psychotic patients and he discussed this in a number of places (see Lacan 1993, p.167; Lacan 1966, p.92).

5   Foreclosure – *forclusion* in French – is the word Lacan uses to translates Freud's term *Verwerfung*. He uses it to describe the mechanism at work in psychosis.

6   Following Heidegger's distinction between discourse (*Rede*) and chatter (*Gerede*), Lacan refers to speech as either *pleine* (full) or *vide* (empty).

7   The concept of an educational therapeutic community is not new, of course. Indeed, Malcolm Pines, one of the founders of the Association of Therapeutic Communities, in the Maxwell Jones Lecture for 1998, said that while the therapeutic community

method is rightly regarded as an important contribution to modern hospital psychiatry, 'its antecedents are to be found in pedagogy, therapeutic education...' (Pines 1999, pp.23–24).

8   We are still familiar with the using the word 'master' – in the sense of teacher – in the context of 'master builder' or 'Zen master'. In later Latin, the words *magister* (master) and *doctor* were synonyms. Both mean, quite simply, teacher – hence our use of the academic term 'doctorate'. From this point of view, we can say, if slightly tongue in cheek, that within the context of our therapeutic educational approach, the therapist as tutor is, quite literally, the doctor!

9   On the background to this notion of exchange structuring kinship relations and language as gift see Levi-Strauss (1963a, 1963b) and Mauss (1990). On its significance for psychoanalysis see Lacan (1994, pp.153–154).

10   'And to what is one called when one is thus appealed to? To one's *own Self*' (Heidegger 1962, section 273).

11   Parable – *parabole* in Greek – simply meant putting one thing alongside another by way of comparison. Aristotle, for example, defines the word as meaning comparison or analogy (*Rhet.* 11, xx, 2–4).

12   *Mashal* has a number of meanings, often aphorisms or discourse. Notably it is used in relation to a riddle (*hidah* in Hebrew).

13   Behind this idea lies the frequent complaint of the prophets, e.g. Isaiah's ironical comment: 'Hear and hear, but do not understand; see and see, but do not perceive. Make the heart of this people fat, and their ears heavy, and shut their eyes; lest they see with their eyes, and hear with their ears and understand with their hearts and turn and be healed' (Isaiah 6, 9–10).

14   For the early Church the problem was simple. How could the Son of God have met with such repudiation and misunderstanding, unless he had, himself, willed it? Unless he had declared his divine identity in an obscure way which would be unintelligible to the great mass of Jews, not destined for salvation? On this view, Christ's use of parables was one of his ways of preserving his Messianic secret. The explanation that the varied response of different people to Christ was due to the deliberate decree of God, who had willed that some should believe and be saved but others should not, comes through clearly in the passage which follows on from the parable of the sower: 'And when he was alone, those who were about him with the twelve asked him concerning the parables. And he said to them, "To you has been given the secret of the kingdom of God, but for those outside everything is in parables; so that they may indeed see but not perceive, and may indeed hear but not understand."' (Mark 4, 10–12a).

15   'Working through' has, intentionally, a Freudian resonance, and I mean by it to imply unconscious processes as well as just grasping the thing!

16   Narcissism was defined by Freud as the investment of the libido in the ego, rather than in the object. Lacan developed the idea further, defining narcissism as the erotic attraction to the specular image, and brings out the aggressive element in the disorder. As in the myth of Narcissus, the client is strongly attracted to the gestalt or completeness of their own image, yet angered at the contrast of disunity they see in their own lack of bodily coordination (Freud 1914; Lacan 1966). Narcissism has also become the focus of major recent trends in psychoanalysis, notably in self psychology (Kohut and Wolf 1978).

17   In this section I have relied heavily on an unpublished paper by John Gale.

18   In the medieval period we find a number of studies that do not form part of the major writings of a philosopher but which are, nevertheless, invaluable. Some of them are known as *quaestiones disputatae* (disputed questions). Mostly these were the results, formulated by the professor, of regular disputations held at intervals throughout the year. These ordinary disputations or discussions are distinct from *quaestiones quodlibetales* (questions about any subject), which were discussions held at Christmas and Easter.

19   Most of this section is taken from an unpublished paper by Sarah Tucker.

20   In CHT, project managers work as team leaders, heading a group of between five and eight therapists, some of whom are still in training. While the background of staff varies considerably (some having trained in psychology or social work, others in teaching or psychiatric nursing) it is CHT's own in-service training programme which provides the principal formation for all, as therapeutic community practitioners. Fundamentally this is a training for group therapists, although 1:1 counselling also forms an integral part of the therapeutic programme for most clients.

REFERENCES

Alford C.F. (1991) *The Self in Social Theory*. New Haven and London: Yale University Press.

Aristotle (1974) *Art of Rhetoric* (ed. and trans. J.H. Freese). Loeb Classical Library. Massachusetts: Harvard University Press.

Benvenuto, B. and Kennedy, R. (1986) *The Works of Jacques Lacan*. New York: St Martin's Press.

Bloom, L. (1973) *One Word at a Time*. The Hague: Mouton.

Braine, M.D.S. (1976) 'Children's first word combinations.' *Monograph for Social Research in Child Development 31*, 1–92.

Condon, W.S. and Sander, L.W. (1974) 'Neonate movement is synchronized with adult speech.' *Science 183*, 99–108.

Cummings, E.E. (1960) *Selected Poems 1923–1958*. London–Boston: Faber and Faber.

de Villiers, J.G. and de Villiers, P.A. (1978) *Language Acquisition*. Harvard: Harvard University Press.

Dodds, E.R. (1951) *The Greeks and the Irrational*. California: University of California Press.

Evans, D. (1996) *An Introductory Dictionary of Lacanian Psychoanalysis*. London and New York: Routledge.

Foucault, M. (1961) *Madness and Civilization* (trans. R. Howard). London: Routledge.

Freire, P. (1979) *Education for Critical Consciousness* (trans. M.B. Ramos, L. Bigwood and M. Marshall). London: Sheed and Ward.

Freud, S. (1911) 'Psycho-analytic notes on an autobiographical account of a case of paranoia (Dementia Paranoides).' In J. Strachey (ed) *The Standard Edition of the Complete Psychological Works of Sigmund Freud*, Vol. XII, 3. London: Hogarth Press and the Institute of Psychoanalysis.

Freud, S. (1914) 'On narcissism: An introduction.' In J. Strachey (ed) *The Standard Edition of the Complete Psychological Works of Sigmund Freud*, Vol. XII, 160. London: Hogarth Press and the Institute of Psychoanalysis.

Heidegger, M. (1968) *What is Called Thinking* (second edition) (trans. J. Glenn Gray). New York: Harper and Row.

Heidegger, M. (1962) *Being and Time* (trans. J. Macquarrie and E. Robinson). Oxford: Basil Blackwell.

Jaspers, K. (1953) *The Origin and Goal of History*. New Haven: Yale University Press.

Kohut, H. and Wolf, E. (1978) 'The disorders of the self and their treatment: An outline.' *International Journal of Psychoanalysis 59*, 413–425.

Lacan, J. (1966) 'Remarks on psychical causality.' In *Ecrits: A Selection* (trans. A. Sheridan). London: Tavistock.

Lacan, J. (1977) 'The function and field of speech and language in psychoanalysis.' In *Ecrits: A Selection* (trans. A. Sheridan). London: Tavistock.

Lacan, J. (1987) *The Seminar. Book I. Freud's Papers on Technique, 1953–54* (trans. J. Forrester). Cambridge: Cambridge University Press.

Lacan, J. (1988) *The Seminar. Book II. The Ego in Freud's Theory and in the Technique of Psychoanalysis, 1954–55* (trans. S. Tomaselli). Cambridge: Cambridge University Press.

Lacan, J. (1993) *The Seminar. Book III. The Psychoses, 1955–56* (trans. R. Grigg). London: Routledge. (Originally *Le Seminaire. Livre III. Les psychoses, 1955–56*, Jacques-Alain Miller, Paris: Seuil, 1981.)

Lacan, J. (1994) *Le Seminaire. Livre IV. La relation d'objet, 1956–57* (ed. Jacques-Alain Miller). Paris: Seuil.

Laplanche, J. and Pontalis, J.-B. (1967) *The Language of Psycho-Analysis* (trans. Donald Nicholson-Smith). London: Hogarth Press and the Institute of Psychoanalysis.

Levi-Strauss, C. (1963a) 'Language and the analysis of social laws.' In *Structural Anthropology* (trans. C. Jacobson and B.G. Schoepf). New York: Basic Books.

Levi-Strauss, C. (1963b) 'Structural analysis in linguistics and in anthropology.' In *Structural Anthropology* (trans. C. Jacobson and B.G. Schoepf). New York: Basic Books.

Levi-Strauss, C. (1987) *Structural Anthropology*, Vol.2 (trans. Monique Layton). Harmondsworth: Penguin.

Louf, A. (1980) *Teach Us to Pray*. London: Darton, Longman and Todd.

Mauss, M. (1990) *The Form and Reason for Exchange in Archaic Societies* (trans. W.D. Halls). London: Routledge.

Merton, T. (1976) *Thomas Merton on Zen*. London: Sheldon Press.

Nelson, K. (1976) *The Conceptual Basis for Naming*. New Haven: Yale University Press.

Oakley, C. (1993) 'Dangerous liaisons: The rivalrous resemblance of David Cooper and R.D. Laing.' *Free Associations 4*, 2, 30, 277–293.

Pines, M. (1999) 'Forgotten pioneers: The unwritten history of the therapeutic community movement. The Maxwell Jones Lecture 1998.' *Therapeutic Communities 20*, 1, 23–42.

Powell, C. (1992) 'On poetry and weeping.' *Free Associations 3*, 2, 26, 185–198.

Reber, A.S. (1985) *The Penguin Dictionary of Psychology*. Harmondsworth: Penguin.

Rosch, E. (1973) 'On the internal structure of perception and semantic categories.' In T.E. Moore (ed) *Cognitive Development and the Acquisition of Language*. New York: Academic Press.

Rycroft, C. (1968) *Anxiety and Neurosis*. London: Maresfield Library.

Stevenson, R.L. (1892) *Travels with a Donkey in the Cevennes*. London: Chatto and Windus.

Watts, A.W. (1965) *The Way of Zen*. Harmondsworth: Penguin.

Winnicott, D.W. (1978) *The Child, the Family, and the Outside World*. Harmondsworth: Penguin.

CHAPTER 8

The Changing Idea of Community

Nadia Al-Khudhairy

What do we mean by community? Those of us who work as psychotherapists in therapeutic communities should be able to answer that question fairly easily, but it is not as simple as it may at first seem. This is especially true now as we find ourselves working within the context of Care in the Community because we are thrown into working with professionals from other disciplines who see community very differently from the perspective of therapeutic community practitioners. We are faced with a situation today in which society itself is changing so rapidly, all across the globe, that traditional communities and community values are not easy to identify or pin down. I believe that this has huge implications for us in the therapeutic community movement, and I will try to explain why it is vital that we look forward and act in an innovative way in experimenting with new modes of therapeutic living.

'COMMUNITY' AND CARE IN THE COMMUNITY

The term 'community' is used in a number of different ways. Rupert Hoare has discussed five different conceptions of community, which vary in their degree of 'thinness' of the sense of community (Hoare 1997, p.55). Others have tried to cover the same ground but approached it rather differently (Richmond Fellowship 1983, pp.24–25). I wish to discuss some of those definitions of community here and then go on to think about the way in which the term community is used within the rather specialized context of the therapeutic community, and see whether or not this can be stretched to encompass new forms of the therapeutic community. These new forms, I suggest, need to be developed because of the changing nature of contemporary society.

We can think of community simply, and perhaps rather naïvely, as a geographical and administratively defined area – a borough, county, state or nation, or even group of nations (Richmond Fellowship 1983, p.24). Another meaning we often use is to think of a well-integrated district or neighbourhood where the inhabitants know each other. Integration is the key here, and it is a concept often inherent in our use of the term community. We think of this when we think of the village community, and it is often overlaid with rather romantic images. The middle classes often buy up country cottages in villages which they describe as 'charming', 'quaint' and culturally traditional – images which would probably not have been used by the farm labourers who previously lived there (Richmond Fellowship 1983, p.24; Sartorius 1998a, pp.7–8). It is an image that brings memories of a way of life that has seen its light of day. It conjures up a nostalgic image – an image of neighbours knowing each other, assisting one another, sharing each other's joys and aiding each other through difficult times. However, in the last decade this concept is alien to most of us. Relationships with our neighbours are often distant. Most of us consider ourselves fortunate if we get along with them. The media has featured many stories of incidents where individuals have moved house because of difficult neighbours. Local shops are constantly changing staff, so when one walks in to buy a daily paper there is a lack of rapport. In most shops, especially in cities, even if the same staff remain, there is no time to establish a relationship as both the customer and the staff are constrained by time and want to complete the sales transaction as soon as possible. It seems that people in today's society do not want to establish contact with others informally; for example, by talking to each other on a plane, train, bus, in a shop, and so forth. It seems that people in today's society do not want to get involved in situations that do not directly affect them. If there is an accident, then people usually call the appropriate service; for example, the ambulance. If there is a fight, no one will come to help directly; however, help will be obtained indirectly by calling the police. These are facts that do not fit in with our nostalgic image of community. The fact is that we no longer live in the traditional community, yet we nostalgically long for it.

At times we use a related but slightly different concept of community. Here community describes a group of people trying to foster personal relationships – people with a common purpose; a religious community, for example. This kind of definition is interesting, for it necessarily demands exclusion and exclusiveness. To belong means to be set apart, somehow (Richmond Fellowship 1983, p.24). Perhaps the narrowest use, but one which is common amongst mental health professionals, is to define community in terms of any form of living other than inside a psychiatric hospital. According to this view anything other than the hospital is thought to be intrinsically superior to the hospital. From this point of view, discharge from hospital or the prevention of admission to hospital is always viewed as something positive. As long ago as 1983, it was noted that were policy to be based on this assumption it would 'lead to even less satisfactory care than was provided in hospital' (Richmond Fellowship 1983, p.24). The fact is that, however poor the former large psychiatric hospitals were, they did indeed create a form of community. Sometimes, for some people, the most difficult aspect of their transition from years of hospitalization into society, with the advent of Care in the Community, was the veritable loss of a profound and real community membership. This fact is all too often neglected.

The dictionary definition expresses all these four uses:

> People living in one locality; the locality in which they live; a group of people having cultural, religious, or other characteristics in common; a group of nations having certain interests in common; the public society; common ownership; similarity or agreement, community of interest. (*Concise Oxford Dictionary*, 1982)

I would now like to turn to Rupert Hoare's examination of the various meanings of community. According to the first view, community exists where there is independent living (Hoare 1997, p.60). His second meaning of community is a little thicker, but not much so! Here community exists where there is individual choice and personal autonomy, but it is more than the sum of its parts (Hoare 1997, p.60). The third meaning of community is that community exists where self-interest is linked to the self-interest of others in the group and builds a self-interest of the whole. The individual citizen is born when they subordinate their self-interest into that of the wider whole. This self-interest of the whole can then be used to confront power. It is a concept of community which Hoare considers is 'extremely strong'. It is a process view of community, and it is one found in a movement called Community Organising. This movement is supported by the Church Urban Fund, and it works with marginalized people from different faith communities in deprived areas. These include Sikh, Hindu, Muslim, Buddhist and Jewish communities as well as Christian communities (Hoare 1997, pp.55, 61–62). Community Organising works primarily with disadvantaged and marginalized groups of people, seeking to enable them to move themselves from dispersed and powerless fragmentation to vital and powerful community action. From a thin and vacuous experience and concept of community, we are moving here to one which is extremely strong. Community Organising involves a dynamic, process view of community. Religious beliefs often imply that change for the better is possible, that strong community can come into being, and injustices be overcome. These things lie at the heart of its operation, working as it does with faith communities. It does so by building a community where there was none in an organized, active sense, out of one-to-one encounters in which people are brought to identify their own self-interest and to see how it fits the self-interest of the others in the group, in the self-interest of the whole. It focuses on specific matters which are debilitating people's lives. It is 'upfront' in confronting those who wield power, its major instrument of effecting change being the organized assembly of massed groups of people, who by their organization change. In the process they create a strong sense of community, and develop active and direct forms of citizenship. The espousal of self-interest, in such a setting, has a very different value and feel to it than it does where it is all too inward-looking and evident in more affluent areas. To Hoare's mind, the citizen as statesman in the polling booth has to ask what is in the interests of the community as a whole and has to subordinate their own self-interest to that wider interest.

Hoare's fourth image of community is where there is fraternity and participating, because in fraternity and participating, people find their person-hood in relation to others. It is social groups which foster persons-in-relation-to-one-another which can rightly be called community, rather than when they aim towards some external end.

According to the fifth view discussed by Hoare, community exists when power is shared and handed on. Aristotle had said as much (Aristotle, 'The Politics', VI, 2, 1317 b2). This view is also a process view of community. It sees community as always in a state of growth from less shared power to more empowerment. It focuses on the relationship between the individual and the group in terms of the way power is shared. The movement into community is always a healing process because community is empowerment. This does not mean that an individual cannot stand alone. On the contrary, community – real community – makes advocacy possible, and when one person stands up and holds their ground, for the good of others, a deep experience of community is born. Real advocacy is impossibly hard for us because the climate in our society is one of individualism, and individualism is the opposite of advocacy. According to this way of seeing community, the process or movement towards community, which happens when real power-sharing takes place, is always difficult and painful as well as being healing. This is because it is costly.

Empowering others, according to Hoare, overcomes the essence of sin, which St Augustine saw as 'being dominated by the desire to dominate'. The desire by individuals to hold on to power, rather than to pass it on or share it, is ultimately illusory; in the end we all have to let go of it, as we grow older and die. One has to give way to others, otherwise collaboration is inherently unstable. Very interestingly and importantly for us in the therapeutic com-munity, this view maintains that professionals can only release power in those around them when they are prepared to share it themselves (Hoare 1997, pp.62–64). Hoare's fifth view understands community and the individual, and the relation between them. It takes a process view, witnessing to a movement from the here and now to what is to come. It takes very seriously division, alienation and fragmentation in human life, but knows that this can move into a greater unity and harmony. It recognizes very clearly that such healing, or movement into community, is costly and difficult. Indeed, the paradigm it works with is that of the Christ figure, the redeemer losing his place in family and community, and losing his friends (his 'support group') until he was totally isolated and alone. Yet the advocacy relationship, one person standing for and speaking for another, or for groups of others, does not disenfranchise or disempower them but precisely the opposite, as a paradigm for our exploration of the much fuller democratic community which we are in need of. Advocacy shows us a way of re-finding the solidarity of one human being for another which our current individualism makes impossibly hard. When a person continues to hold his or her ground to the point of death and knows themselves to be doing that 'for' someone else, or for others, and those others come themselves to see it to be so, that it was indeed done for them, then the isolation of individualism is overcome and a new way into community comes into being.

'COMMUNITY' FROM A THERAPEUTIC COMMUNITY PERSPECTIVE: A COMMITMENT-TO-STRUGGLE

Therapeutic communities aim not just to provide therapy in a community setting, but to create communities which are themselves therapeutic. That is to say, communities in which the group experience itself is therapeutic (Kennard 1988, p.162). By being part of a community, it is suggested, clients can work through their psychological problems and re-gain enough of a sense of themselves to start living with meaning and purpose. What are the central features of community from a therapeutic community context? Asking this question comes very close to asking for an identification of the central features of a therapeutic community itself.

One way of approaching an answer to these questions is to provide a list of the defining features of a therapeutic community. For example, one might start in the following way. The community of a therapeutic community essentially involves Community Meetings where every member of the community meets regularly. Further, it essentially involves a certain structuring of time as, for example, in therapeutic groups. There should be a range of roles for clients and staff to take. Members run the community in which they live. The tasks members take on will vary from everyday domestic tasks and increasing levels of responsibility in the day-to-day running and management of the community, to engaging within therapy groups, to outside employment and college courses. The list of defining features could be extended along these lines. From a list like this, we would then extrapolate core components. For example, we would end up saying that a community, according to the principles of the therapeutic community, exists when all members meet together regularly, when time is structured, roles defined and where clients share with staff the running of the place. Alternatively, rather than looking at the specific practice found in therapeutic communities, we can look at the underlying principles which seem to govern therapeutic community practice, even when that practice varies in the detail from institution to institution. An early example of this approach was Rapaport's study of the Henderson Hospital, which suggested that the four characteristics of therapeutic communities were democratization, permissiveness, reality confrontation and communalism (Rapaport 1960). One of the difficulties of attempting to articulate the essential features of a community which serve to make it therapeutic, by providing a defining list of practices, is that it will always be open to counter-examples of organizations which fulfil everything in the list but which manifestly fail to provide an environment in which therapeutic change takes place for clients. This is because the 'community' from the therapeutic community perspective is not so much captured by what tasks go on amongst the group of people, though it is important that some tasks do go on, but rather it is captured by the *way* in which the tasks are carried out amongst the group of people.

Central to the notion of 'community' from a therapeutic community perspective is the idea that each individual in the community does what they do within the context of a commitment-to-struggle. This is the struggle which the client has with himself or herself in-relationship to the others. It is a struggle which will be manifest in all aspects of community life, in the practical tasks of everyday living, within therapy groups, in individual counselling sessions and in informal time. It marks the client's stay in the community, and they do not escape from it even when they withdraw into the solitude of their own room. In essence, this struggle is the struggle to learn a new language, not just in order to be able to speak to the others and to understand them, but in order to articulate themselves to themselves as well. This commitment to a personal struggle binds us to our fellow strugglers in a linguistic community and creates a sense of belonging and membership (see Buber 1965, p.31).

The commitment-to-struggle involves the decision on each person's part not to rest, to be ever-attentive to our motives and intentions and to refuse to accept only superficial social contact, and to radically open ourselves both to ourselves and to others. It is to enter the place that in Zen Buddhism is called 'the cave of the heart' (see Lacan 1987, p.1). This is the place where there is no façade and where a person is confronted with their insincerity and selfishness, their egotism and ambition. If one can work through this, the experience is cathartic and life-giving. However, it is a minefield because we resist honesty in ourselves pathologically. This is often because when we are honest with ourselves, we are forced to face up to the meaninglessness of our existence, to face up to our transience, our finitude and the reality of death (see Heidegger 1962, sections 46–53).

Clients are constantly battling to open up to themselves and others and to confront themselves with aspects that are terribly painful. This might be in a therapy group where they find they cannot speak, or it might be in a gardening group where they find they cannot face mowing the lawn. To do this they need to be committed to asking questions of themselves and others, to articulating those questions, to thinking and to staying with the fact that all too often those questions are not met with responses or answers immediately. They need to struggle to stay with uncertainty as their questions are met with further questions. Similarly, staff are committed to this struggle in their attempt to understand the clients, as they help them articulate themselves. Therapists are constantly using dialogue to confront clients with what they understand from the clients' direct spoken dialogue or indirect dialogue of their actions (or lack of them). Therapists are also faced with having to confront themselves and their relationships with eachother. As with clients, this can also be difficult and painful. Therapists and clients are joined by this commitment-to-struggle to speak. It is this joining which creates the community where members belong, and in which they can find a place to begin to make their own choices.

NOT EVERY COMMUNAL LIVING EXPERIENCE IS A THERAPEUTIC COMMUNITY EXPERIENCE

Even when our communities have all the defining features of therapeutic communities, and all the ideal therapeutic community practices, they may not, then, capture 'community' from a therapeutic community perspective. This is so when it is forgotten that, before all else, it is the culture of struggle which is essential. When this is forgotten a community can drift into a therapeutic 'institution'. The community can go through the motions of a therapeutic programme but the clients in it do not discover any meaning:

> There seems to be an unspoken assumption by its adherents that the therapeutic community must be a good thing. To question whether it follows any guiding principles of empowerment – let alone whether it rehabilitates clients – is a topic close to heresy! (Allen 1992, p.254)

Here Allen echoes the sentiment that therapeutic communities can drift into institutionalization. Therapeutic communities, even if they have all the key features of therapeutic communities in their programmes, are not immune to institutionalization.

Indeed, it is not uncommon for a therapeutic community to develop a culture in which therapists and clients behave institutionally, in which they are not affected by other people and in which they do not want or have a sense of responsibility. Here there is no sense of community – rather, simply a collection of individuals occupying the same quarters. For example, a member of a community in which I worked had both a history of drug abuse and a diagnosis of borderline psychosis. He had not used drugs for about two years prior to joining our community. After about six months he met up with an old friend at the college where he had recently started to re-train. This friend was still using drugs and became inseparable from the client, spending all his time with him in the community. It became clear that the two were using drugs together in the project. However, despite discussion of this, facilitated by the therapists in community meetings and an apparent agreement by all – including the client – to support the client by excluding the friend from the project, the community took absolutely no interest in whether or not the friend came into the project at night when therapists were not present. This was the beginnings of the client group drifting into institutionalization. Again, while there may be a written policy in line with therapeutic community principles that therapists and clients eat together as part of the non-hierarchical therapeutic ethos, it is not uncommon for staff to congregate together and for clients to congregate together. An unwritten institutional segregation of 'the healthy' from 'the ill' emerges. Unless staff and clients, together, are willing to struggle with, challenge and look at the real questions underlying this dynamic as it arises in the community, the community will stagnate and drift into institutionalization.

Through no desire of their own, therapists may be driven by external constraints (in the form of 'care standards' from external local authorities) to keep the place clean, to ensure that medication is taken, and so on. This and the pressure on time can result in a loss of meaningful and mutual exchange between therapists and clients and an unreasonable use of their power to exclude clients from the community in order, simply, to get the result they need quickly. Unless therapists face these constraints honestly and openly with clients in a mutual commitment to overcoming them, they will not be creating a community which can genuinely be called a therapeutic one.

Therapeutic communities drift into institutionalization not just by virtue of the fact that such things begin to happen – this is probably inevitable anywhere. Rather, they drift into institutionalization when these things are not spoken about within a culture and atmosphere of enquiry, questioning, thinking and, above all, a commitment-to-struggle through the ensuing dialogue. Hinshelwood identifies 'bureaucratic rigidity' and 'ossification' in therapeutic communities as dynamic responses to the 'deep-seated nature of the anxiety about fragmenting' that can arise within a community (Hinshelwood 1987, pp.195–198). If the community can recognize this and then begin in the struggle to face that anxiety verbally, the essence of community can be maintained. If not, institutionalization will pervade.

Living together, meeting together on a daily basis, cleaning, shopping, cooking and talking together, running and turning up to community meetings and therapy groups, and believing one is adhering to therapeutic community principles, are not enough to ensure that there is a meaningful community in which clients can engage in a journey of change by being a member of it. These things are not enough to ensure that people will have a sense of belonging together. Rather, what is important is that these things are done within the context of a culture of commitment-to-struggle with oneself and others in learning a new language, the language of the spoken unconscious.

THERAPEUTIC COMMUNITIES DO NOT REQUIRE LIVING TOGETHER

Our world is changing dramatically and more rapidly than ever before. In thirty years or so, four-fifths of the world population, in developed and developing countries, will be living in urban areas. This change will bring new health problems or magnify those currently facing health care (Sartorius 1998b, pp.3–13). This will mean that our cities will continue to grow, possibly dramatically:

> Judging from tendencies already visible in some developing countries the cities of the future will grow to unprecedented sizes – to agglomerations of dwellings of 20 or 30 million people. Megalopolises are not only cities grown big: they are likely to be different creatures – in the same vein as adults are not big children although they continue to belong to the same biological species when they are children and when they grow up. (Sartorius 1998b, p.3)

This will inevitably mean that big changes will need to take place in the way health and social care is organized, and it is likely that international strategies will be developed. Urban growth is already much faster in developing countries than it is in industrialized countries. Rural people in Third World countries often perceive urban life, with all its dangers and problems, as still far better than the life of the village. Towns draw the country folk to them with the promise of the easy availability of things which contrasts with the rural struggle to make ends meet amid failing crops, corrupt bureaucracy and increased mechanization in farming, which reduces the need for a large workforce of agricultural labourers. Villagers do not migrate to towns any longer in small numbers and slowly: their move to cities is massive. This migration does not, of course, only affect towns and cities, it affects the countryside too. The younger and able-bodied often migrate first, and this leaves the villages with an increased proportion of disabled and elderly people who live with those too young to leave home. This is often underlined by the fact that those who fail in the town or become injured as a result of working conditions return to their village. The point to notice here is that all of this contributes to the inability of Third World rural areas to function independently (Sartorius 1988, pp.4–5). Rural areas in developed and under-developed countries alike are increasingly inhabited by middle-class and richer people who have weekend or holiday homes there. This pushes house prices up, and with the practical disappearance of tithed cottages the local people cannot afford to buy properties there.

Generally, we no longer live in a 'tribal' community, in the context of extended family networks or locally situated community, even if we have been born into any of these forms of community. Technology has changed the manner in which we live. Where people live will depend on factors such as work opportunities. Our communities are dispersed, with family and friends living and working in disparate places. Those in an adequate financial position are able to maintain contact with their dispersed community via the phone, fax, the internet, planes, cars and trains. In today's society, people also move around the globe. For some, this reflects positive changes in their lives, a better job, the financial capacity to return home and visit friends and relatives. Others, such as refugees and economic immigrants, move and are dislocated from their original community through no choice of their own, due to events outside their control.

The prevalence of mental disorders in cities differs from that in rural areas (Cooper and Sartorius 1996). This is not only the case in Third World countries, as studies of the situation in the UK have shown (Meltzer *et al.* 1995). The fact is that there are more lonely chronic mentally ill people and more homeless mentally ill people in urban areas in industrialized countries. Studies of schizophrenia show differences in course and outcome of mental disorders between developing and developed countries. Systematic comparisons of course and outcome of schizophrenia and other mental disorders in urban and rural areas of developing and developed countries are lacking.

Does the fact that contemporary communities are ever more dispersed mean that it is not possible to have a real community at all? Does it mean that it is not possible to belong and be a member of a group of people who are committed-to-struggling together with themselves and with others? Does it mean that in reality Care in the Community cannot be care in a real community because the community is dispersed? I believe the answer is 'no', as I shall explain.

The loss of the geographically local community may indeed be a loss. Perhaps the close proximity allowed its members to be 'just' there. Perhaps its components enabled a person to turn to their immediate community for support and allowed the community to intervene when it saw that one of its members required aid. However, as I have explained in the previous section, living in close proximity, as is the case for clients sometimes in therapeutic communities, does not ensure a proper sense of community in and of itself. Living in close geographical proximity is not sufficient for creating a creative community for people. Living in the same house does not ensure that the people who live there are committed-to-struggling together, and it is this, I have suggested, that provides the essence of community from a therapeutic community perspective.

Do the various problems with Care in the Community stem from the fact that the contemporary community is dispersed? To answer this we need to ask not only whether living in close geographical proximity is sufficient for a community but, further, whether it is necessary at all. If living in close proximity is not necessary for a community to properly exist, then the problems with Care in the Community are not caused by the dispersed nature of contemporary communities. I suggest that it is not necessary for people to live in close proximity to each other in order for them to belong to a community and thus that people living in a dispersed community can become members of a proper community from a therapeutic community perspective. This is because, as I have discussed, being part of a community means being part of a culture where there is a commitment-to-struggle together to speak and this does not require that we literally live in the same place..

People today have many technological ways of keeping in contact, and these may provide a sustaining way of keeping one's membership of a community in between actually meeting with people. Meeting with people is important but one need not even be in the same town as them on a daily basis given modern technology. Second, while most current therapeutic communities create a space for this commitment-to-struggle through engagement in ordinary everyday tasks, it is the way in which people engage in these tasks rather than the tasks themselves which is important in terms of them belonging to that community. It is not necessary that these tasks form the medium through which the community functions. In a dispersed community, people can engage in a commitment-to-struggle together in different ways.

On these grounds I propose that, given that we do live in dispersed communities, the therapeutic community approach can be implemented in the context of a dispersed community. I now turn to a description of a dispersed housing scheme for homeless people which I have recently set up. I believe it is an innovative model of a dispersed therapeutic community.

HOME: A SENSE OF BELONGING

According to Kennedy, home is a place in which we feel safe, secure, warm, dry and protected. A place to rest, to eat, sleep, love, laugh, argue, cry, read, watch TV, and the like (Kennedy 1998, pp.99–106). We all have a need for a place like this. However, for some people, home is beyond their grasp because something has happened in their lives that has separated them from their home and they are unable to create a place of their own where they feel safe and at ease. Kennedy defines people who find themselves like this as people who are going through a 'transition' in their lives. For example, perhaps they are moving from one home to another and have somehow got stranded in between; perhaps they are in transition from their family home to adult independence, and something has gone wrong for them; perhaps they have mental health problems and are in transition, trying to cope with this, and have not found a new place or community; or perhaps they are fleeing from violence, war or abuse and are trying to find a hiding place.

Kennedy discusses the dangers facing people in transition. People in transition can sometimes get trapped in the transitional phase of their lives and never make it to the place they set out for. People faced with major life changes can lose their way. The problems arise when they are not able to find themselves and their way. What began as a phase of life becomes a crisis, and these major changes can result in unfortunate occurrences. If there is nobody to give them a helping hand at this crucial stage in their lives, they may easily slip into a way of life that is without hope.

Homeless people have no possession and no security. Homelessness results in them eventually losing their self-respect, and they are often bitter and angry. This may result in them being destructive towards themselves and others. Providing a homeless person with a bed for the night is one positive step in the right direction. However, it still does not provide a home. People need shelter, but they also need security, warmth and to belong. Kennedy gives an example of this by referring to Charles Dickens's book, *Nicholas Nickleby*. In the story Nicholas befriends a young disabled boy whilst working at a children's home. When the boy discovers that Nicholas is leaving the home, he wants to go with him, but Nicholas is poor and is unable to offer the boy a proper home. The boy, however, was not thinking of practical matters, like food, clothes or shelter; instead, he turns to Nicholas and says with passion: 'You are my home.' Kennedy points out that to the boy the home he sought was not physical shelter but the feelings of safety, security and belonging he felt with Nicholas. The notion of the home, in this sense, has little to do with bricks and a roof. As that old saying goes, home is where the heart is. Home is a place with support, inner security and a feeling of safety and belonging – and above all it is the place in which everyone speaks the same language.

Kennedy refers to homeless people as displaced. By this she means people who have lost their place in our world. They have no home, they are displaced and do not belong. In this sense all the clients in our therapeutic communities are homeless. I believe what we need to try and achieve, in caring for people who are displaced or have lost their way in their transition, is to help them create their sense of belonging, to find a place where they feel they belong in society, and this means teaching them to find meaning in dwelling. What I think we need to think about now is how to achieve this. How do we support people in transition in the community so that they settle, find their home, their threshold?

HOME BASE: CHT'S DISPERSED THERAPEUTIC COMMUNITY

I remember being approached by a number of colleagues to apply to work on a new dispersed therapeutic community our organization was aiming to set up. This was a new concept for me. All the literature I had read about therapeutic communities and my own experience was of people living together. How could it work if this vital ingredient of living in one place was missing? But when I thought about it a little deeper, I questioned the term community. I first looked at what community meant to me in my own life. My community was definitely dispersed. Most of my closest friends and family not only did not live near where I lived but were scattered all around the world. As I have discussed earlier in this chapter, I gained insight into the fact that I did belong to a community, but not in the traditional sense. My community was dispersed, but although separated in geographical terms, modern technology enabled all of us to be involved in each other's lives, sharing our success, supporting one another through problems and difficulties. Furthermore, although I love my home, its warmth and its shelter, I realized that it was not the physical structure of bricks and mortar that made me feel it was home. Rather, my sense of belonging and feeling at home were much deeper than this and akin to what Dickens points to in *Nicholas Nickleby*. If the people in my dispersed community – family, friends, colleagues at work – were suddenly not part of my life, then I would lose my sense of belonging. I would be in a state of transition and would need to re-create a new status for myself.

Home Base is aimed at working with a specific group: homeless or potentially homeless ex-service people. This in itself was an interesting idea for a therapeutic community organization which saw a resonance here of the seminal development made at a military hospital at Northfield. The project was set up in response to a research study which indicated that around 25 per cent of the homeless in London alone were ex-service people. Apparently service people were finding it difficult to re-settle back into the community. Some of the difficulties were due to poor living skills, no network of friends or family, no transferable skills, and high emotional support needs. The aim is to place these individuals in their own flats. The placements are for six months. All clients are allocated a keyworker as soon as they are allocated a flat. The keyworker aims to explore with each client the reasons why they have become homeless, explore their skills, explore with them what they want to work in, help them establish their own network, and re-establish links with their family and friends. The underlying aim is to help them gain practical skills as well as to help them gain a sense of belonging, a sense of home that can be taken with them when they move on to their own permanent accommodation.

The key idea here is the notion of belonging. By belonging I mean, in the first instance, becoming part of a community which is formed by its common language. The feature of the common language which characterizes the dispersed therapeutic community is therapeutic discourse. This discourse, which belongs to the group of which each individual is a member, is internalized at the most basic level. That is, even if an individual were never to meet their fellow group members, they would still know that the members exist, that they belong to Home Base and CHT. For example, news of a member moving on is discussed with each member of the dispersed community. Members are encouraged to explore their own feelings about, and relationship to, this separation. Other members who live in the same area are encouraged to make contact. This contact is inevitably permeated by each member's struggle to find meaning in relation to each other. Arguments and minor incidents happen regularly, and staff at Home Base work with this in a positive way to help members understand their place in the Home Base community and in relation to the community outside. Even members living at quite a distance from each other are encouraged to provide ongoing support for each other. For example, one member living in Fulham, whose relationship with his girlfriend had ended, was supported by another member living in Paddington, through visits involving therapeutic dialogue. This was facilitated by staff at Home Base.

After six months of operation in the dispersed scheme, I can see very clearly why 25 per cent of the homeless in London are ex-service people. On leaving the services, most of these people are leaving behind a whole community that has clear rules and boundaries. On entering civilian life, they are exiled, isolated as if in foreign territory, at a loss, lost. In this, they are similar to many of the mentally ill clients I have worked with who have been placed in flats with little support after years of living in hospitals where they were part of a community. They, too, have left a community which consists of individuals living together within a boundary with rules and with a common language.

I would like to draw on a case study to describe this model in operation. James was a 26-year-old man. He had been homeless for two years since he was discharged from the services. His mother moved to Australia when he was a child. He did not want to go with her and stayed behind with his father. James's father was an alcoholic. At the age of 16 James had a major argument with his father, left home and joined the army. James left the army because all his friends were doing so. He had no transferable skills and nowhere to live. He described these two years as a period in which he just drifted. He had slept on friends' floors but disliked having to do this as it made him feel like he was a burden. Having joined Home Base, James began to feel he had gained a great deal. He felt he had gained confidence from his keywork sessions. He felt that these sessions helped him talk about his feelings; the keyworker helped him learn how to do things by showing him, so that he could do them for himself. He felt he had more confidence to talk to civilians. James said this in itself increased his confidence, as it taught him how to talk and establish a relationship with people. James did not know how to shop, budget or cook. At the time of writing he is still not a very good cook but he tries and is improving gradually. He has got a job now with an agency moving furniture. He never gets into debt but is working on how not to spend all the money he saves. He has used keyworking sessions to explore what he would like to re-train in. At first, he had a number of ideas of what he wanted to do. After much exploration, he came to the decision he wanted to be a tree surgeon. He has applied to do a course in this and has been accepted.

However, it has not been an easy ride for James. During Christmas, after much discussion in keyworking, James decided to re-establish contact with his father. Unfortunately, his father did not want to know and rejected him. This set him back. He avoided his keyworker and would not respond to letters or attend sessions. Eventually, he asked another client to inform his keyworker to give him space – he would see her after the New Year. James contacted his keyworker immediately after the New Year, but avoided talking about his father and wanted to block out his feeling about the whole thing. James has contact with his mother who lives in Australia. He is now thinking of going and visiting her after he completes his course. He is making some civilian friends, dates women, has joined a library, goes out with friends – some he has known from his army days, others he has met at work or whilst out socializing. James still has a lot to learn and needs to grow in a lot of ways. He still sometimes acts out rather than talking about his difficulties. For example, he misses sessions when he is worried. During sessions he tries to avoid talking about areas of his life that he finds very painful. He still misses the army and the sense of comradeship he had there. However, with all the issues that James is struggling with I see a big difference. I see a young man who is much more confident and responsible – in his work, in his house-keeping, in his payment of rent, towards his neighbours. Most importantly, James has gained a sense of belonging, he has a home, he is not drifting, he is no longer in total transition and not displaced. James has become a member of a community consisting of his mother in Australia, his new civilian friends, his old army friends, his friends back in his home town, his work, his relationship with his landlady and his neighbours, his keyworker and, importantly, other members of the Home Base community.

Building a community of relationships is the core component of our dispersed therapeutic community. In belonging to the dispersed therapeutic community, client and staff members have committed themselves to working through the struggles of their past and present and facing them together. As in residential therapeutic communities, meetings are called which have an administrative and therapeutic function. Home Base consists of a community of individuals who live separately, have different paths, different aims, different problems, but who share membership of a committed and boundaried group which has rules and structure. Although clients live their own lives (they may spend their days at work, voluntary work, supported schemes, and so on), they are also required to maintain contact with other members and with staff. While this does involve meeting, great emphasis is also placed on telephone, e-mail and fax contact.

A central theme of the dispersed therapeutic community is that clients should use phones and visit one another for support. In this manner, clients are learning the basis of how to gain support in a dispersed community format. The staff carry a bleeper or a mobile phone so that clients can contact them, but this is only for emergencies, as a last resort. Clients are continually encouraged to give and obtain support from other members of their dispersed community. This helps them to cope independently when they eventually are no longer members of the community. In this way they learn the skills of how to live in today's world rather than how to live in a traditional community.

As well as in group meetings, clients are also seen individually in their accommodation. Staff aim to support clients in the responsibilities of being a tenant, help them to develop relationships and to network, support them in re-training and in finding employment. The overall aim is to encourage clients to make decisions for themselves and to develop their place within a community of friends and colleagues. In order to achieve this acquisition of a common language, individual counselling sessions are an essential feature of the programme. Through dialogue the client learns to share his or her thoughts, feelings, fears, aims and ambitions and learns to express and be in touch with their emotions.

CONCLUSION

In order to provide appropriate care within society, an essential feature is common understanding and agreement on the meaning of terms and concepts used. In the example of Care in the Community, the meaning of the term 'community' has to reflect changes in society. The dispersed therapeutic community model outlined in this chapter *is* formulated on the basis that society has changed. Strategies for social care need to continuously take into account how cities, towns and villages are evolving and how urbanization is altering lifestyles across the globe. I have suggested that these changes do not exclude the possibility of applying a therapeutic community model to contemporary Care in the Community. On the contrary, they invite such an application for two important reasons. First, 'community' is about our commitment-to-struggle together, and this does not require geographical proximity. Second, given the nature of contemporary life, the need for such community is needed more than ever.

REFERENCES

Allen, P.D. (1992) 'User involvement in a therapeutic community.' *Therapeutic Communities 13*, 4, 253–262.

Aristotle (1941) 'The Politics.' In R. McKeon (ed) *The Basic Works of Aristotle.* New York: Random House.

Buber, M. (1965) *Between Man and Man.* New York: Macmillan.

Concise Oxford Dictionary (1982) (ed. J.B. Sykes). Seventh edition. Oxford: Clarendon Press.

Cooper, J.E. and Sartorius, N. (eds) (1996) *Mental Disorders in China. Results of the National Epidemiological Survey in 12 Areas.* London: Gaskell.

Heidegger, M. (1962) *Being and Time* (trans. J. Macquarrie and E. Robinson). Oxford: Basil Blackwell.

Hinshelwood, R. (1987) *What Happens in Groups: Psychoanalysis, the Individual and the Community.* London: Free Association Books.

Hoare, R. (1997) 'A platform – Moral and spiritual values.' In P. Askonas and S.F. Frowan (eds) *Welfare and Values: Challenging the Culture of Unconcern.* London: Macmillan.

Kennard, D. (1988) 'The therapeutic community.' In M. Aveline and W. Dryden (eds) *Group Therapy in Britain.* Milton Keynes: Open University Press.

Kennedy, S.S. (1998) *Now is the Time.* Dublin: Town House Publishing.

Meltzer, H., Gill, B., Petticrew, M. and Hinds, K. (1995) *The Prevalence of Psychiatric Morbidity among Adults Living in Private Households.* London: HMSO.

Lacan, J. (1987) *The Seminar. Book I. Freud's Papers on Technique, 1953–54* (trans. J. Forrester). Cambridge: Cambridge University Press.

Rapaport, R.N. (1960) *Community as Doctor.* London: Tavistock.

Richmond Fellowship (1983) *Mental Health and the Community: Report of The Richmond Fellowship Enquiry.* London: Richmond Fellowship Press.

Sartorius, N. (1998a) 'Universal strategies for the prevention of mental illness and the promotion of mental health.' In R. Jenkins and T.B. Ustun (eds) *Preventing Mental Illness – Mental Health Promotion in Primary Care.* Chichester: John Wiley.

Sartorius, N. (1998b) 'Nearly forgotten: The mental health needs of an urbanised planet.' In D. Goldberg and G. Thornicroft (eds) *Mental Health in our Future Cities.* Maudsley Monographs 42. London: Psychology Press.

White Paper (1989) *Caring For People.* London: HMSO.

The Contributors

Nadia Al-Khudhairy is the project manager of CHT's project Home Base and has a postgraduate degree in psychology from the University of London. She trained in group psychotherapy with the Institute of Group Analysis and before joining CHT worked in research for UNICEF where she supported refugees. Nadia has established Home Base this year in partnership with Central and Cecil Housing Trust. Nadia completed a research project for CHT's Campaigning Group and presented its findings in a paper at the 1998 International Conference of the Team for the Assessment of Psychiatric Services (TAPS). This year she also presented a paper at the Cassel Hospital Conference on psychotherapy. Currently Nadia edits the ATC newsletter and is completing her chartership to qualify in counselling psychology at City University.

John Gale is director of social work for CHT and was formerly a Benedictine monk. He studied theology at the University of Kent and took a postgraduate degree in Rome. Soon after ordination to the priesthood he served as a dean, and on a number of theological commissions, lectured in early Church history and has published a number of papers on patrology. He studied counselling with the Clinical Theology Association and trained in psychiatric social work, group consultancy and supervision with the Richmond Fellowship (RF) and in psychotherapy at Metanoia Institute. John worked as a trainer for RF and as a manager of a number of mental health projects before taking up his present post. He recently joined the editorial board of *Therapeutic Communities*. Currently John is also a trustee and director of The Homeless Fund and a manager under the Mental Health Act at two psychiatric units operated by Cygnet Health Care.

Kirsty Handover is project manager of Lexham House in Notting Hill. Kirsty has a degree in community studies with art and design from Exeter University and studied art therapy at City University. She is working to promote the use of art therapy in CHT and has been involved in organizing a number of exhibitions of clients' work.

Anne Salway is the project manager of Dainton House in Surbiton. Anne has a joint honours degree in drama and English and a postgraduate diploma in dramatherapy from Roehampton Institute. Before coming to CHT Anne worked for two years in France working on community based theatre projects with the local church. Each summer Anne leads a team of volunteers who work with a Palestinian community of young people in Israel, using drama and the arts to help them to discover and express their place. Anne has presented papers at the 1998 and 1999 Windsor Conferences and at a dramatherapy conference in Italy last year that was organized by the Italian association of therapeutic communities.

Clare Saxon has worked as an apprentice therapist and therapist at Lytton House in Putney. She has a degree in social studies from University of Newcastle and is currently a postgraduate social work student at Royal Holloway, University of London.

Emma Smith has worked as an apprentice therapist and therapist at Lexham House in Notting Hill. She came to CHT after A-levels for a one-year student placement. She currently has a place at Sheffield University where she is studying for a degree in social work.

Sarah Tucker is training coordinator for CHT. She is secretary of the ATC and has convened a working group to look at the development of training programmes for TC staff. Previously she worked as a university lecturer and for CRUSE. Sarah has Cambridge University postgraduate degrees in the philosophy of language and psychology. Her first interest in TCs emerged while training in psychotherapy with the Philadelphia Association. She has participated in training at the Institute of Group Analysis. She is an occasional lecturer at the Tavistock Clinic, a facilitator of ATC 'living learning experience' residential workshop and has published articles on therapeutic community theory and practice.

Subject Index

Author Index